Labor Politics in Latin America

LABOR POLITICS IN LATIN AMERICA

Democracy and Worker Organization in the Neoliberal Era

PAUL W. POSNER, VIVIANA PATRONI,
AND JEAN FRANÇOIS MAYER

University of Florida Press
Gainesville

Printed in the United States of America on acid-free paper

This book may be available in an electronic edition.

23 22 21 20 19 18 6 5 4 3 2 1

Library of Congress Cataloging-in-Publication Data
Names: Posner, Paul W., author. | Patroni, Viviana, 1957– author. | Mayer, Jean François, author.
Title: Labor politics in Latin America : democracy and worker organization in the neoliberal era / Paul W. Posner, Viviana Patroni, and Jean François Mayer.
Description: Gainesville : University of Florida Press, 2018. | Includes bibliographical references and index.
Identifiers: LCCN 2017060697 | ISBN 9781683400455 (cloth : alk. paper)
Subjects: LCSH: Labor policy—Latin America. | Labor laws and legislation—Latin America. | Labor unions—Latin America. | Latin America—Politics and government.
Classification: LCC HD6530.5 .P67 2018 | DDC 322/.2098—dc23
LC record available at https://lccn.loc.gov/2017060697

UF PRESS
UNIVERSITY OF FLORIDA

University of Florida Press
15 Northwest 15th Street
Gainesville, FL 32611-2079
http://upress.ufl.edu

Contents

Figures

Tables

Abbreviations

AD—Democratic Action (Acción Democrática)

APPO—Popular Assembly of the Peoples of Oaxaca (Asamblea Popular de los Pueblos de Oaxaca)

ASI—Independent Trade Union Alliance (Alianza Sindical Independiente)

ASSA—Union of Flight Attendants (Asociación Sindical de Sobrecargos de Aviación)

C-CURA—United Revolutionary Autonomous Class Current (Corriente Clasista, Unitaria, Revolucionaria y Autónoma)

CCC—Classist and Combative Current (Corriente Clasista Combativa)

CGT—General Confederation of Labor (Confederación General de Trabajo)

CHA—comparative historical analysis

CLT—Consolidation of Labor Laws (Consolidação das Leis do Trabalho)

CNE—National Electoral Council (Consejo Nacional Electoral)

CODESA—Confederation of Autonomous Trade Unions (Confederación de Sindicatos Autónomos)

COPARMEX—Employers' Confederation of the Mexican Republic (Confederación Patronal de la República Mexicana)

COPEI—Independent Electoral Political Organization Committee (Comité de Organización Política Electoral Independiente)

CPC—Confederation of Production and Commerce (Confederación de la Producción y del Comercio)

CPI—consumer price index

CPME—Council of Small and Medium-Sized Business (Consejo de la Pequeña y Mediana Empresa)

CROC—Revolutionary Confederation of Workers and Peasants (Confederación Revolucionaria de Obreros y Campesinos)

CROM—Regional Confederation of Mexican Workers (Confederación Regional Obrera Mexicana)

CST—Socialist Workers' Central (Central Socialista de Trabajadores)

CT—Labor Congress (Confederación del Trabajo)

CTA—Argentine Workers' Central (Central de Trabajadores de la Argentina)

CTB—Brazilian Workers' Central (Central dos Trabalhadores e Trabalhadoras do Brasil)

CTC—Confederation of Copper Workers (Confederación de Trabajadores del Cobre)

CTEP—Confederation of Workers of the Popular Economy (Confederación de Trabajadores de la Economía Popular)

CTM—Confederation of Mexican Workers (Confederación de Trabajadores Mexicanos)

CTV—Workers' Confederation of Venezuela (Confederación de Trabajadores de Venezuela)

CUT—Sole Workers' Confederation (Central Única dos Trabalhadores) (Brazil)

CUT—United Workers' Central (Central Unitaria de Trabajadores) (Chile)

EAP—economically active population

ECLAC—Economic Commission for Latin America and the Caribbean

EPZ—export processing zone

FADESS—Autonomous Employment Salary and Trade Union Defense Front (Frente Autónomo en Defensa del Empleo, el Salario y el Sindicato)

FAPUV—Federation of University Professors of Venezuela (Federación de Asociaciones de Profesores Universitarios de Venezuela)

FEDECAMARAS—Federation of Chambers of Commerce and

Production (Federación de Cámaras y Asociaciónes de Comercio y Producción)

FEDEPETROL—Federation of Oil Workers (Federación de Trabajadores Petroleros)

FEDESSP—Democratic Federation of Unions of Public Servants (Federación Democrática de Sindicatos de Servidores Públicos)

FENAJUPV—National Federation of Retired Persons and Pensioners of Venezuela (Federación Nacional de Jubilados y Pensionados de Venezuela)

FENASINTRASALUD—National Federation of Regional, Sectoral and Allied Trade Unions of Health Workers (Federación Nacional de Sindicatos Regionales, Sectoriales y Conexos de Trabajadores de la Salud)

FENASTEI—National Federation of Unions with Workers in the Informal Economy (Federación Nacional de Sindicatos con Trabajadores en la Economía Informal)

FpV—Front for Victory (Frente para la Victoria)

FrePaSo—Front for a Country in Solidarity (Frente País Solidario)

FSBT—Bolivarian Socialist Workers' Force (Fuerza Socialista Bolivariana de Trabajadores)

FSM—Mexican Union Front (Frente Sindical Mexicano)

FSTSE—Federation of Public Service Workers' Unions (Federación de Sindicatos de Trabajadores al Servicio del Estado)

GDP—gross domestic product

IACHR—Organization of American States' Inter-American Commission on Human Rights

IADB—Inter-American Development Bank

IFI—international financial institution

ILO—International Labor Organization

IMF—International Monetary Fund

IMSS—Mexican Social Security Institute (Instituto Mexicano de Seguridad Social)

ISI—import substitution industrialization

ISSSTE—Social Security and Social Services Institute for State Workers (Instituto de Seguridad y Servicios Sociales de los Trabajadores del Estado)

JCA—Boards of Conciliation and Arbitration (Juntas de Conciliación y Arbitraje)

LFC—Downtown Light and Power (Luz y Fuerza del Centro)

LFT—Federal Labor Law (Ley Federal del Trabajo)

MINPPTRAS—Ministry of Popular Power for Labor and Social Security (Ministerio del Poder Popular para el Trabajo y la Seguridad Social)

MOBASE—Trade Union Movement of the Base (Movimiento de Sindicatos de Base)

MPPEC—Ministry of Popular Power for the Community Economy (Ministerio del Poder Popular para la Economía Comunal)

MTA—Movement of Argentinean Workers (Movimiento de Trabajadores Argentinos)

NAFTA—North American Free Trade Agreement

OECD—Organization for Economic Cooperation and Development

PAN—National Action Party (Partido Acción Nacional)

PCdoB—Communist Party of Brazil (Partido Comunista do Brasil)

PCV—Venezuelan Communist Party (Partido Comunista Venezolano)

PDVSA—Venezuelan state oil company (Petróleos de Venezuela, S.A.)

PJ—Justicialist Party (Partido Justicialista)

PJJHD—Program for Unemployed Heads of Family (Programa Jefes y Jefas de Hogares Desocupados)

PRD—Party of the Democratic Revolution

PRI—Institutional Revolutionary Party (Partido Revolucionario Institucional)

PROVEA—Venezuelan Program of Education and Action in Human Rights (Programa Venezolano de Educación Acción en Derechos Humanos)

PSI—Public Services International

PSUV—United Socialist Party of Venezuela (Partido Socialista Unido de Venezuela)

PT—Workers' Party (Partido dos Trabalhadores)

SAP—structural adjustment program

SINTRAFERROMINERA—Orinoco Iron Miners' Union (Sindicato de Trabajadores de Ferrominera Orinoco)

SITUAM—Independent Union of Workers at the Metropolitan Autonomous University (Sindicato Independiente de Trabajadores de la UAM)

SME—Mexican Union of Electricians (Sindicato Mexicano de Electricistas)

SNTE—National Teachers' Union (Sindicato Nacional de Trabajadores de la Educación)

SNTMM—National Union of Miners and Metal Workers (Sindicato Nacional de Trabajadores Mineros y Metalúrgicos)

SNTP—National Union of Press Workers (Sindicato Nacional de Trabajadores de Prensa)

SNTSS—National Union of Social Security Workers (Sindicato Nacional de Trabajadores del Seguro Social)

STPRM—Mexican Oil Workers' Union (Sindicato de Trabajadores Petroleros de la República Mexicana)

STPS—Secretariat of Labor and Social Welfare (Secretaría de Trabajo y Previsión Social)

STUNAM—Union of Workers of the National Autonomous University of Mexico (Sindicato de Trabajadores de la Universidad Nacional Autónoma de México)

SUNEP-INN—Single National Union of Public Employees of the National Institute for Nutrition (Sindicato Único Nacional de Empleados del Instituto Nacional de Nutrición)

SUNEP-SAS—Single National Union of Public, Professional, Technical, and Administrative Employees of the Ministry of Health and Social Development (Sindicato Único Nacional de Empleados Públicos, Profesionales, Técnicos, Administrativos del Ministerio de Salud y Desarollo Social)

SUTERM—Sole Union of Electrical Workers (Sindicato Único de Trabajadores Electricistas de la República Mexicana)

TNC—transnational corporation

UASG—Labor and Trade Union Action Unit (Unidad de Acción Sindical y Gremial)

UCR—Radical Civic Union (Unión Cívica Radical)

URD—Democratic Republican Union (Unión Republicana Democrática)

UIA—Argentine Industrial Union (Unión Industrial Argentina)

UNT—National Union of Workers (Unión Nacional de Trabajadores) (Mexico)

UNT—National Workers' Union (Unión Nacional de Trabajadores) (Venezuela)

VAT—value-added tax

Acknowledgments

We are thankful to the University of Florida Press for its steadfast support during the writing of this book. We would like to particularly emphasize the work done by our editor, Stephanye Hunter, who provided us with guidance, encouragement, and enthusiasm, especially during the last phases of the writing and review process. We are also thankful to the reviewers, who invested significant time and effort in helping us to improve the original manuscript. Their commitment and insightful critiques were instrumental in enhancing the analytical focus of this book. We are also grateful to the Latin American Studies Association (LASA) and the Ford Foundation, from which we received a Special Project Grant that was instrumental in advancing our thinking on some of the conceptual matters that underpin this book. Additionally, we are grateful to Shana Yael Shubs for her assistance in formatting the manuscript for final submission.

Jean François Mayer would like to thank Concordia University, which provided financial and logistical support during the rather extensive research and writing periods this book involved. Mayer is grateful to Dr. André Roy, Concordia University's dean of the Faculty of Arts and Sciences, and Dr. Graham Carr, provost–vice-president Academic Affairs, for their backing and the key role they played in making Latin American studies a vibrant and dynamic research field at Concordia and in the city of Montréal. A part of the research conducted by Mayer for this book was funded by a grant he received from the Social Science and Humanities Research Council (SSHRC). Mayer thanks Dr. Jorge P. Gordin, editor of the *Journal of Politics in Latin America*, for the permission to utilize an article he published in that journal, which constitutes the bulk of chapter 6. Mayer would also like to thank his spouse and colleague, Tina Hilgers, for her enduring support, patience, and encouragements. Mayer feels particularly proud to not have to write in this section that he apologizes to his two wonderful daughters, Elsa Raphaëlle and Fleur Emmanuelle, for having missed out on some of their childhood because of work-related concerns. Mayer hopes to be able to continue this often seemingly impossible juggling act of coordinating work and family life, as the results are well worth the sacrifices supposed by this endeavor.

The Centre for Research on Latin America and the Caribbean and the Global Labour Research Centre, both at York University in Toronto, have been welcoming spaces where we have shared with colleagues many of the ideas in this book. Viviana Patroni would like to thank colleagues and friends in these institutions and, also, York University's Faculty of Liberal Arts and Professional Studies for the generous support extended during the preparation of this book. Beyond York, Ruth Felder has been a constant source of much intellectual engagement and encouragement for Patroni. Similarly, Jean François Mayer and Paul W. Posner were the perfect collegial companions in the laboring for this book. Closer to home, Patroni wishes to acknowledge very specially the personal and intellectual support of Pablo Idahosa, her partner and colleague, for his unwavering support, insightful comments to the text, and for always being ready to listen to the many ideas that come and go throughout the writing process. Pablo, Bruno, and Isabel bring the joy that makes all efforts gain renewed meaning. For that Patroni is endlessly thankful.

Paul W. Posner gratefully acknowledges financial support from Clark University, through the Oliver and Dorothy Hayden Junior Faculty Fellowship, which facilitated field research in Venezuela and Chile, and the Department of Political Science's Francis A. Harrington Public Affairs Fund, which provided resources that were helpful in preparing the manuscript for publication. He thanks John Wiley and Sons, publisher of *Latin American Politics and Society*, for permission to reprint "Laboring Under Chávez: Populism for the Twenty-first Century," and Taylor and Francis, publisher of *New Political Economy*, for permission to reprint, "Labour Market Flexibility, Employment and Inequality: Lessons from Chile." He is immensely grateful to the Turner family, Benner, Irene, and Juan Andres, for their support during his field research in Venezuela. To Viviana and Jean François—great colleagues and friends—who could imagine better collaborators? Finally, Posner would like to express his deepest gratitude to his son, Sam, for challenging him daily with his intellectual curiosity, and to his wife, Heather, for being an ever-present sounding board and constant source of care and support.

1

Introduction

Labor Politics in Latin America

Conditions for workers in Latin America have undergone a sea change since the latter decades of the twentieth century. Starting with the rise of repressive dictatorships in the 1960s and 1970s, followed by the painful adjustment of the 1980s and the consolidation of structural change in the 1990s, workers in Latin America have seen both labor rights and living standards erode. In countries like Chile, the deterioration of labor rights was the result of the enactment of new, flexibilizing labor legislation. In others, like Mexico, the preservation of protective labor regulations was no match for the brunt of changing economic conditions. Early in the new century, several countries in the region veered away from these trends. Yet nowhere was the eroded political and economic power of workers and their unions fully restored.

Workers' rights, and the specific ways in which they had structured labor relations in many Latin American countries, became a critical subject of contention as consensus for the prevailing inward-oriented development strategies in the region unraveled. By the end of the 1980s, one of the central items in the reform agenda put forth by major international financial institutions (IFIs) for the region and elsewhere was precisely the need to "modernize" labor market institutions to make them compatible with more globally integrated production strategies. Moreover, institutions like the International Monetary Fund (IMF) and World Bank insisted on the basic neoclassical premise that unions, negotiating on behalf of workers for higher wages and more stable jobs, were not only an obstacle to economic growth but also actually acted as barriers to the incorporation of larger numbers of workers into the formal economy.

Thirty years later, however, there seems to be some major rethinking about the soundness of this advice. Prompted by crisis and the stubborn malaise that has afflicted the global economy since 2008, IFIs have considerably revised their conception of labor flexibilization. The World Bank dedicated its 2013 *World Development Report* to the issue of employment and the potential of jobs for spreading the benefits of economic growth and, hence, reducing poverty (World Bank 2012). Equally relevant, Goal 8 in the United Nation's post-2015 Development Agenda affirms the need to "[p]romote sustained, inclusive and sustainable economic growth, full and productive employment and decent work for all" (United Nations 2015, 14). The International Labor Organization (ILO) responded to the threat of growing unemployment under the current global crisis with the adoption of a Global Jobs Pact, with the understanding that the challenge is not only to generate employment, but also to extend social protection and respect for labor standards (ILO 2010a).

Yet this change in orientation is nowhere more visible than in the IMF. After its long stand in favor of labor flexibilization, its April 2015 *World Economic Outlook* acknowledges that a study of 16 countries in the G20 failed to show any strong evidence linking labor market deregulation and economic growth (IMF 2015). This study follows another IMF publication that identifies the decline in unionization, one of the direct consequences of labor flexibilization, as the culprit for the growth of inequality in more developed countries (Jaumotte and Osorio Buitron 2015). The common theme in these reports is the IMF's recent preoccupation with the negative consequences of inequality for sustained economic growth (Dabla-Norris et al. 2015; Ostry, Berg, and Tsangarides 2014).

The reorientation of both social and economic policy in Latin America and economic consensus within major IFIs might point toward a new era in development thinking. However, the structural changes forced upon the economies of the region and their wide range of social, political, and economic consequences will not be easily reversed. Thus, notwithstanding the considerably more sympathetic view some governments in Latin America have exhibited toward the plight of workers in the new century, labor has maintained tense relationships with these administrations. Moreover, in addition to being weakened by labor reforms and deteriorating economic conditions, workers' organizations have been fragmented under the weight of new trends—including increasingly precarious employment, more heterogeneous working classes, and shifting party alliances—emerging from a deeply transformed social structure.

Countries in the region embarked on the pattern of IFI-promoted labor reform because there was widespread agreement among policymakers that it could become an effective means to temper the power of unions at a moment when controlling economic demands appeared critical for the execution of structural reforms. However, the deep social, political, and economic dislocations resulting from the undermining of unions' power were at the core of the negative trends—particularly growing poverty and inequality—that ultimately prompted a broad rejection of structural reforms. And notwithstanding labor's enormous losses during this period and the marked heterogeneity of the political movements that responded to the neoliberal challenge, workers were certainly no minor force in the shift away from market-oriented reforms led by several countries in the region starting in the late 1990s.

Our book addresses the complex processes, myriad political motivations, and often insurmountable obstacles governments in the region have encountered in undertaking labor legislation reform, starting in the 1970s and continuing into the new century. This discussion of labor legislation places the state at center stage, revealing its critical, although not always coherent, role in molding the spaces where struggles between workers and their employers take place. Ultimately, our book assesses the capacity of working-class organizations to represent and advance working people's demands in an era in which capital has reasserted its power on a global scale. Our premise is that the longer-term sustainability of development strategies for the region is largely connected to the capacity of working-class organizations to secure a fairer distribution of the gains from growth. To begin to develop this argument, this introductory chapter presents our goals, explains the justification for the selection of our case studies, and provides a summary of the volume's findings and theoretical contribution.

Laboring in Latin America: Overview of the Project

Project Goals

Broadly speaking, we attempt to achieve three interrelated goals in this book. First, we seek to assess the capacity of working-class organizations and workers to advance their demands and secure a more just distribution of the gains from economic development in an era in which capital has reasserted its power on a global scale. Second, we attempt to determine the factors that shape this capacity; in particular, we want to understand the causes and consequences of changes in labor movements and labor organization since 1990. Third, we attempt to evaluate the purported beneficial effects of making labor markets more flexible. In this regard, our objective is to go beyond a narrowly economistic assessment to explain both the circumstances under which labor flexibilization has been implemented and to assess how this transformation has conditioned the potential of labor as a political force. In short, we seek to explain the variations in the adoption of flexibilizing labor reforms as well as the consequences for workers that these variations have produced.

Cutting across these three objectives is an enquiry about the specific connection between workers and the parties that either historically represented them or that emerged more recently in opposition to neoliberalism. This topic is particularly significant for us in this book, since this relationship conditioned the role labor movements have played in contesting, accommodating, and accepting changes in labor markets since the 1990s. The party-labor relationship has been the focus of a number of studies that have sought to account for the political variables that facilitated or obstructed reforms in labor regulation. Some of these contributions focused on the way in which party-union links worked to shape structural reforms generally and labor reform more particularly (Etchemendy 2004; Murillo 2001, 2005; Murillo and Schrank 2005; Paczyńska 2009). Other studies lent a more critical lens to labor reform as a political process through which governments strived to reconcile pressures for economic deregulation in the midst of the democratic expectations the downfall of authoritarianism generated (Bensusán 2006; Cook 2007; Roberts 2007a).

In our view, however, most studies on labor reform do not address in a fully satisfactory fashion the impact of the much wider structural and political transformations the region underwent at this time.[1] Moreover, as our discussion of specific cases shows, these transformations conditioned labor's response to governments in the post-neoliberal period as well. This is a subject that has received some attention, but much still remains to be explored.

These are the gaps our study endeavors to fill. It is our premise that it is only through an analysis of the complex set of factors that transformed labor capabilities that a more productive enquiry into the position of organized labor in the process of labor law reform can be undertaken. In other words, rather than taking as a given labor's weakened position during this critical period in Latin America, our intention is to account for the intricate process leading to it. In particular, our country studies show the substantial impact that neoliberal reforms exerted on workers and labor unions. Even when in some cases these unions succeeded in protecting a substantial portion of their institutional capabilities, economic restructuring inflicted a very heavy toll on their structural and organizational powers. The end result was that they became increasingly less influential politically, a reality that conditioned their relationship even with the more progressive governments that took office in several of our case studies in the new century. It is this attention to labor's relative power that gives concrete meaning to our enquiry about the direction of deregulation and flexibilization of labor markets. We build on existing scholarship on labor reform with the aim of advancing questions that transcend their focus on processes of struggles and negotiation around the implementation of flexibilization as shaped mostly by short-term political calculations. Our analysis suggests the need to take into consideration the wider structural transformations that reconfigured the political maps of the countries we study, i.e., globalization and its impact on democratic transformation in the region, operating within longer time frames. It is precisely this wider structural analysis and historical narrative that allows our country studies to show that, even in the uncovering of substantial variation, what becomes evident in the study of Latin America over the last three decades is the overwhelming reality that for most workers in the region, labor reform—or the lack thereof—implied in essence increased precarity, informality, and weaker labor movements.

Explanation of Methods and Justification of Case Study Selection

In order to realize these research goals, we examine five cases in depth: Argentina, Brazil, Chile, Mexico, and Venezuela. Our approach in undertaking these country studies, and in developing our comparative work, draws from two somewhat overlapping but distinct main methodological strategies that are bridged in some ways by Collier and Collier (1991). The first, following Gerring (2007), is informed by our understanding of the potential utility that in-depth analysis of a small number of case studies holds in identifying causal connections in complex phenomena, in this instance the transformation of labor relations in contemporary Latin America. Our approach to case selection here was guided by the desire to explain the deteriorating working conditions confronted in most countries of the region regardless of key distinctions in their political trajectories while recognizing the variations in the nature of labor reform derived from the different paths followed.

The second methodological approach relies on key elements of the comparative historical analysis (CHA) (Collier and Collier 1991, 5; Huber and Stephens 2012, 47–49; Thelen and Mahoney 2015). We use CHA to explain outcomes that in our view cannot be fully comprehended without consideration of macro processes of transformation, for example, globalization. In so doing, we acknowledge the pragmatic and ontological points, "where structural features play a key causal role there is nothing to be gained—and much to be lost—by insisting that every outcome be traced back to the actions and strategies of individual agents" (Thelen and Mahoney 2015, 6–7), as is often demanded of the explicit or tacit forms of methodological individualism that guide certain forms of enquiry. Furthermore, our approach also provides the means for within-case analysis through which we seek to "solve real-world puzzles" (12) by identifying historical sequences and their temporal locations. The combination of these methodological tools of analysis informs the causal analysis at the level of individual case studies and their broader comparative implications.

Following Collier and Collier (1991, 15) we adapt a combination of the "most similar" and "most different" strategies of comparison proposed in their study.[2] All of our cases are "broadly matched" in that after the 1930s they adopted state-led development in the form of import substitution industrialization (ISI), a transformation that gave rise to a substantial industrial working class. The labor movement played a critical political role in the five countries we study, very often backed by labor-based parties. These countries also underwent substantial economic and political regime changes in the past several decades, ushering in an era in which neoliberalism became the predominant development model. Thus, they have experienced the increased openness to global competition and vulnerability to boom/bust cycles, the adoption of labor flexibility practices, and the substantial transformation of party-labor ties and the related fragmentation and lack of efficacy of labor organizations.

The examination of these broad similarities allows us to identify some substantial differences among the five cases in terms of the timing, extent, and impact of reform. This variation constitutes the basis for the "most different" method of comparison. For example, our analysis suggests that both Chile and Mexico adopted structural reforms under authoritarianism and as a result were able to adopt more extensive reforms than was the case in either Argentina or Brazil. In comparison to the Chilean and Mexican cases, the Argentinean authoritarian regime was much more equivocal in its commitment to neoliberal reforms, and the Brazilian military regime remained committed to ISI throughout its reign in power. Thus, extensive market-oriented labor reforms were not adopted in either case until the post-transition period, ultimately making those reforms less sweeping, less securely entrenched, and thus less detrimental to labor than in Chile and Mexico. Finally, in Venezuela the Punto Fijo regime's adoption of structural adjustment policies in response to economic crisis in the 1980s and 1990s precipitated a popular backlash and facilitated the rise to power of a so-called radical leftist regime under the leadership of Hugo Chávez. Accordingly, examination of labor politics in Venezuela provides insight into the extent to which this "radical leftist" model supports workers' rights and organizational capacity. More broadly, comparison of these five cases, which differ in terms of the timing, depth, and impact of labor reform, allows us to assess the purported benefits of flexibility and to determine the causes and consequences of changes in labor movements and labor organization since 1990.

Summary of Findings and Theoretical Contribution

Among the most significant of our findings relates to the issue of flexibility. Analysis of our case studies provides scant support for claims regarding the purported benefits of flexibilization, particularly with respect to its promise of employment generation and the reduction of inequality. Indeed, as chapter 3 illustrates, contrary to the predictions of labor flexibility's proponents (e.g., Cox Edwards 2007; Heckman and Pagés 2000, 2004; Sabatini and Farnsworth 2006), Chile's high degree of labor market flexibility—the highest among our five cases—has not led to reduced levels of income inequality or increased levels of employment, particularly for Chile's poorest citizens. In none of our case studies did flexibilization of labor reduce levels of informality. Thus, analysis of our case studies suggests that flexibilization is best understood, not as a means of reducing informality or inequality, but instead as a means of subverting the organizational strength of workers, thereby reducing both wage and nonwage costs to employers. In this sense, we argue that flexibility reforms shift the balance of power in favor of employers at the expense of workers.

Additionally, one of the central findings of our research is that there exist multiple ways in which labor flexibilization can be imposed. While some analysts focus on de jure protections of collective labor rights (Murillo and Schrank 2005) as evidence of improved organizational capacity for workers across Latin America, we observe that flexibilization—and thus the subversion of worker organizational capacity—has been achieved in ways other than the legal reform of the labor code. In particular, firms acquired an increased power to enact flexibilizing measures through the negotiation of collective agreements at the plant level, even when labor legislation continued to protect centralized forms of bargaining. This was a central strategy in labor flexibilization in countries like Argentina and Mexico. Moreover, our case studies demonstrate that the economic consequences of structural adjustment—including poor rates of employment generation, rising unemployment, and, given the lack of a significant safety net, the parallel growth of the informal economy—were central to employers' capacity to impose extensive de facto flexibilization. As our case studies analyze in further detail, the hardships inflicted upon workers through the economic changes restructuring brought about—in particular the constant threat not only of unemployment but also of the elimination of jobs that had previously secured the protection extended by the law—acted as a very powerful mechanism to impose new conditions on workers, whether the law changed or not. It is simply impossible to develop a comprehensive view about the full impact of the labor reform neoliberal regimes sought in Latin America without taking into account the many ways in which flexibility was imposed on workers and its disciplinary impact.

In this regard, our case studies also reveal that the imposition of flexibilization, whether de facto or de jure, has had a significant impact on labor organization and party-labor ties. We observe a general pattern in which the more severe the structural adjustment and repression carried out pre-transition or pre-regime change: (1) the weaker organized labor is post-transition or post-regime change; and (2) the weaker the linkage between organized labor and political parties, whether these be newly ascendant leftist parties such as the United Socialist Party of Venezuela (Partido Socialista Unido de Venezuela, PSUV) in Venezuela or historical allies of the labor movement such as the Socialist Party in Chile.[3] As chapter 3 demonstrates, the severity of the Chilean military regime's structural adjustment policies and repression undermined the historical ties between organized labor and parties of the left and center; these conditions have continued post-transition, leaving workers without political leverage to reverse the legacy of Augusto Pinochet's labor reforms.

Chapter 4 demonstrates a similar pattern in Mexico as occurred in Chile. As in Chile, structural reforms carried out under Mexican authoritarianism were perpetuated after the country's democratic transition. Thus, despite important differences between the Mexican and Chilean cases, particularly in terms of the countries' respective forms of authoritarianism, the analysis in chapter 4 of Mexico indicates that, like Chile, the legacy of structural adjustment and authoritarianism persists post-transition and plays a significant part in shaping party-labor relations and in constraining labor's political leverage under democracy.

Chapter 5 indicates that Argentina's authoritarian regime's equivocal adoption of neoliberal reforms and its disgraced exit from power allowed organized labor a degree of leverage to shape the nature and extent of labor reform under democracy not seen in Chile and Mexico. Nonetheless, neoliberal reforms adopted in Argentina produced a major restructuring of the economy. As a consequence, even with high rates of economic growth in the new century, informality and other forms of precarity remain very high. Therefore, while the General Confederation of Labor (Confederación General de Trabajo, CGT) retained the bases of its considerable power, the existence of a large mass of unorganized workers continues to limit both the confederation's structural power and influence within the party.

Chapter 7 reveals similar dynamics at play in Venezuela. By substantially increasing informality and producing a related decline in unionization, the economic crisis and subsequent adoption of neoliberal reforms under the Punto Fijo regime in the 1980s and 1990s precipitated a fundamental restructuring of party-labor ties in Venezuela. This restructuring deepened under the Chávez regime, as it pursued the unorganized masses that comprise the urban informal sector as its primary base of support.

With a majority of workers in the informal sector, the Chávez regime realized that it could build a winning electoral block without relying on the organized labor movement, thereby freeing it from constraints the organized labor movement sought to impose on its power and policymaking. Rather than deliver on its promise to empower workers through some form of radical participatory democracy, the Chávez (now Maduro) regime has instead fragmented and weakened the labor movement and in the process fundamentally altered party-labor ties in Venezuela to the detriment of unions and workers.

In contrast to prevailing debates in the literature, in which scholars either conflate populism and leftism (Castañeda 2006; Castañeda and Morales 2008; Weyland, Madrid, and Hunter 2010) or see them as distinct (Cameron and Hershberg 2010; French 2009; Levitsky and Roberts 2011), we argue that, as the Venezuelan case demonstrates, they are not only distinct but in tension with one another. More precisely, we argue that analysis of labor politics in contemporary Venezuela indicates that the populist drive to concentrate political and economic power subverts the leftist goals of eroding hierarchical forms of domination of marginalized groups, including most prominently both formal and informal sector workers. In this regard, our analysis of the Venezuelan case offers insights that promise to deepen our understanding of the fate of workers and labor reform in other so-called radical leftist regimes in Bolivia and Ecuador.

Additionally, we observe in Venezuela a vicious cycle that is also evident in Chile and Argentina: the decline in the size and strength of organized labor—whether as a result of authoritarian repression, structural adjustment, or both—prompted parties historically aligned with labor to deemphasize this alliance and to shift their focus to unorganized workers in the informal sector. To the extent that this shift occurs, analysis of these case studies indicates that it is problematic for all workers since in none of these countries has the relative decline in influence of formal sector workers been accompanied by empowerment of the masses in the informal sector.

The analysis presented in chapter 6 indicates that Brazil is an exception to this pattern. In stark contrast to the Venezuelan case, our examination of the Brazilian case reveals the positive gains workers have experienced under a more moderate form of leftism. Chapter 6 details how positive party-labor relations in Brazil were facilitated by institutional reforms adopted under successive Workers' Party (Partido dos Trabalhadores, PT) governments. In contrast to these other cases, PT governments supported organization and improved legal protections for informal sector workers. Nonetheless, the political activation of segments of the informal sector did not change the fundamentals of the PT's relationship with organized labor and the dominant labor confederation, the Sole Workers' Confederation (Central Única dos Trabalhadores, CUT). Our analysis of the Brazilian case reveals the exception that affirms the general pattern noted above regarding the importance of the timing and nature of regime change and economic liberalization in determining the fate of labor reform and organization. In other words, if the Chilean and Mexican cases demonstrate the negative impact severe structural adjustment and repression under authoritarianism have on party-labor ties in the post-transition period, the Brazilian case demonstrates that adopting less extreme neoliberal reforms and adopting them in the post-transition period allows for the development of more positive party-labor ties.

In chapter 8, we summarize in greater detail our findings with respect to Brazil and the other cases examined in this volume and more fully develop our comparative analysis. As Latin American countries reevaluate the full consequences of past and present development decisions, it is essential to analyze the ability of workers' organizations to actively engage in the construction of alternatives. What has been the extent and legacy of the political losses experienced by the working class in the emergence of post-neoliberal regimes? In what ways does the heterogeneity in working conditions engendered through the reforms of the 1980s and 1990s remain an obstacle for labor to engage more assertively with politics? Are there new opportunities for the renewal of labor movements as representative organizations? These are the questions that inform our analysis in the following chapters.

2

Historical Overview

VIVIANA PATRONI

> All too often we succumb to the temptation to explain historical processes as the abstract unfolding of forms, as rigid, timeless "systems." We subsume the struggles through which certain groups impose their domination over others under rigid systemic logics that make the outcome of conflict seem almost inevitable, when in fact what is significant is movement itself, the alliances that maintain structures while at the same time opening the possibility of their transformation.
>
> Juan Eugenio Corradi, "The Politics of Silence" (1978)

This chapter offers the background, through historical and comparative analysis, to understand the global and regional transformations that affected labor in Latin America during the critical 1990s and their aftermath in the new century, which is the focus of this book's country-specific discussions of Chile, Mexico, Brazil, Argentina, and Venezuela. In the development of this background, key concepts are also explored that are essential to understanding the case studies presented. I begin this analysis by examining the origins of working-class organizations in these countries and the responses they elicited from the state.

A particular focus is placed on the first attempts to create legislation specifically aimed at regulating the relationship between labor and capital;

this is the subject of the first section below. I follow in the second section with a discussion about the rise of mass politics in Latin America, in particular the consolidation of two forms of regulation of class conflict that had enduring power in the region: populism and corporatism. The third section of the chapter addresses the deep economic, political, and social changes the region has undergone since the 1980s, which in turn constitute the conditions under which labor struggles have unfolded during this critical moment in the region's development. Here, a discussion of the transnationalization of Latin America's economies is included to situate the case studies' analyses of the changes pursued by governments, employers, and IFIs in the arena of labor relations. The conceptual discussion about the meaning and implications of labor flexibilization is framed in this context. This section concludes with a discussion about the emergence of "pink-tide" governments, their search for alternative forms of insertion into the world economy, the pivotal role of extractive industries in fueling economic growth, the expansion of social welfare benefits, and also the somewhat paradoxical distance that has grown between pink-tide governments and the working class.

Latin American Working Classes: Class Identities and the Politics of Social Change

In this section I outline some general trends for the region. However, while considering these general trends, it is essential to bear in mind not only the heterogeneous nature of the working classes within each country but also the diversity across the region in terms of composition, political practices, and relative strength. What follows is a brief discussion to identify some of the patterns and conditions that favored greater degrees of working-class organization and also the relevance of labor legislation in this regard.

The rapid industrialization of Europe by the mid-nineteenth century created new economic opportunities that countries in the region seized with great vigor. Growing demand for new raw materials and foodstuffs for which Latin America had a comparative advantage acted as a major incentive not only for economic growth but also for the consolidation of national states. Interactions between national dynamics and the conditions of commodity production—such as patterns of investment and ownership, labor requirements, and competition in the international markets—help to explain the trajectory of social, political, and economic change in Latin American countries. They also partly account for the particular strength of workers in export-producing sectors and in those other sectors and activities that grew along with them.

It warrants mentioning that while this discussion focuses on unions in the urban sector, this period of transformation in Latin America also produced very high levels of conflict among the rural populations most affected by the development of export economies. A high concentration of workers in enclave economies in the mining, petroleum, and agricultural sectors, along with the harsh working conditions prevailing in these settings, created a charged environment for the development of class conflict and organization. In turn, struggles demanding better working conditions became an additional factor in the consolidation of a common identity among these workers. Similar conditions existed for the organization and mobilization of workers in the transportation systems developed to service the export sector (Collier and Collier 1991, 64). Perhaps no other event of the period provides a better illustration of the scope of the political and social responses to the dislocations modernization produced among peasants and workers, both in rural settings and rapidly expanding urban centers, than the Mexican Revolution of 1910–17, which so radically transformed Mexican politics and society.

In several countries in the region, export-led economic growth promoted a process of rapid urbanization, and with it, the development of a range of economic activities, including an early industrialization process demanding a growing number of workers. These workers organized early on to form unions and made cities the setting of a significant number of labor conflicts. While early industrial production was undertaken mostly in small-size firms—places notoriously challenging for labor organizing—workers in the industrial sectors were nonetheless key participants in the emerging labor movement, particularly in those countries where by the early twentieth century they were a sizeable proportion of the economically active population (EAP), as was the case in Argentina and Uruguay (Collier and Collier 1991, 64).

The labor movement in Latin America was influenced in important ways by the tradition of labor struggles that had developed in Europe with the rise of industrialization. This experience was transmitted in very direct ways through the large inflow of European immigrants who began to arrive in the region in the last quarter of the nineteenth century. The greatest impact of European immigration was felt in Argentina, southern Brazil, and Uruguay, but countries like Chile, Venezuela, and Mexico also received a large body of immigrants (Weaver 2000, 68). These immigrants, particularly those coming from countries like Italy and Spain, were the bearers of a long tradition in socialism, anarchism, communism, and anarcho-syndicalism that contributed in crucial ways to the political direction of early labor movement struggles in the region.

It was against this backdrop of rising labor organization in industry, cities, and export enclaves, along with the struggles workers sustained against employers, that early labor legislation was implemented in the region. Through it, governments attempted to provide some protection to workers in the expectation that this would reduce the level of conflict that had both disrupted key economic activities and prompted violent state responses with detrimental political consequences (Banuri and Amadeo 1991, 184; Bronstein 1997, 7). This latter concern was particularly important in countries like Argentina and Chile, where ascending urban middle classes sought workers as potential political allies in their bid to challenge the existing distribution of political power. Nonetheless, beyond the recognition that the state could play a role in addressing some of the demands workers pressed for through mobilization, early labor legislation was also often intended as a tool to co-opt, control, or undermine unions. When this failed, governments in the region did not hesitate to continue to use all necessary force against unions. The enactment of individual labor protection measures thus did not contradict the relentless hardline approach that governments continued to adopt toward labor unions (Bronstein 1997, 7–8).

Initial legislation during the first two decades of the twentieth century addressed weekly rest, the work of women and children, industrial accidents, and some aspects of occupational safety. By far, the most important achievement in this period was the promulgation of Article 123 in the Mexican Constitution of 1917, establishing extensive rights for workers. Its codification, however, had to wait until 1931 with the enactment of Mexico's labor code. This document, along with the Chilean labor code of 1924–25, was considerably influential in the sanctioning of other labor codes and laws in countries of the region during the 1930s and 1940s. In the group of countries in the book's case studies, labor laws approved in Venezuela (1936), Brazil (1943), and Argentina (1946) represented a thorough attempt to extend workers' rights and, as discussed below, regulate and control the actions of unions. Enacted during or after the Great Depression of the 1930s, these legal instruments acquired fundamental significance during the next broad range of transformations, triggered by the decline of export economies in the region.

While not all Latin American countries were equally affected by the downturn of the 1930s, most of them were hit very hard as export earnings fell precipitously. Economic hardship led to crisis for many workers in the export-producing sectors and other closely connected areas of the economy. In many cases, these were the same workers who had managed to achieve higher levels of organization. Thus, they also possessed the capacity to respond to the hardships the crisis imposed on them with resolve. Moreover, as mentioned above, in some countries the state had already attempted to respond to growing labor mobilization through co-optation rather than repression. Thus, while the 1930s presented some increased challenges to securing social stability, there was an effort in many countries to assert state power in ways that would reduce the impact of the economic decline on workers. Of course, governments still utilized repression to discipline workers, but in countries where the export economy had fostered economic diversification and urbanization, the political cost of such an option was very high (Weaver 2000, 119).

Both the impact of the crisis on the economy and the predisposition of the state to seek means other than repression to respond to workers' demands are important variables in accounting for the variation in the responses that Latin American governments implemented during the 1930s. The one common transformation during the 1930s in the case studies was the significant, but incomplete, shift in the distribution of economic and political power away from traditional export elites toward emerging urban-based economic groups—a change that would be critical for the labor movement in the decades to come. In the case of Venezuela, reliance on petroleum exports meant that the country was somewhat shielded from the worst of the downturn in international markets. Yet, the death of dictator Juan Vicente Gómez in 1935 initiated a period of important—if still uncertain—change for the working classes. While new labor legislation was passed, it effectively became an instrument for controlling unions, very much in the vein of other early corporatist experiments in the region. And although the state supported unionization, the increasing influence of the opposition within the labor movement resulted in the use of repression and an increasing antiunion stance on the part of the government (Collier and Collier 1991, 253). It was only with the rise to power of Democratic Action (Acción Democrática, AD) in 1945 that a full-fledged approach to labor emerged in the form of populism.

In comparison with Venezuela, Brazil felt the impact of the Great Depression sooner and more severely. Between 1930 and 1945, under the rule of Getúlio Vargas, the government in this country cemented a new alliance between its traditional export elites, now clearly displaced from the gravitational center of political power, and emerging middle-class sectors. The model called for the state to take an active lead in the process of modernization, in which a program to secure social peace through the control of working-class organizations was a prominent feature. Starting with the creation of a Department of Labor in 1931 and the sanctioning of a complex body of labor legislation, the state sought to bring labor organizations under its tutelage in order to ensure their subordination to its reform program. This paternalistic approach to labor control during this first Vargas period changed considerably after 1935, when in response to growing opposition by some segments of the labor movement, the government increased repression against the working class in general, making attempts to organize more difficult and costly (Roxborough 1998, 231). The corporatist model of state control was tightened during the Estado Novo period between 1937 and the fall of Vargas in 1945. As shown below, there were some heavy costs for the labor movement during this transformation, particularly in terms of its autonomy.

The critical question about the potential, and also the dangers, of collaborating with the state confronted Chilean workers in the 1920s. Chile's markets for its main export at the time, nitrate fertilizer from guano, contracted sharply as the result of the invention of synthetic alternatives, sending tremors throughout the economy and contributing to political instability. Between 10 and 15% of the population had been employed in nitrate production, and along with those employed in the new industries fostered through forward and backward linkages, they formed a new working class in the country (Valenzuela 1995, 75–76). The mobilization of this new working class and its political allegiance to new parties more closely linked to working-class identity generated concern among conservatives, who came to see increasing social protection as a means to preempt further radicalization (Collier and Collier 1991, 189). As in other countries at the time, labor policy was also related to the modernization project, which was in many respects reminiscent of some of the ideals of fascism, particularly in its focus on how to address the "social question." Emerging political elites saw the use of state benefaction to regulate labor conflict as a way to safeguard the country against further working-class radicalization.

The Great Depression only aggravated the challenges Chile confronted, as exports fell abruptly, resulting in very high levels of unemployment in the affected sectors, particularly mining. As a result, the 1930s in Chile was a decade of political turbulence that promoted a much more radical political perspective among the working class, leading to a substantial growth of unionization, a process that consolidated the control of socialists in the movement (Roxborough 1998, 235). As in the case of Brazil, the unionization drive and the extension of protective labor legislation in Chile had been focused on urban workers. Under the tutelage of the Popular Front government from 1938 to 1941, further legislation provided additional benefits for these workers, while at the same time, legislation was approved to restrict the right of rural workers to organize and strike (Weaver 2000, 124).

The 1930s were also difficult times for Argentina. The decline in export earnings produced a significant domestic economic setback. The travails of the country were compounded by a military coup and later a series of right-wing governments elected through fraud. The CGT was founded in 1930 and would play a central role in Juan Domingo Perón's rise to power in the following decade. When the economy recovered after the first half of the decade, unions once again were able to launch an active campaign to improve wages and working conditions. The active role of unions also reflected the important economic and social transformation the country had undergone by then and that continued as industrialization proceeded during the 1940s.

However, workers and their unions were not particularly successful in obtaining significant concessions from a very recalcitrant economic and political elite. By the 1940s, workers had developed a common identity, closely linked to their experience of economic exclusion and political marginality (Murmis and Portantiero 1971, 76). This experience was to change quite dramatically with the rise of Juan Domingo Perón in a military coup in 1943 and his actions in the decisive couple of years that followed. For labor unions, Perón represented the most powerful ally imaginable for helping them attain a larger share of the national income. As in the other countries analyzed in this study, what made Argentine workers and their organizations a subject of concern for governing elites were the same features that made them an appealing political ally. The issue for aspiring political elites was how to bring workers into an alliance while retaining the power to set the limits of social conflict.

Bringing workers into a governing alliance was a key component of post-conflict governments in Mexico, though the consolidation of such an alliance was not secured until the second half of the 1930s, under the administration of Lázaro Cárdenas (1934–40). Article 123 of the 1917 Constitution extended levels of protection unparalleled in its time. However, broad internal variations in the codification of Article 123 prompted labor organizations to press for a federal law that would eliminate these discrepancies. Congress only approved this law after the relationship between government and organized labor had reached an impasse, as the distance between governing elites and labor organizations made it more difficult to control the growing labor unrest that accompanied the recessionary process that began in 1929. Thus, it was not until 1931 that the government was able to obtain congressional approval for the enactment of a federal labor law, which then became the central legal instrument regulating employers and workers' disputes and workers' organizational rights. In the hands of President Cárdenas, this legislation became an invaluable tool, allowing industrial workers to be brought into an alliance that was key to securing the president's supremacy within his party.

For workers in these and other countries in the region, the extension of protection through labor legislation signaled the state's willingness to acknowledge both the legitimacy of the demands at the core of labor conflicts as well as its own role in compensating for the asymmetry in power between capital and labor. However, labor legislation was also an instrument through which the state exercised some control over workers and their organizations. Labor legislation and the increasing ability of the state to regulate social conflict at the site of production became the basis for particular forms of state-labor relations. The modalities of these relations conditioned the political inclusion of labor in the modernization project emerging as mass parties began to advance in the 1930s.

As elsewhere, labor legislation provided the state with an instrument to strengthen its capacity to act as an arbiter in the struggle between capital and labor. As an essential part of this process, the state also needed to acquire the administrative capacity to employ the legal arsenal at its disposal. To do so, most countries in the region at this time developed specialized bodies within the state apparatus in the form of government secretaries and ministries aimed at addressing the complexity of labor relations. Having the legal and administrative means to regulate labor conflict at its disposal also allowed the state to use coercion in a more selective way, demonstrating both the costs of confrontational approaches pursued by the more radical political factions within the labor movement and the potential rewards of using the channels legitimized through state policy.

As the discussion below shows, the consequences of engaging under such terms were at the heart of the dilemma, as they posed a threat to the autonomy of workers' organizations. The scope for union autonomy was further compromised by the heterogeneity of working experiences and its adverse impact on the consolidation of strong collective identities (Oxhorn 1998, 221).[1] Below, I explore how these phenomena affected the relationship between the state and the labor movement, particularly through the consolidation of corporatism as the institutional mechanism for controlling the participation of labor movements in politics.

Labor and the Age of Development: Inclusion and Exclusion

The economic, social, and political changes Latin American countries had experienced up to the 1930s transformed organized labor into a crucial political force. As industrialization proceeded during the 1930s and especially after the 1940s, the industrial working class grew rapidly, and with this transformation, the central question of workers' political place in modernizing societies acquired a critical significance. More importantly, working-class struggles, previously focused almost exclusively on the extension of labor rights, soon encompassed a much broader set of demands for the recognition of basic citizenship rights. In carrying forward the demands of other subaltern groups, workers, through their unions, acquired a pivotal role as representatives of a much broader segment of the population, which—through this process and at this critical time in the political history of the region—became constituted as "the people" (Roxborough 1998, 227). The principal features in this construction of citizenship included notions of social justice and also, in societies so hierarchically organized, a defense of the basic premise of the value of workers' contributions and their intrinsic dignity as equal citizens.

The populist movements that sprang up in Latin America in the 1930s and 1940s provided new language to these aspirations and granted them political legitimacy. Addressing the conditions of exclusion through redistribution was both the fundamental goal of the populist regimes at the time and a key pillar for the multi-class alliances supporting them. Redistributive policies, the transformations brought about by mass politics, and the personalistic nature of the leaderships that commanded these movements to power met with fierce opposition from traditional elites and the conservative forces that represented them. Mass mobilization played a critical role in creating momentum to both advance reforms and neutralize opposition to them. However, it was in the essence of populist leaders to exercise as tight a control as possible over popular mobilization, a trend that betrayed their fear and distrust of the unforeseeable consequences of subaltern groups' political spontaneity.

Organizing, directing and controlling the demands arising from "the people" and some of their organizations thus became a pivotal initiative under populist regimes. Because workers' organizations did possess a substantial capacity for mobilization relative to other subaltern groups, they were the subject of a concerted effort to ensure both their support and compliance with the new populist alliance. The emergence of this very particular form of relationship between the state and the organizations of the working class had the power to transform labor unions along the lines of what is understood in this study as corporatism, a concept to which I return in the paragraphs below.

This top-down control exercised by populist leaders over the organizations and demands of the working classes was also evident in the mode of economic reform they pursued. In response to the economic turmoil wrought by the Great Depression and the Second World War, populist leaders across Latin America restructured their economies to promote local industries with a set of policies known as import substitution industrialization (ISI). State-led industrialization, as an alternative to reduce the impact of often highly unstable international markets for primary commodities, offered an option to exercise greater control over the variables affecting economic growth and, with it, the expectation of avoiding the social turmoil that afflicted countries at the time. It also provided the language that gave development substance to rising nationalist concerns.

Starting with the larger and more industrialized economies, in one way or another, all countries in the region embraced import-substituting industrialization as the main pillar of their development strategy.

Indeed, some variant of ISI became a fundamental feature of the populist experiments. However, even in moments of retreat of populist regimes, ISI remained central as an economic strategy because, notwithstanding all its shortcomings, ISI provided the possibility of accommodating conflicting class interests. The proviso was that these interests needed to be shaped and negotiated to fit the confines of a pattern of accumulation based mostly on what remained limited domestic markets. That the region achieved very high rates of economic growth during the ISI period is probably the best testament to the effectiveness of the state and the political apparatus it developed in reshaping working-class demands and aspirations.

Local political conditions affected the specific ways in which industrialization unfolded, but overall, shielding local markets from international competition allowed for the extension of protection to workers, as increasing labor costs could be transferred to the price of locally produced industrial goods. Not surprisingly, the state's predisposition to promote the institutionalization of labor regulation reached its most expansive phase under populism. The state became central not only as the most logical site for the articulation of workers' demands but also as labor's principal interlocutor (Collier 1996; Collier and Collier 1977; Schmitter 1982). There were country-specific conditions that determined how labor movements found new spaces for accommodation within political parties and the state, but the main practices came to form a constellation identified as corporatism.

The notion of corporatism, and more precisely state corporatism, has been used extensively in studies of Latin American labor, often to depict forms of interest representation where the state—via labor legislation and other forms of legal and administrative control—acquired the capacity to sanction and regulate the existence of organizations representing sectoral interests, in particular labor and capital.[2] Among the instruments the state used to exercise control was its capacity to grant these organizations a monopoly of representation and provide them with other legal, political, and economic advantages that reinforced their organizational power and upper hand against opposition. There was a trade-off, of course, and this has usually been understood to be the weakening of the autonomy of these organizations, which was a result of the influence the state was able to exercise on their leaderships, and also because, eventually, the very way in which demands and objectives were formulated became molded to fit the parameters of the relationship with the state (Collier and Collier 1977, 493). In this sense, then, more than representing workers, corporatist unions became intermediaries between their rank and file and the state, making the demands of one and the political exigencies of the other somewhat compatible and viable within a given development model or project, as was the case with ISI. It was the political alliances thus cemented that also limited organized labor's ability to challenge those development options that did not address the high levels of heterogeneity in working conditions, particularly informality. As a result, a substantial portion of the benefits populism extended to lower classes accrued mostly to organized workers in the formal sector (Oxhorn 1998, 223).

State corporatism was ostensibly a system of labor control, but it was neither completely effective as such nor did it prevent labor from achieving some very significant rights. On the one hand, it needed to be constantly strengthened against frequent challenges from opposing segments within the working class. Indeed, an accurate depiction of the political trajectory of labor in Latin America must start by recognizing that, while corporatist organizations may have been predominant in some countries, they were far from being the only representatives of the working class. State corporatism was often a way of displacing and isolating the more radical political currents that have been influential within the working class. As the book's case studies show, corporatist practices clearly discriminated against those sectors of the organized labor movement that were less open to cooperation by benefiting others relatively more willing to comply.

On the other hand, labor leaderships did not surrender all of their autonomy in exchange for the benefits the state could dispense. Since their legitimacy rested on their ability to address the concerns and aspirations of their rank and file, they often confronted both the state and employers in their struggles to secure and extend workers' rights. In the countries we analyze, the record of labor movements in securing improvements in working conditions or a higher share of the national income, at least for formal workers, remained a function of their capacity to exercise direct pressure on the state and employers through both their participation in corporatist institutions and their mobilization capabilities.

In most cases, the strength and viability of labor corporatism was related not only to the scope of the rights workers enjoyed or the legal framework that supported such rights but also fundamentally to the working class's political identification with the party whose intervention was critical in establishing both. Corporatism in Latin America thus possessed a powerful political component that imbued it with ideals—such as social justice and the dignity of work and workers—that transcended the immediate interests of the working class but were central to the identity of workers. Populism cemented this relationship in ways that later allowed populist parties to withstand their transformation in the 1990s, when they became the main conduit for neoliberal reforms. Thus, although corporatism as a system of state-labor relations was consolidated in most countries during the period of populism, it was also compatible with a number of other types of political regimes.

Latin America Transformed: Market Fundamentalism and Labor

The transformation of capitalism in Latin America starting in the early 1970s was brought about by various momentous changes. The catalysts of the economic structural transformation in the region included the relocation of industrial production toward low-wage countries; the debt crisis of the 1980s and the power IFIs attained under the new conditions to determine domestic policy in debtor countries; the ascending power of financial capital; and, most importantly, the decisive local and global political victory of capital to roll back many of the concessions working classes and underprivileged sectors had previously obtained. By the 1990s these reforms had redefined the political economies of the region.

The terms "market reforms," "market-friendly reform," "structural reforms," and "neoliberalism" are utilized in this book to refer to the transformations that took place in the case studies sometimes as early as the 1970s. It is this last term, though, that most thoroughly captures the direction and depth of the transformation that took place in Latin America. Throughout, the term neoliberalism is utilized to indicate the set of policies first pursued through what became known as the Washington Consensus, including privatization, trade liberalization, labor flexibilization, and economic deregulation. There was also a general understanding that the state needed to have a less active role as a regulator, but it was clear, too, that the state was central in securing the viability of the reforms pursued. Following G. Harrison (2005, 1306), I find it useful to think of neoliberalism as "*a project to expand and universalize free-market social relations*" (italics in original), where the notion of "project" invites an analysis of those actors with the capacity to implement change and those with the power to contest it. Thinking of change in the context of "free-market social relations" enables us to examine how neoliberalism seeks to "shape the economy, the state and society" (1306).

As the case studies make evident, there was a large degree of variation in when and how Latin American countries implemented neoliberal policies and the results they produced. In the 1970s the dictatorial regimes in Chile and Argentina initiated the implementation of economic reforms that advanced the content of neoliberal structural adjustment. In these cases, neoliberal structural reforms constituted a key component of the societal reorganization these regimes pursued to overcome the dangers of political subversion and economic disorder. Later during the transition away from military rule in the 1980s, Argentina and Brazil evaded the most draconian restructuring policies then supported by the U.S. government and major IFIs in favor of more "heterodox" approaches to stabilization in the hope of addressing some of the distributional concerns that had emerged as a response to authoritarian policies. In these two cases, fully fledged neoliberal restructuring was entrenched only by the early 1990s. Mexico followed an alternative route, incorporating orthodox adjustment policies early in the 1980s that quickly became the basis for its own ongoing neoliberal transformation. A similar pattern unfolded in Venezuela; however, in this country the consequences of adjustment produced major social upheavals by the end of the decade and substantial regime change by the end of the 1990s. Chile remained consistently committed to neoliberalism, even after its democratic transition.

While the changes neoliberal restructuring brought about were expressed in myriad ways—affecting a broad range of social, cultural, and political aspects in the lives of Latin Americans—here I discuss three categories that best summarize both the challenges and opportunities workers in the region have faced. The first is the depth of the region's economic transformation, which has a direct bearing on the capacity of workers to protect some of their hard-won rights. The second relates to the consensus emerging in the 1980s justifying the case for greater labor flexibilization. Third and finally, I consider the critical transformation of South American countries with the onset of the primary export boom in the first decade of the new century, which coincides with the rise to power of a wave of more progressive governments in the region.

The Transnationalization of Latin America

Latin America has become significantly more integrated into the circuits of global financial, commercial, and industrial capital. With respect to financial capital, there has been a growing integration of the region's capital markets with global finance, as well as an entrenchment of financial capital as the key sector in the economy, dictating and modifying the conditions for productive investment (Epstein 2005). Increased public and private debt was also an integral component of reforms in the 1990s. The heavy reliance on external financial resources and the volatility of capital flows produced several financial crises in the region during this period. In contrast, economic growth since early in the new century has facilitated a reduction in the debt burden in many countries. On average, the debt-to-gross-domestic-product (GDP) ratio declined in ten Latin American countries from 59% in 2003 to 32% in 2008 (IMF 2009, 56) and allowed them to weather the global downturn of 2008–9 considerably well. Nonetheless, the power of national and international financial institutions remains a conditioning factor in the quest for development options.

Changes in consumer and retailing patterns have been equally profound. Robinson (2012) notes that big retailers like Walmart, Carrefour, and Costco, along with fast food chains, inundated domestic markets, radically changing the retail sector in many Latin American countries. This retailing revolution introduced new consumer practices that, as elsewhere, have placed a new premium on consumption, even among the poorest sectors of the population. These retail conglomerates were the conduit for the large inflow of consumer imports that began in the 1990s and so negatively affected domestic production and employment. They have also inflicted very heavy losses on small local traders. Nonetheless, space inevitably remains for the informal producers and petty traders who satisfy the consumption needs and appetites of large sectors of the population so impoverished by "market-friendly" reforms that their consumption lies outside of mainstream retailing (Abrahamer Rothstein 2007). For these large segments of the marginalized population, commodities produced and traded within the informal economy provide the only way to meet their basic needs. This informal economy is the site of the most extreme forms of precarity for workers, including non-salaried family members in small workshops, self-employed workers, and informal workers toiling under subhuman conditions in sweatshops across the continent. While the informal economy has been a long-standing feature in the region, it has grown rapidly since the 1980s (ILO 2003, 33; Portes and Hoffman 2003, 50), as is considered in further detail below.[3]

The industrial transformation in the region has not been any less marked. As noted above, one important change was the relocation of industrial production from developed countries to Latin America, which has brought with it an expanding presence of assembly plants. In countries like Mexico, for example, at the end of the 1960s, transnational corporations (TNCs) took advantage of very low wages to assemble manufactured exports produced with mostly imported inputs (Cypher and Delgado Wise 2010; Kopinak 2004; de la O and Quintero 2001). Since the late 1980s, this maquila system has undergone rapid expansion, as the sector became the linchpin of the export-led model Mexico pursued as an alternative to ISI. Growth in the maquila sector reached its peak in the period between 1994 and 2001, seeing a rise in employment of 123% during those years. Even during this period of exponential growth, though, wages remained 52% lower than in non-maquila manufacturing (Cypher and Delgado Wise 2010, 80–82).

Export processing zones (EPZs) have since sprung up in several other countries of the continent as part of TNCs' strategies to consolidate production chains with global reach. One of the central characteristics in the spread of this form of segmented industrial production has been the very concrete power of investors to threaten relocation when confronted with labor strife. It is not surprising, then, that the growth of EPZs has weakened the capacity of workers—most of whom are young women—to organize and gain basic rights. The capacity of global manufacturers to access an international tiered network of contractors and subcontractors has also increased their power to avoid accountability over labor practices. The literature on global value chains and global production networks provides a useful conceptualization of shifts in the organization of production on a global scale, the role of emerging economies in them, and the implication for economic growth and employment in the region (Arnold 2010; Blyde, Volpe Martincus, and Molina 2014; Gereffi 2014).

Within the hemisphere, the growth of EPZs was closely tied to the U.S. market. Thus, with the economic slowdown in the early 2000s and the 2008–9 recession, the performance of the export-oriented assembly sectors in Mexico and Central America was seriously and negatively affected. Their prospects as industrial exporters have been further complicated with the emergence of China as an industrial powerhouse, particularly after it joined the World Trade Organization in 2001. Between 2001 and 2006 alone, Chinese-manufactured commodities for the United States displaced probably as much as 11.4% of Mexican industrial exports to that country (Jenkins 2010, 821), and Mexico's share of world manufacturing exports fell from 3.3% to 2.5% in the same period (Santiso and Dayton-Johnson 2012, 252–53).

These changing patterns of trade reflect the relocation of TNC investment away from Mexico and Central America to China. In Mexico as in other countries in the region, the dismantling of a domestic industry that, until the 1980s, had satisfied a large portion of national demand for consumer goods and provided a large number of protected jobs, has not given rise to development strategies capable of providing either long-term sustained growth or conditions for better-quality employment. This continues to be the case even when the acceleration of growth in the United States after 2013 has been reflected in the strengthening of Mexico's export performance.

Labor Flexibilization

Closely connected to the transnationalization of the region's economies just described, one of the most visible changes neoliberal globalization has brought about is a profound transformation in the relation between capital and labor, which has been for the most part detrimental to workers, as indicated by the rise in informal and precarious jobs (Álvarez 2005; Biles 2009). Indeed, the ILO estimates that 66% of the jobs created in Latin America during the 1990s presented the characteristics of informal employment (ILO 2003). Volatile and weak economic growth during the 1980s and even in the 1990s at least partly explains the increasing lag in employment creation during these decades, a problem that in turn contributed to the surging informal economy. Along with unemployment and informality, between 1982 and 1998 most workers in Latin America also faced declining wages and, with the exception of Chile, deterioration in the participation of wages in total income (Meeks 1999, 155–56). In the most unequal region in the world (Gootenberg 2010, 3; Hoffman and Centeno 2003, 365–66), these changes translated into growing poverty and social polarization (Klasen and Nowak-Lehmann 2008; Robinson 2003, 19).

According to proponents of neoliberal reforms, the way out of the conundrum was to introduce legal and institutional changes to make labor markets more flexible, with the expectation to encourage two main transformations. First, flexibilization would promote greater economic growth, as it would allow for new gains in the competitiveness of local production, again because the costs of labor were a major consideration in globally integrated markets. Therefore, less "rigid" labor practices would promote higher rates of labor absorption, as employers would face lower direct and indirect labor costs.[4] Second, job creation under these more flexible conditions would provide a solution to the incorporation into the formal sector of the large mass of workers within the informal sector and also reduce the high levels of inequality that existed between protected and unprotected workers. The centrality of these issues in the promotion and justification of labor flexibilization is discussed in more detail in chapter 3. The more pervasive unemployment became during the 1990s, then, the greater was the emphasis governments placed on the need to change existing legal provisions to facilitate the establishment of more flexible working conditions.

However, not only did labor flexibilization, either de jure or de facto, fail to provide a solution to the problem of unemployment at the aggregate level but also the high regional levels of informality and precariousness increased further. The cases of Argentina, Chile, and Brazil in this study are evidence of the ineffectiveness of labor flexibilization as a strategy for the promotion of employment. Moreover, nowhere in the region or among our case studies did the flexibilization of labor relations reduce the levels of informality. The phenomenon is not new or unique to the region. As Thomas (1996) noted, increasing labor flexibility induced transformations in the labor market that resulted in greater pressure toward informality. This pressure was exerted either top-down (i.e., the institutionalization of new forms of work such as subcontracting and temporary contracts) or bottom-up (i.e., the heightened competition created among workers as unemployment grows and the ranks of those informally occupied increase).

Just as flexibilization may lead to informality through distinct types of pressures, flexibility itself may take different forms. Drawing on Cook (2007) and Munck (2004), we identify two key forms of flexibilization. First, there is functional flexibility, which involves the power of employers to change work organization within the firm to adapt to technological innovation; this kind of flexibilization is aimed at overcoming the impediments to assigning workers to different tasks within the firm. Employers also seek greater flexibility in the deployment of their labor force by acquiring new capacities to change the length of the work day and week, to schedule shifts without regard to workers' needs or demands, and to reduce overtime rates. Second, there is external numerical flexibility, which seeks to make it easier for employers to hire and fire workers, particularly through the extension of atypical labor contracts (temporary or fixed-term) and eliminating or reducing severance payments.

Most forms of flexibilization aim ultimately at facilitating a reduction in the price of labor since they tend to exercise a downward pressure on both wage and nonwage costs. Some of these changes can be imposed via labor legislation reform and reducing employers' contributions to payroll taxes and social security. Individual employers also have the power to reduce labor costs directly, as firms can impose wage restrictions through plant-level collective agreements, even against the government's formal minimum wage regulations and rates of indexation. Moreover, inflation can be an effective informal means of reducing the real cost of wages, as was the case in most countries in the region during the 1980s.

Employers and IFIs pushed for formal changes to existing labor legislation to ensure that more flexible labor relations could not be readily overturned. As our case studies show, however, this was not always easily achieved, or at least not without heavy political costs. Labor code reforms were thus avoided in some cases for a very long time, as in Mexico, or were implemented only to be reversed when political conditions demanded it, as was the case in Argentina. The severe reforms introduced in Chile under the Pinochet dictatorship, in contrast, remained largely unaffected by the democratization of the country.

On the whole, changes in labor legislation were aimed at modifying the legal framework that regulated either individual employment conditions (i.e., contracts, working conditions, and salary levels) or collective labor rights (the right to organize, bargain collectively, and strike). These changes to employment legislation explain the rising "precarity" of employment, as workers increasingly confront the problem of jobs that "incorporate job insecurity, very low pay and lack of access to social security coverage, union representation or other legal benefits like holidays and family allowance" (Felder and Patroni 2016). The weakening of collective rights was an important objective of labor reform for at least two reasons. One was that ideologically, unions were seen as presenting a concrete obstacle for the more fluid adaptation of labor markets to changing economic conditions and demands. The other was the more practical necessity of reducing the capacity of labor unions to respond to the new challenges posed by neoliberalism to the greatest extent possible.

The case studies are diverse in terms of the reforms implemented in these two spheres of labor legislation. For example, while individual rights have been strengthened in Chile and collective labor rights remain very weak, the opposite is the case in Argentina and Brazil. In general, as the case studies also show, challenging and transforming union power were taxing undertakings. Murillo and Schrank (2005, 974) argue that even while individual labor legislation was transformed in some countries to accommodate employers' demands for flexibility, the same cannot be said of collective labor legislation. On the contrary, according to these authors, by and large, neoliberal governments in Latin America advanced union-friendly labor reforms. What is paradoxical in their view is that reforms were consolidated at a time when pressure to reduce labor costs—through more flexible working conditions or reductions in wages—was very high. However, as Cook (2007, 39) correctly observes, collective legislation is inevitably undermined when individual employment standards deteriorate. Moreover, while the separation between collective and individual rights is a very useful distinction for the purpose of analytical clarity, they cannot be treated in isolation from one another. A failure to characterize the multiple ways in which one set of rights might affect the other runs the risk of limiting one's understanding of the scope and significance of labor legislation transformations. Equally important, the actual exercise of rights granted through legislation cannot be assumed to be exclusively the consequence of the existence of the law itself. Law enforcement (the case of labor inspection) is also clearly a factor, as are labor market conditions that hinder the exercise of rights (de facto flexibilization).

These two factors are central in Anner's (2008) study of labor law reform in Latin America. As he notes, it is certainly fundamental to dispute the notion that labor legislation reform proceeded unchallenged during the 1990s. Nonetheless, one must also recognize that regardless of how effectively labor movements limited the scope of labor reform, unions in the region have become weaker over the period of market-oriented restructuring (33–34). According to Anner, two main factors account for this: one is the incapacity of "union-friendly" labor legislation to offset the negative impact of market-oriented structural reforms, and the other is connected to the weak mechanisms that exist in most countries of the region to enforce existing legislation (ibid.).

Preserving labor legislation that protected individual or collective rights did not prevent the flexibilization of labor relations, as the case of Mexico shows most clearly. Indeed, one of the central conclusions cutting across all of the case studies we examine is precisely that the impact of labor reform for workers in general, and their organizations in particular, cannot be measured only in terms of the extent to which the letter of the law was modified. Flexibilization was achieved through changes imposed in various spheres and through various means. Firms imposed flexibilization through the negotiation of collective agreements at the plant level, for example, as was the case in Mexico and Argentina. Moreover, the economic consequences of structural adjustment and neoliberal policies—in particular poor rates of employment generation, rising unemployment, and, given the lack of a significant safety net, the parallel growth of the informal economy—were central to employers' capacity to impose extensive de facto flexibilization. Bleak job prospects motivated workers to accept unregistered jobs not only in the informal sector but also in the formal economy, while the same conditions fostered a climate of weak legal enforcement and noncompliance with existing legislation (Cook 2007, 45).

Informality in Latin America, then, is not limited to low-productivity activities but rather traverses the entire economy. The notion of "informal employment" was incorporated into labor statistics and studies precisely to denote the existence not only of workers within the informal sector—waged, self-employed, or nonwaged family members—but also unregistered salaried workers in formal firms. Unregistered workers cannot benefit from the legal protection extended by existing labor legislation or obtain access to social security (Felder and Patroni 2016). Informal employment represents an extreme form of flexibilization, and it adds to the uncertainty workers face in labor markets where other precarious forms of labor are widespread.

The net result of the changes neoliberalism introduced was the inability of the economy to reincorporate those who had been displaced from their jobs in the public sector or in the industries undermined by imports into the formal labor market. Informal activities offered these workers some refuge from the burden of unemployment, and by the end of the 1990s, informal employment as a proportion of total urban employment was close to 47% for the region as a whole. In several countries, such as Brazil and Venezuela among the case studies, the informal sector accounted for over half of the employment in the EAP (ILO 2005, 11). Women were particularly affected by this transformation of working conditions in Latin America, as their participation in an increasingly less favorable labor market more than tripled between 1960 and 1990, climbing from 18 to 57 million (Munck 2004, 9), with an especially large concentration in the service sector (ILO 2012). In short, far from addressing the challenges of already large informal sectors, market reforms and labor flexibilization compounded the problem, strengthening the structural conditions that have historically fostered economic polarization in Latin American countries (Reygadas 2010, 38–39).

The drop in formal employment and the growing diversity of working experiences for Latin Americans created a radically different situation for unions. To fully grasp the significance of this change, the book's case studies consider the shifting political realities faced by organized labor, from the market reforms of the 1980s and 1990s to the new challenges of post-neoliberal governments. Labor's weakened structural position clearly affected its organizational capacities. At the same time, though, the political trajectory of the labor movements in several countries of the region also hindered labor's ability to respond to the detrimental consequences of these political changes. Either because of their links to the parties that imposed the reforms or because of the heavy losses suffered during the extremely repressive regimes in the 1970s and 1980s—or a combination of both—it became increasingly difficult for labor to retain the political prominence it had once enjoyed. The contemporary trajectories of the labor movements in Chile, Mexico, Venezuela, and Argentina are good cases in point.

Post-Neoliberal South America

By the end of the 1990s several countries in the region confronted severe economic and social crises that soon translated into extensive political turbulence. As our case studies address in more detail, by this time, the merits of neoliberalism came to be questioned by large segments of the population. Their discontent provided the basis for a substantial political shift toward governments whose immediate preoccupation was to address the several problems neoliberalism had precipitated. Many of the policies that governments conceived of as alternatives were influenced by a critique articulated by the Economic Commission for Latin America and the Caribbean (ECLAC).

In contrast to the neoliberal policies governments had followed, ECLAC suggested the region could only overcome the challenges it confronted by seeking new, more progressive and equity sustaining alternatives of insertion into world markets. The postulate was in tension both with neoliberal economic objectives and with the understanding that ECLAC structuralism had advanced previously. The term "neo-structuralism" came to represent the new theoretical and policy approach developed by the institution. In very schematic form, neo-structuralism as a development option was articulated around three fundamental principles: economic growth, social equity, and political democracy. To foster them, Latin America needed to find new forms of insertion into the world economy that took full advantage of the opportunities it had to offer (Leiva 2008, xvii). The proposition was certainly attractive for the rising wave of the so-called pink tide in the region that sought pragmatic ways of addressing the broad and pressing need to increase economic growth and reduce poverty.[5]

Finding new and economically progressive opportunities in global markets implied fundamentally moving away from the heavy reliance on cheap labor or the export of primary resources, the historical cornerstones of the region's comparative advantage. To achieve this fundamental transformation governments were called to create the conditions for what could be conceptualized as dynamic comparative advantage or "systemic competitiveness." The essential tasks of the state involved facilitating technological change, investing in human capital, and creating the institutional setting to ensure that economic growth could fuel greater social equity. Labor flexibilization was not in tension with neo-structuralist principles, but the understanding was that overcoming rigidities in labor markets involved substantial investment in training and in creating a highly skilled labor force capable of adapting to the constant changing demands of highly competitive international markets (Leiva 2006, 344).

Notwithstanding the commitment countries expressed to seek more dynamic forms of insertion into the global market, and the appeal of ECLAC's premise that such a transformation held the secret to greater economic stability, wellbeing, and social cohesion, in practice the policy recommendations were not equally influential among countries of the region. In practice also, very little has changed in the new century when it comes to new forms of insertion into international markets. For Mexico, as was also the case for Central American countries, the search for expanded forms of insertion into the world economy focused on their cheap labor—made even cheaper by the transformation of labor markets since the 1980s.

Countries in South America saw their opportunity in the international commodities boom that began in the 1990s. Growing demand in rapidly industrializing Asian countries, particularly the very large Indian and Chinese economies, accounts for the rapid expansion of extractive industries and their growing centrality in the economic strategies of the South American countries studied in this book. The relevance of primary exports is certainly not new in any of them. In Venezuela and Chile, for example, petroleum and mining, respectively, have been fundamental since early in the twentieth century, as have agricultural exports in the cases of Brazil and Argentina. However, late in the last century, the substantial expansion of the primary producing sectors took on a new dimension, partly as a result of the now thoroughly transformed economic structures.

The most telling aspect of the primary export boom in the case studies, though, is the relevance of this economic strategy for pink-tide governments in the region—a reality at odds with strategies progressive forces in the region had usually advanced. While these governments sought alternatives to veer their countries away from the neoliberal policies they had followed, the growing reliance on primary exports remained a constant. This development pattern has come to be known as "neo-extractivism," a term denoting the centrality of primary extraction—petroleum, mining, and intensive monoculture—as an economic and export activity upon which countries have become overly dependent as both the engine of economic growth and a source of funding for redistributive social programs (Gudynas 2010).

Extractive industries—and increasingly among them, mining—started to develop at a very fast pace in the 1990s. While investment in mining exploration increased by 90% worldwide between 1990 and 1997, over the same period in Latin America it grew by 400% (Svampa and Antonelli 2009, 15). However, as has happened so many times in the past, periods of boom in the demand for primary commodities are followed inevitably by bust. And, unfortunately, it is no different this time, as changes in international markets for petroleum and the slowing of the Chinese economy have triggered new economic difficulties in the region. Moreover, the tendency in trade with China has been toward an increasing share of unprocessed primary products (Jenkins 2010, 814–15). In the case of Argentina, for example, while the export of unprocessed soybeans has increased, there has been a parallel decline in the export of soybean products, as the Chinese government seeks to develop its own oilseed industry (Jenkins 2010, 823).[6] Thus, not only are extractive industries traditionally poor generators of employment but also their capacity for creating employment has recently begun to decline even further.

Certainly, the primary export boom provided new fiscal opportunities to several regional governments attempting to steer their economies away from neoliberalism, and in this capacity, extractive activities are central to understanding the political and economic capabilities of leftist governments in the book's study samples. First, the performance of the extractive sector was central to the very high rates of economic growth achieved by many countries in the region until at least 2012. In contrast with countries whose exports relied heavily on sustained demand from the North American market—as is the case with manufactured exports from Mexico, Central America, and some Caribbean countries—resource-rich South America withstood the financial crisis of 2008–9 with considerably less pain. Yet while primary resource exporters recovered very quickly from the economic downturn, they have nonetheless been unable to escape the difficulties that would subsequently emerge, in particular the drop in the price of oil and the declining demand for other key exports from the region.

Second, the expansion of extractive activities and the high rate of economic growth it brought about provided these governments with a historical opportunity to address the social deficit created by neoliberalism. It is precisely this inclination of leftist governments to allocate some of the revenue accruing from primary exports to social programs that differentiate recent extractivist programs in the region from traditional forms of extractivism. Nonetheless, critics identify the persistent reliance on extractive activities not only as a key area of continuity with the previous neoliberal decade but also as one of the most discouraging weaknesses of the new left in Latin America (Acosta 2013; Gudynas 2012).[7] As has happened in the past, extractive industries have not provided the stimulus to further the kind of economic diversification that might provide more sustainable and reliable opportunities for growth. Changes in international markets for primary commodities leave countries in the region, and several of the countries analyzed in this book, once again with very little means at their disposal to compensate for this vulnerability.

Finally, as the cases of Argentina, Brazil, and to some extent, Chile show, following the losses suffered by workers throughout the 1990s, more progressive governments in Latin America have brought about some positive changes. However, while economic growth in the new millennium translated into less unemployment and better wages, reversing the labor market transformations analyzed in the following chapters will take considerably more effort, especially because it will require the reconstitution of labor's power to struggle for crucial reforms. During the critical years between the end of the twentieth century and the beginning of the second decade of the twenty-first, post-neoliberal regimes appeared to hold promise for addressing some of the most pressing demands of large sectors of the population affected by the neoliberal legacy.[8] This window may have now closed as countries face both substantial economic challenges and uncertain political change.

As the following chapters illustrate, one of the most critical manifestations of the economic resources the export boom generated for countries in the pink tide was the growing distance between the parties in power and the labor movement. As the book shows, the move beyond neoliberalism was an expression of a growing capacity for state autonomy. That is, the growing distance between post-neoliberal governments and labor movements is a reflection of the desire of national governments in countries like Venezuela, and to some extent Argentina and Brazil, to consolidate and legitimize their power by mobilizing support from new allies outside of organized labor, particularly sectors within the informal economy and other groups marginalized by the transformations of the 1980s and 1990s. These sectors lie beyond the grasp of traditional unions and most political forces. Unlike traditional populism, then, government policy in the new century has been directed at building support among these segments of the population, particularly through the implementation of a number of social policy initiatives (Mazzuca 2013). Yet, as the country studies show, the vulnerability of the labor movement to such strategies can only be fully explained in the context of political transformations dating back at least to the 1990s.

3

Labor Market Flexibility, Employment, and Inequality

Lessons from Chile

PAUL W. POSNER

Labor reform in Latin America has taken on increased urgency in recent years as democratic governments struggle to contain perennial economic and social problems exacerbated by structural adjustment and global market fluctuations. Yet, while there is widespread agreement on the need for labor reform in Latin America, there is no consensus regarding the type of reform necessary. Policy options fall into two broad categories: those designed to promote labor market flexibility and those intended to strengthen labor standards and the bargaining leverage of workers. The proponents of labor market flexibility assert that Latin American labor markets are plagued by rigidity, which impedes economic expansion and job growth. Accordingly, as Sabatini and Farnsworth suggest, "the keystone of reform has to be the updating of outmoded labor codes, especially insofar as these make the cost of dismissing workers unreasonably and destructively high. Unreformed, these laws will continue to act as a deadly drag on new hiring, investment, economic expansion and prosperity" (2006, 62). Other analysts argue that heightened flexibility, produced through liberalized labor codes, exacerbates inequality among workers and has little, if any, positive impact on job creation (Behrman, Birdsall, and Székely 2007; Portes and Hoffman 2003; Marshall 2004; Standing 1999; Vega Ruíz 2005). From this perspective, the appropriate remedy to precarious employment and inequality in the region is the establishment of institutional reforms that strengthen labor's bargaining power relative to capital.

The Chilean case provides a valuable opportunity to assess the merits of these competing perspectives. Chile's macroeconomic and political stability since its 1990 democratic transition are the envy of many of its Latin American neighbors. Moreover, labor reforms adopted during the Augusto Pinochet dictatorship and largely maintained since the democratic transition are consistent with the flexible labor policies advocated by IFIs such as the IMF, World Bank, and Inter-American Development Bank. As a result, one should expect over time increased formal sector employment, particularly among the least skilled Chilean workers. In other words, labor market flexibility should promote economic efficiency, which in turn should stimulate the expansion of formal sector employment and the reduction of wage inequality.[1] In fact, however, the rate of unemployment among least-skilled workers in Chile remains essentially unchanged since the democratic transition, and income inequality has abated only marginally, if at all. These conditions persist despite a high degree of labor market flexibility. Thus, in essence, labor flexibility in Chile has perpetuated, if not exacerbated, the very conditions its proponents have argued it would ameliorate.

Consequently, Chile's continued adherence to a flexibilized labor market should be understood not in terms of its capacity to reduce inequality or generate employment. Rather, it should be understood as the product of several interrelated factors: (1) the business sector's ability to protect its interests through the leverage it accrued with policymakers over the course of the dictatorship; (2) the center-left Concertación's conscious limitation of threats to the business sector's interests in order to maintain political and economic stability; and (3) the weakness of organized labor, resulting from the perpetuation of the Pinochet-era labor regime and its own failure to adapt to Chile's profoundly altered labor conditions.

To substantiate the preceding argument the analysis is structured as follows. The chapter provides a brief critique of the literature on labor flexibility substantiated by an empirical assessment of the impact of labor flexibility in Chile. Subsequently, it presents a historical overview of business-state relations in Chile during the military regime. The analysis then evaluates labor reform under the post-transition governments of presidents Patricio Aylwin, Eduardo Frei, Ricardo Lagos, and Michelle Bachelet, respectively. The chapter concludes by assessing labor reforms and conditions in the post-transition period. From this assessment a general lesson from the Chilean case is drawn, which we extend to the analysis of other cases in this volume, namely that flexibilization is best understood, not as a means of reducing informality or inequality, but instead as a means of subverting the organizational strength of workers and thereby enhancing the institutional power and economic advantages of employers.

Labor Flexibility in Theory and Practice

The debate over labor flexibility is rooted in the larger debate concerning the benefits and detriments of structural reform. Since the mid-1980s, advocates of structural reform, including IFIs such as the World Bank, IMF, and Inter-American Development Bank (IADB) and market reformers within individual Latin American countries, have asserted that the full benefits of market liberalization cannot be achieved without a commensurate flexibilization of labor markets (IADB 1997, 60). Proponents of labor market flexibilization argue that "rigid" labor legislation inhibits job creation, promotes the substitution of capital for labor, increases informal sector employment, and exacerbates inequality between protected and unprotected segments of the labor force. They assert that minimum wage and job security provisions are inefficient because they keep wages artificially high by distorting market forces. The costs involved with hiring—high wages and benefits along with high dismissal costs (e.g., mandatory severance payments based on length of service)—drive up labor costs to employers, thereby reducing formal sector labor demands and increasing income disparities between formal and informal sector workers. Therefore, the solution to generating more formal sector employment is to reduce wage and dismissal costs by establishing flexible labor institutions (Cox Edwards 2007; Heckman and Pagés 2004; Maloney and Nuñez 2004; Sabatini and Farnsworth 2006). Such institutions would lower the costs involved in hiring and firing by, for example, allowing employers to hire workers through temporary labor contracts and to dismiss them in response to declining market conditions.

Critics of these polices have assailed labor flexibility on a number of grounds. They note, first and foremost, that the evidence linking labor flexibility to reduced unemployment is weak or contradictory. Cook observes, for example, that Argentina, Brazil, and Spain all experienced high, if not increased, rates of unemployment subsequent to adopting flexible policies for labor contracting and dismissal (2007, 36). Other analysts assert that decentralization of production and weakened labor protections negatively affect wage dispersion and formal sector employment. For example, Harrison argues that decentralization of large firms through subcontracting has not reduced these firms' power but rather has led to greater labor market segmentation as low-wage, insecure employment has proliferated in the smaller firms (1997, 210, 213). Similarly, Katz and Darbishire, in their comparative study of labor conditions in seven developed countries, emphasize the role of national institutional structures such as labor codes and rules governing unionization in shaping employment patterns and outcomes (2000, 264, 280). Accordingly, they note that institutional arrangements that weaken unions also tend to exacerbate wage inequality (4, 283). Other analysts, focused on labor conditions in developing countries, observe a relationship between increased labor flexibility and higher levels of informality. In this regard, intensified market pressures originating from increased labor flexibility result in what Thomas (1996) has referred to as "top-down" and "bottom-up" informalization. In top-down informalization, the state and capital impose flexibility on workers through promotion of subcontracting and short-term contracts. In bottom-up informality, workers expelled from or unable to find work in the formal sector are compelled to find work or generate self-employment in the informal sector (Thomas 1996, 99). From this perspective, critics suggest that labor flexibility policies increase job insecurity without increasing formal sector employment or reducing inequality.

Chile offers a valuable case by which to assess the relative merits of these competing perspectives on labor flexibility for two reasons. First, the labor reforms enacted by the military regime under General Augusto Pinochet (1973–90) created a highly flexible labor market. Second, these labor reforms were largely preserved after the 1990 democratic transition. Before the military takeover, the legislation regulating employment security, the so-called job security law, stipulated that workers could not be fired without just cause. With the implementation of Decree Law 2,200 in 1978, the military regime undermined this guiding principle in Chilean labor relations. The military regime's law allowed employers to modify work contracts unilaterally on such things as the duration of employment, conditions of dismissal, and level of remuneration (Ruiz-Tagle 1989, 81). The military regime's labor code further strengthened the employers' hand by allowing them to lock out workers and hire replacement workers during strike action (Decree Law 2,758). Moreover, the law circumscribed the legal length of strikes to sixty days, after which time workers had to return to work or face dismissal (Haagh 2002a, 39–40; Martínez and Díaz 1996, 60).

The objective of these reforms was to make the utilization of labor more flexible in relation to the employers' economic interests (Cárdenas 2005, 6). To facilitate the achievement of this objective, employers developed new modes of contracting workers. These included permanent (indefinite) and impermanent (definite) contraction, with the latter being divided into a number of different types of temporary contracts, for example, seasonal contracts, or contracts for specific jobs or services (5). To reinforce the impact of these new forms of contraction, the military regime's labor code prohibited collective bargaining by temporary workers. The relevant provision of the Labor Code, Article 305, states that "workers subject to apprenticeship contracts or those that are contracted exclusively for the performance of a determinant job or transitory or temporary task" are prohibited from negotiating collectively (Tapia Guerrero and Domínguez Soto 2011, 140; my translation). In addition to being prohibited from engaging in collective bargaining, temporary employees are not entitled to severance payments when they are terminated and employers are not obligated to pay social security taxes to insure them against injury. As a result, employers have had strong incentives to maintain or expand their reliance on temporary workers.[2]

The Pinochet regime further weakened the relative position of labor by creating *grupos negociadores* (bargaining groups) to compete with, and to thereby undermine the power of, unions. These were groups of any number of workers that assembled for the purpose of bargaining and dissolved once a labor agreement was signed. Unlike unions, bargaining groups had no legal right to information. Moreover, these groups would typically sign a convention rather than a contract, the distinction being that conventions did not grant them the right to strike or other minimal rights normally entailed in collective bargaining. Worker use of bargaining groups

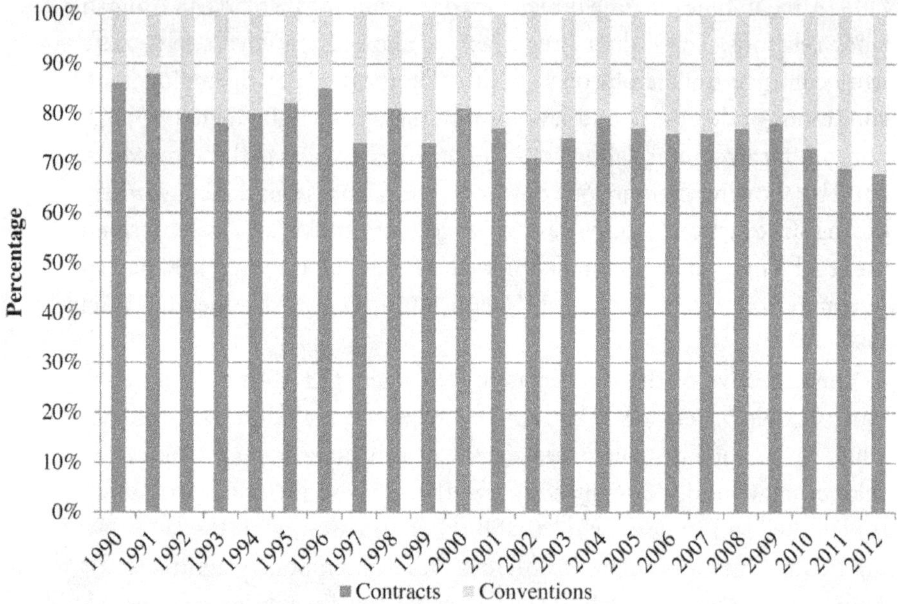

Figure 3.1. Annual Proportional Distribution of Collective Bargaining Instruments Negotiated by Unions. Source: Dirección del Trabajo 2013, 191.

and conventions increased significantly throughout the 1990s (Haagh 2002b, 103) and has remained high since 2000, resulting in a relative decline in the strength of unions. (Figure 3.1 illustrates unions' proportional increase in use of conventions relative to contracts from 1990 to 2012.)

The precipitous decline in unionization among Chilean workers, from a pre-coup rate of 35% to approximately 10% throughout the 1980s, epitomized the detrimental impact such reforms had on the labor movement (Roberts 2002, 15, 22; see table 3.1 for unionization rates 1970–2012). Such reforms had a similar impact on labor flexibility. In this regard, Levinsohn's research on Chile's economic liberalization (1979–85) notes the high rate of job creation and destruction during this period. With about a quarter of all workers changing jobs in every year of this period except 1985, Levinsohn observes that "If one associates Japan with the notion of lifetime employment, Chile during liberalization is at the other end of the spectrum" (1999, 342).

Given that the features of the military regime's labor reforms described above remained intact until the implementation of the most recent labor reforms in April 2017, one should expect that Chile's labor regime remains

Table 3.1. Rates of Unionization and Average Union Size, 1970–2012

Year	Unions	Active Unions	Population Affiliated w/ Unions	Total Employed Labor Force	Rate of Unionization	Average Union Size
1970	4,758	**	628,396	2,719,900	23.1	132
1971	5,401	**	789,621	2,808,200	28.1	146
1972	6,326	**	883,188	2,836,000	31.1	140
1973	6,692	**	939,319	2,784,300	33.7	140
1980	4,597	**	386,910	3,331,000	11.6	84
1981	3,977	**	395,951	3,453,100	11.4	100
1982	4,048	**	347,470	3,124,000	11.1	86
1983	4,401	**	320,903	3,284,500	9.8	73
1984	4,714	**	343,329	3,433,400	10.0	73
1985	4,994	**	360,963	3,671,300	9.8	72
1986	5,391	**	386,987	3,862,850	10.0	72
1987	5,883	**	422,302	4,001,290	10.6	72
1988	6,446	**	446,194	4,285,440	10.4	69
1989	7,118	**	507,616	4,463,420	11.4	71
1990	8,861	**	606,812	4,525,530	13.4	68
1991	9,858	7,707	701,355	4,630,670	15.1	71
1992	10,756	8,323	724,065	4,877,430	14.8	67
1993	11,389	7,974	684,361	5,109,290	13.4	60
1994	12,109	7,891	661,966	5,122,760	12.9	55
1995	12,715	7,505	637,570	5,174,410	12.3	50
1996	13,258	7,476 (est.)	655,597	5,298,680	12.4	49
1997	13,795	7,446	617,761	5,380,190	11.5	45
1998	14,276	7,439	611,535	5,432,350	11.3	43
1999	14,652	7,057	579,996	5,404,480	10.7	40
2000	14,724	7,659	595,495	5,381,460	11.1	40
2001	15,192	7,410	599,610	5,479,390	10.9	39
2002	16,310	8,149	618,930	5,531,260	11.2	38
2003	16,987	8,967	669,507	5,675,130	11.8	39
2004	18,047	9,414	680,351	5,862,900	11.6	38
2005	**	9,148	676,368	5,904,999	11.5	**
2006	**	9,424	703,706	6,410,982	11.0	**
2007	**	9,365	724,606	6,567,241	11.0	**
2008	**	9,340	801,251	6,740,408	11.9	**
2009	**	9,776	837,055	6,710,990	12.5	**
2010	**	9,871	858,571	7,353,835	11.7	**
2011	**	10,310	892,365	7,564,346	11.8	**
2012	31,294	10,585	940,603	7,699,431	12.2	30

Sources: For 1954–68 data: Valenzuela 1978, 28, 31, and Stallings 1978, 246. For 1970–85 data: Cortázar 1997, 240. For 1986–2012 data: Dirección del Trabajo 2013.

** Data not available.

highly flexible. A wealth of empirical evidence supports this conclusion. For example, Berg and Contreras (2002) identify a wage curve—a negative relationship between unemployment and pay—in Santiago between 1974 and 1996, which is indicative of labor market flexibility. They identify a wage curve of -.08 during the period in question, meaning that a twofold increase in unemployment leads to an 8% decline in wages (Berg and Contreras 2002, 13). In short, since Chile's economic liberalization, unemployment has had a negative and significant effect on workers' wages, an effect that did not exist under ISI (10–11). Thus, Berg and Contreras conjecture that under Chile's economic liberalization more flexible labor laws, especially those related to worker dismissal, intensified workers' fears of job loss and thus made them more willing to accept lower wages. In contrast, under state-led development, the political-economic system provided Chilean workers much greater protections, enabling them to better resist wage reductions. Noting that Chile's wage curve under a liberalized economy is comparable to findings in the United States, the United Kingdom, Australia, and Germany, the authors conclude that Chile's labor market is as flexible as that of other Western, capitalist economies (13).

Research conducted under the auspices of the Bank of Chile reaches a similar conclusion. The authors of the bank study assess the flexibility of the Chilean labor market between 1986 and 2002 by measuring how quickly after a macroeconomic shock the unemployment rate returns to its natural rate (i.e., the prevailing rate before the shock) (Albagli I., García S., and Restrepo L. 2004, 29). The more quickly the unemployment rate returns to its natural rate, the more flexible the labor market. Despite the adoption of labor reforms in the 1990s—which increased severance costs, sanctions for unjustified termination of labor contracts, the minimum wage, and the capacities of unions in collective bargaining and strikes—the authors' analysis indicates that among a comparison group of eighteen countries, including the Organization for Economic Cooperation and Development (OECD) and emergent economies, Chile's labor market demonstrated itself to be among the most flexible. Indeed, among this comparison group, only labor markets in South Korea and Hong Kong proved to be more flexible, with the United States and Mexico following Chile (31). Thus, the authors conclude that, in spite of reforms that could have introduced labor market rigidities, Chile's labor market is relatively flexible in the international context (45).

Recent research and data published by the Chilean government reinforce the finding that Chilean labor markets are highly flexible. For example, under the auspices of the Labor Bureau, Echeverría and López observe that Chilean enterprises employ a full range of flexible labor practices, "producing a degree of labor flexibility that is considerable" (2004, 150; my translation).[3] In drawing this conclusion, Echeverría and López distinguish between external and internal flexibility. External flexibility refers to the capacity of firms to hire and fire workers in response to their changing personnel needs; internal flexibility refers to the freedom firms exercise over the use of their employees in the production process. The authors note that Chilean firms utilize these two forms of flexibility in complementary fashion. For example, internal flexibility allows firms to take full advantage of workers hired on short-term contracts (external flexibility) through the promotion of longer workdays, shift, and weekend work (39% of firms utilize shifts; 25% regularly operate on Sundays) (150). Moreover, workers continue to be subject to significant wage dispersion, with most workers at the medium-low range of the pay scale (Dirección del Trabajo 2011, 385). Finally, it should be emphasized that workers with indefinite (i.e., permanent) work contracts do not necessarily experience greater job security than workers with contracts of limited duration. Of all indefinite contracts, 20% are less than one year old, while 44.6% are less than three years old, indicating significant employment turnover among workers with permanent contracts (384).

Given these flexible features of Chile's labor market regime, one should see over time, as advocates of labor market flexibility have argued, a greater absorption of lesser-skilled workers into the labor force and a reduction in income inequality. Empirical evidence, however, does not support these expectations. Rather, as table 3.2 illustrates, government data tracing the evolution of Chile's income distribution from 1990 to 2013 indicate high and persistent disparities over time.[4] While these data suggest that there has been some modest reduction in income inequality over time, a number of caveats are in order. First, this modest reduction is largely, if not wholly, explained by the provision of monetary subsidies by the state rather than an improvement in real wages for low-income workers. Note, for example, that without the addition of government subsidies, the top 10% of wage earners in 1990 earned 30.5 times more than the bottom 10% while in 2013 the top 10% earned 35.4 times more than

Table 3.2. Distribution of Income, 1990–2013

Year	1990	1992	1994	1996	1998	2000	2003	2006	2009	2011	2013
10/10[a]	30.5	28.1	30.9	33.0	34.7	34.2	34.4	31.3	46.0	39.9	35.4
10/40	3.5	3.3	3.4	3.5	3.5	3.5	3.4	3.0	3.4	3.1	3.0
20/20	14.0	13.2	14.0	14.8	15.6	14.5	14.5	31.1	15.7	14.2	13.7
Gini	0.57	0.56	0.57	0.57	0.58	0.58	0.57	0.53	0.54	0.54	0.53
Income with Government Subsidies and Transfers											
10/10	27.1	25.2	27.7	28.7	28.4	29.5	27.3	23.9	25.9	24.3	21.7
10/40	3.3	3.2	3.3	3.4	3.3	3.3	3.2	2.8	2.9	2.8	2.6
20/20	13.0	12.3	13.1	13.6	13.9	13.3	12.8	11.5	11.9	11.3	10.7
Gini	0.56	0.56	0.55	0.56	0.57	0.58	0.56	0.53	0.53	0.53	0.52

Sources: Ministerio de Desarrollo Social 2011, 2013.

[a] These figures indicate income ratios of wealthier segments of Chilean society proportionate to poorer segments. Thus 10/10 indicates the income ratio of the wealthiest 10% of Chilean society to the poorest 10%, 10/40 indicates the ratio of the top 10% to the bottom 40% and so forth.

the bottom 10% (Ministerio de Desarrollo Social 2013). Thus, as Gammage, Alburquerque, and Durán (2014) observe, while poverty fell consistently in Chile from the early 1990s through the late 2000s, income inequality increased. Moreover, reductions in poverty and inequality have been achieved through targeted social spending, taxes, and transfers, not through redistribution secured in the labor market.

Second, while government figures suggest a modest improvement in the Gini index in recent years, these figures are skewed due to the high rate of tax evasion on the part of Chile's wealthiest citizens. Factoring in these evasion rates raises the relative share of Chile's top 1% in national income substantially, from 15.1% to 21.1%, reflecting an underestimation in government figures of nearly 40%.[5] Similarly, using these revised income calculations to determine the Gini index raises the average for 2004–10 from 0.55 to 0.58 (López, Figueroa B., and Gutiérrez C. 2013, 13–14). If revised capital gains figures for Chile's top 1% are utilized to calculate the Gini index, one sees a substantial increase over the government-calculated average for 2004–10, from 0.55 to 0.63 (25, 28).[6] This revised Gini coefficient indicates a much higher concentration of income in Chile than previous calculations suggested. Moreover, in comparative international terms the relative shares of national income for Chile's wealthiest 1.0% (30%), 0.1% (17%), and 0.01% (10%) are the highest known based on available data (28).

Chile's extreme level of income inequality is further reflected in the high and growing disparity of real wages among different levels of workers. Between 1986 and 2005, the real wages of managers grew 1.5% above average real wages, 2.1% above skilled workers' wages, and 1.5% above unskilled workers' wages. A similar pattern of wage increases for professionals vis-à-vis skilled and unskilled workers occurred between 1990 and 2005 (Solimano 2007, 16–17). Though economic growth was relatively high during this period, averaging 5.6% between 1990 and 2005, the average rate of employment growth was 1.8% while real wage growth averaged 3.0%, with above average increases going to managers and professionals and at and below average increases going to unskilled and skilled workers respectively. Thus, rapid economic growth during this period led to modest increases in employment growth and unequal wage increases that favored the more privileged employment categories of managers and professionals over skilled and unskilled workers.

Finally, it is important to emphasize that contrary to the predictions of labor flexibility's proponents, Chile's high degree of labor market flexibility has not led to increased levels of employment, particularly for Chile's poorest citizens, those in the first two deciles of income. The failure of the Chilean economy to significantly lower its unemployment rate is striking given the high rate of economic growth Chile has experienced over more than two decades. Between 1990 and 2013 Chile's growth rate averaged 5.3%, while its per capita GDP increased nearly fivefold, from $4,388 to $21,911 (World Bank 2014). During this same period, however, unemployment averaged 8.3%. Though Chile's 2009 unemployment rate of 9.7% during the height of the global financial crisis steadily declined to 5.9% in 2013, the rate of unemployment for the poorest Chileans remained high and relatively constant between 1990 and 2011 (the latest year for which comparable data are available).[7]

As table 3.3 indicates, the 2011 rate of unemployment for Chile's lowest decile of income, 28.6%, was only marginally better than the 1990 rate of 31% and the average first decile unemployment rate during this period of 29.9%. Moreover, the unemployment rate for the second decile from 1990 to 2011 showed an upward trajectory, averaging 17.9% from 2000 to 2011, compared with an average of 13.2% between 1990 and 1998. These figures reflect the fact that firms perceive the creation of employment as a threat to their survival and profitability, which motivates them to more fully exploit existing workers rather than hire new ones. Thus, contrary

Table 3.3. Unemployment Rate by Decile of Family Income, 1990–2011

Year	I	II	III	IV	V	VI	VII	VIII	IX	X	Total
1990	31.0	14.4	11.9	11.3	6.8	5.6	4.6	3.4	2.9	1.9	8.3
1992	20.3	10.3	7.7	6.6	4.9	4.2	3.2	2.8	2.2	1.1	5.6
1994	24.2	12.3	9.2	7.6	6.0	5.1	4.0	3.0	2.4	1.8	6.7
1996	21.8	10.7	7.7	6.4	5.9	3.7	3.1	2.5	2.1	0.9	5.7
1998	38.4	18.4	13.6	8.8	9.1	6.3	5.4	4.8	3.2	2.3	9.9
2000	34.1	18.6	14.0	11.0	9.2	7.0	6.4	4.4	3.7	1.7	10.4
2003	34.7	18.8	13.9	10.6	8.6	6.7	5.2	4.5	3.2	2.3	9.7
2006	26.6	14.7	10.1	7.3	6.6	4.8	4.4	3.6	3.2	2.4	7.3
2009	39.1	19.8	15.8	10.5	8.8	7.7	6.0	5.2	4.5	4.1	9.7
2011	28.6	17.4	10.9	8.4	7.8	5.4	4.4	4.1	3.1	2.2	7.1

Sources: Ministerio de Desarrollo Social 2011; Ministerio de Planificación 2006.

to the predictions of labor flexibility's proponents, Echeverría and López conclude that "flexibility does not generate more employment but instead leads to an increase in the utilization of available labor" (2004, 152; my translation).

Therefore, as the preceding analysis makes clear, while Chile clearly has a highly flexible labor market, this high level of flexibility has not resulted in increased employment for the nation's poorest citizens or lower income inequality. In fact, the evidence suggests that Chile's labor market flexibility has, in large measure, precipitated and perpetuated the very economic and social ills for which, its proponents argue, it is the cure. As the following analysis substantiates, the continued vulnerability of low-skilled workers to unemployment, coupled with high levels of employment insecurity and stratification among Chilean workers in general, results from the flexibilized labor market regime instituted under the military regime and largely preserved under post-transition governments.

From this perspective, Chile's continued adherence to a flexibilized labor regime should be understood not in terms of its capacity to reduce inequality or promote employment. Rather, its perpetuation should be understood in terms of the interaction among several factors: (1) the business sector's ability to protect its advantages vis-à-vis labor, institutionalized in the labor code, through leverage accrued with policymakers during the dictatorship; (2) the commitment of the center-left Concertación (1990–2010) to limit threats to the business sector in order to maintain investment levels and the stability of Chile's political economy; and (3) the weakness of the organized labor movement, resulting from the perpetuation of Pinochet-era labor regime and its own failure to adapt to Chile's radically altered labor conditions. The following two sections substantiate this argument. Section 3 delineates the manner in which the business community elevated its influence with policymakers during the military regime while section 4 examines the Concertación's response to business and labor pressure in the post-transition period.

Business-State Relations under the Military Regime (1973–1990)

The period preceding the military regime, under socialist president Salvador Allende's Popular Unity government, marked the high point of Chilean organized labor's membership, organization, influence, and power. Union membership grew substantially during this period, from a total of 628,396 union affiliates in 1970 to 939,319 affiliates in 1973, equaling approximately a third of the labor force (see table 3.1). The Allende government consulted labor leaders on national policy issues and gave them the opportunity to shape labor relations. Indeed, Allende named national labor leaders as ministers of labor and appointed them to key government posts. As a result, the Popular Unity government interpreted and applied the existing labor code in ways that favored unions and workers (Winn 2004, 17).

Following the 1973 military coup, unions and workers suffered a profound reversal of fortune. The Pinochet regime reacted to Chile's economic and political crises in two ways. First, through armed repression, the shutdown of democratic institutions, and the banning of political activity, it attempted to eliminate all channels of individual and collective political expression. Second, the regime attempted to stabilize the economy, dismantle the statist policies and programs adopted under previous administrations, and implement a neoliberal development regime designed to substantially increase market pressures on workers. The convergence of economic and social policy along neoliberal lines occurred in two distinct phases: an initial period of radical neoliberal development that evolved between 1973 and 1982 and a subsequent period of pragmatic neoliberalism that developed between 1983 and 1990. One can distinguish between these two phases of neoliberal development in terms of changes in the relationship between competing factions within the business community as well as the shifting relationship between the business community, on the one hand, and the military regime and neoliberal technocrats (the so-called Chicago Boys) on the other. These relationships were, in turn, shaped by economic crises in 1974–75 and 1982–83 and the related political and social crises within the country. Ultimately, the manner in which these crises were resolved led to historically unprecedented cohesion within the business community, which gave business significant political leverage to promote and protect its economic interests at labor's expense, both during the final years of the dictatorship and in the post-transition period.

The radical neoliberal phase was marked by the adoption of extreme free market policies promoted by an ascendant group of neoliberal technocrats within the Pinochet government and their consequent marginalization of both small- and medium-sized entrepreneurs and big business. The lack of cohesion and unity between small- and medium-sized producers, represented by the Council of Small and Medium-Sized Business (Consejo de la Pequeña y Mediana Empresa, CPME), and the larger entrepreneurial organizations, represented by the Confederation of Production and Commerce (Confederación de la Producción y del Comercio, CPC)—based in fundamental differences over economic policy and political strategy—facilitated the ascendance of the Chicago Boys.

Historically, conflict occurred frequently between Chile's small- and medium-sized entrepreneurs and big business. Though these two competing entrepreneurial factions were briefly united by their opposition to Allende's Popular Unity government and shared fears that it would usurp private property, such unity was short-lived. Once the Pinochet regime toppled the Allende government and firmly established itself in power, the CPME sought to gain institutionalized influence over social and political policy and to convince the regime to continue state protection of domestic enterprises (Campero 1991, 132). However, the 1974–75 economic crisis thwarted the CPME's ambitions. Fear that the crisis would reinvigorate and mobilize the social forces associated with the Popular Unity government led the business class to coalesce in its support of the military regime. General Pinochet, in turn, transferred all positions of economic responsibility to the neoliberal technocracy, granting it autonomy from the immediate interests of competing capital class factions (Martínez and Díaz 1996, 86).

The Chicago Boys' autonomy allowed them to ignore protectionist pressures from small- and medium-sized producers and to pursue a radical opening of the Chilean economy. This strategy favored business sectors with external comparative advantage, and beginning with the reactivation of the economy in 1976, facilitated the formation of new economic conglomerates with access to international credit (Martínez and Díaz 1996, 87). These conglomerates concentrated their investment in internationally competitive industries such as food processing and paper and export activities such as mining, fishing, and agriculture. The transformation of the state's core constituency under the dictatorship led to a shift in development focus from industrialization and production for domestic consumption to the export of primary and manufactured products. This shift undermined the economic, and thus the political, leverage that workers enjoyed under the previous mode of development. Since the domestic market is insignificant for the forms of enterprise in which the large conglomerates concentrated their investment (e.g., copper, fruit production, wood pulp and timber, and fish meal), policymakers within the military regime had little incentive to be concerned with raising wages or social benefits. Rather, in addition to liberalizing the economy and privatizing most state-owned industries, military leaders, in cooperation with neoliberal technocrats and business interests, restructured the social welfare system and rewrote the labor code in ways that would increase the susceptibility of workers to global economic competition.

Initially, the large economic conglomerates were ensured representation of their interests through a revolving door relationship with the military regime. Many important executives and directors from firms controlled by these conglomerates joined the government after the military took power (Schamis 2002, 54–55). Thus, "key policymakers of the Pinochet government served on the boards and in the executive offices of large economic conglomerates before and after holding cabinet and central bank positions, leading to collusion between economic and political power" (65). José Piñera, a Harvard University–trained economist and executive at the Cruzat-Larraín conglomerate before joining the military government in 1978, best personified this collusion. As minister of labor and social security, he designed the military regime's labor code and oversaw the privatization of social security.

This cozy relationship between big business and the military government initially appeared to work well for the conglomerates and the economy as a whole, leading to the rapid growth of economic sectors in which Chile had a comparative advantage. However, when international liquidity dropped precipitously and interest rates spiked in the early 1980s, over-indebtedness led to a wave of bankruptcies across the country (Silva 1996, 307). The ensuing economic crisis provoked a political crisis for the regime. Within the business community, the small- and medium-sized entrepreneurs sought to utilize their organizational strength to challenge the authority and policies of the neoliberal technocrats within the government.

While they had complained for some time that the large entrepreneurs were the primary beneficiaries of the new economic model, now that even the most successful entrepreneurial groups were suffering from the economic downturn, the small- and medium-sized entrepreneurs tried to recruit their larger counterparts to join the mobilization against the government. The Pinochet regime thwarted this opposition by imposing economic and political pressure against its most vocal antagonists while attempting to co-opt more moderate critics. The small- and medium-sized entrepreneurs succumbed to this pressure, which as a result reinforced the more pragmatic approach taken by the large entrepreneurs, represented by the CPC (Campero 1991, 137). In this way, the large entrepreneurs reasserted their historical dominance over organizations representing small- and medium-sized entrepreneurs and initiated the pragmatic phase of neoliberal policy under the military regime. Through the CPC, disenchanted segments of the business community demanded greater flexibility in policymaking and better access to policymakers.

To counter the influence of the Chicago Boy radicals, the leadership of the CPC sponsored a series of meetings during the 1982–83 economic crisis designed to build a consensus among Chile's business leaders over a national economic policy. The proposals that emerged from these meetings departed only moderately from neoliberal orthodoxy, indicating much of the business community's acceptance of the fundamentals of the military regime's economic policy. The more significant change reflected in the outcomes of these meetings was an emphasis on unity among Chile's diverse business sectors, with large producers in the dominant position and small- and medium-sized producers subordinate to them. Major lobbying efforts had to be conducted in the name of the CPC rather than individual sectoral organizations lest government technocrats reject them as too narrowly defined and thus threatening to the general health of the economy. Pleasing government technocrats became increasingly important since by 1985, once Chile's economic and political upheavals had subsided, the military regime recruited top economic policymakers almost exclusively from the ranks of experienced technocrats rather than business leaders. As a result, it became increasingly necessary to present policy proposals in terms of their likely impact on the economy as a whole rather than the benefits they might produce for specific economic sectors (Silva 1996, 309–10).

The consultation and coordination of economic policy between business and government established at this time set the pattern for business-state relations that have continued through the democratic transition to the present. These relations were founded on a unified business community that was committed to using its political clout to protect its economic interests. These interests were defined first and foremost in terms of the perpetuation of neoliberal economic and social policy and a strong desire to prevent any reversion to statism. The increased cohesion of the business community and its increased autonomy from state control in the context of a liberalized economy, gave it considerable leverage over government policy. The return to electoral politics, first with the 1988 plebiscite and then the 1989 elections, strengthened this leverage by putting added pressure on government to work with business to ensure positive economic outcomes in terms of employment and growth (Silva 1996).

Meanwhile, the ascending power and influence of business were mirrored by the relative decline and fragmentation of the labor movement and popular sector opponents to neoliberalism. The transformation of party-labor relations, which occurred over the course of the dictatorship, compounds the impact of structural reforms on labor's organizational capabilities. In the early years of the dictatorship, authoritarian repression coupled with the regime's ban on political activity sundered the traditional symbiotic relationship between organized labor and political parties of the center and left. As the labor movement regrouped and opposition to the military regime mounted, labor's role in organizing mass demonstrations, work stoppages, and other forms of resistance against the dictatorship was successful in forcing an opening in civil society. This opening allowed political parties and their leaders to reemerge (Garretón 1989, 173–75).

However, this reemergence did not lead to a reestablishment of the close ties with labor that existed before the coup. Instead, the parties that led the democratic opposition and that now form the Concertación distanced themselves from the labor movement and committed themselves to the preservation of the market economy and related state reforms established under Pinochet. The Christian Democratic and Socialist parties, the dominant parties in the democratic opposition and the governing Concertación, concluded that excessive state intervention in the economy and excessive party intervention in civil society were the primary causes underlying the collapse of Chilean democracy. On the basis of this assessment, they committed themselves to the preservation of the market economy and related state reforms established under Pinochet and distanced themselves from the labor movement (Roberts 1998; Walker 1990).

As a result, labor policy under democracy has been substantially the same as it was under authoritarianism. Though the four Concertación governments that held office between 1990 and 2010 increased social spending, the state's economic model continued essentially unchanged, and the organizational strength and influence of labor on the state and state policy remained severely compromised while business maintained its privileged position. Moreover, despite the return to democracy, linkage between political parties and the labor movement remains weak, limiting organized labor's political influence. The Concertación's failure to adopt pro-labor policies even after achieving a majority in the Chilean Congress in 2005 points to the influence of dominant business interests as a primary determinant of its labor policy. The following section elaborates this argument more fully by examining in detail key policies and institutional arrangements.

Flexible Labor and Precarious Employment under Democracy (1990–2010)

Before the democratic transition the prospects for meaningful labor reform looked promising. At that time, the leaders of the Concertación and labor's peak association, CUT, agreed upon the necessity of reforming the Pinochet labor code to redress the extreme inequities precipitated by the military regime's neoliberal development policies (Haagh 2002b, 93). However, this agreement proved to be short-lived. Both the Concertación and the CUT had to contend with a highly cohesive business sector fully committed to maintaining the labor movement's fragmentation and evisceration achieved during the dictatorship (Haagh 2002a, 61).

Structural changes in the global economy, which increased competition for both Chilean exporters and domestic producers, heightened the business community's opposition to reforming the Pinochet regime's labor reforms. As other countries followed Chile's lead and lowered their trade barriers in the late 1980s and early 1990s, foreign firms at the upper end of the value chain were able to lower their prices by increasing their suppliers. This intensified global competition severely constrained the ability of Chilean export firms to raise prices and increase rents. Chilean firms selling to the domestic market faced a similar dynamic. With multinational firms aggressively pursuing expansion in the Chilean market, domestic producers were forced to keep prices low to maintain market share.

Thus, whether focused on export or domestic markets, Chilean firms confronted increased competitive pressures from free trade. They responded by reducing labor's share of rents, a goal accomplished in large measure by hiring subcontracted and temporary employees. As previously noted, temporary employees were prohibited from engaging in collective bargaining. While subcontracted workers had some collective bargaining rights, they were limited and ultimately dependent on the willingness of employers to negotiate.[8] In this way, the Pinochet-era labor code enabled Chilean employers to force the brunt of cost-savings onto low-skilled workers. The flexibility provisions of the labor code made such workers easily replaceable and gave them little leverage to increase job security or improve wages (Berg 2004, 134–35). In a global economic environment of increasing competition, Chilean firms were determined to maintain this flexibility vis-à-vis workers.

Accordingly, the CPC strongly opposed any curtailment of labor flexibility or expansion of workers' bargaining rights. Through implicit threats of destabilizing the democratic regime, the business sector was able to extract from the Concertación legislative concessions on key labor reform issues (Haagh 2002b, 94). In the process, it precipitated division between the Concertación and the CUT and helped to expose organized labor's weaknesses. These weaknesses were apparent at the plant level, at the national federation level under the CUT's leadership, and more broadly in terms of the persistent detrimental impact of Chile's neoliberal labor regime on worker organization and mobilization.

At the plant level, competition between unions pursuing partnership strategies with management and more militant unions undermined the labor movement in at least two ways. First, rather than increasing union density, such competition led to union raiding, in which unions with close ties to management, and thus which appeared to offer workers better employment protection or quicker resolution to workplace problems, siphoned off workers from more militant unions. Having expanded their membership by raiding other unions, these "partnership" unions had little incentive to organize unorganized workers, thus stymying the growth of the labor movement (Palacios-Valladares 2010, 93). Second, more militant unions found themselves excluded from labor relations, which exacerbated inter- and intra-union factionalism. Thus, while unions that sought partnerships with management may have been able to advance their own interests, at least in the short term, they did so at the expense of other unions and labor solidarity more broadly (ibid.).

Compounding these problems at the plant level was the CUT's failure at the national level to adapt to the radically altered labor environment brought about by neoliberal reform. In particular, the CUT failed to develop effective strategies to organize and represent the increasing numbers of Chileans subject to flexible and precarious employment, including the growing number of women. As Leiva argues, while labor in Chile has become increasingly feminized and flexibilized, the CUT has continued to adhere to a model of labor activism forged between 1936 and 1973 (2012, 8). Given that this model was developed to address labor conditions under ISI, it was predicated on outdated assumptions that have impeded the CUT's efficacy in expanding the labor movement. For example, the original model presumed a worker identity based on the predominance of the male wage-earner working in mining and manufacturing. Moreover, it was based on the notion that union leaders could further labor's goals by operating through established political party representation in Congress. However, with the decline in manufacturing, the exponential growth of women in the labor market since 1973, the growth of forms of labor contraction (e.g., temporary and subcontracted) that did not exist prior to the military regime's adoption of neoliberal reforms, and with the deterioration of traditional party–labor ties, the CUT was left with an understanding of how to pursue labor organization at odds with actual labor conditions (Leiva 2012, 8).

Plant and national-level factors along with the impact of neoliberal reforms led to a stagnant, feckless labor movement, incapable of compelling government to promote its core interests. The primary obstacles to a more robust labor movement imposed by the Pinochet labor regime included: (1) the prohibition of collective bargaining beyond the plant level; (2) the

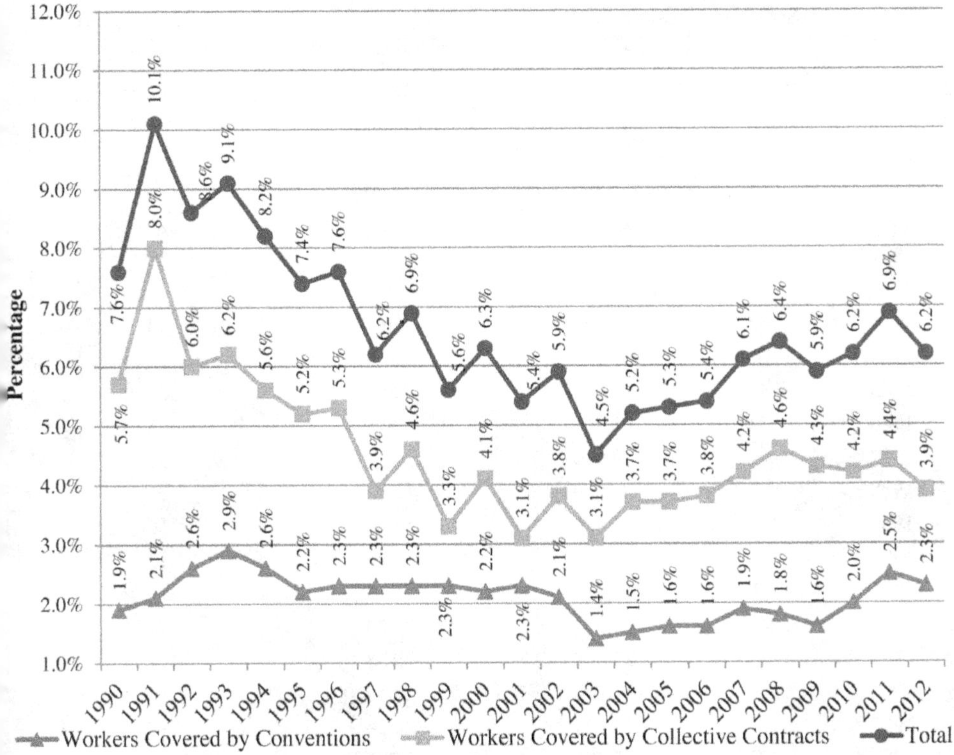

Figure 3.2. Percentage of Private Sector Wage Workers Involved in Collective Bargaining (Contracts and Conventions). Source: Dirección del Trabajo 2013, 222.

exclusion from collective bargaining of all workers except those with indefinite contracts (i.e., workers hired to complete a particular job, under apprenticeship, or with temporary contracts were prohibited from collective bargaining); (3) the exclusion from collective bargaining of all issues having to do with the management of the firm; (4) the power of employers to replace striking workers from the first day of a strike; (5) the ability of employers to extend the benefits gained through collective bargaining to nonunionized workers, if those workers pay 75% of the dues unionized workers pay, a disincentive for union organization and collective action; and (6) the perpetuation of parallel entities to unions, bargaining groups, that undermine union influence and efficacy (Durán Sanhueza 2013, 85–86). These factors combined led to declining rates of unionization, union density (table 3.1), and collective bargaining (figure 3.2), as well as low strike levels (table 3.4).

Table 3.4. Strike Activity, 1970–2012

Year	Strikes[a]	Workers Involved	Total Days Duration	Average Days Duration
1970	1,819	656,170	**	**
1971	2,709	304,530	12,461	4.6
1972	3,289	397,142	13,814	4.2
1973	**	**	**	**
1979	28	10,700	560	20
1980	68	22,500	1,428	21
1981	57	14,900	1,197	21
1982	31	6,900	589	19
1983	36	3,600	468	13
1984	38	3,600	456	12
1985	42	8,500	882	21
1986	41	3,900	615	15
1987	81	9,900	1,134	14
1988	72	5,600	1,008	14
1989	101	17,900	1,616	16
1990	176	25,010	2,643	15
1991	219	45,910	2,725	12.4
1992	247	26,962	2,975	12.0
1993	224	25,098	2,578	11.5
1994	196	16,209	2,640	13.5
1995	187	24,724	2,324	12.4
1996	183	25,776	1,795	9.8
1997	179	19,278	1,850	10.3
1998	121	12,608	1,204	10.0
1999	108	10,667	1,308	12.0
2000	125	13,227	1,121	9.0
2001	86	11,591	805	9.4
2002	117	14,662	1,363	11.6
2003	92	10,443	802	8.7
2004	125	13,013	1,586	12.7
2005	101	11,209	1,131	11.2
2006	134	15,602	1,501	11.2
2007	146	17,294	1,593	10.9
2008	159	17,473	1,701	10.7
2009	171	21,915	1,961	11.5
2010	174	31,799	2,178	12.5
2011	183	22,698	2,227	12.2
2012	161	30,035	1,886	11.7

Sources: For years 1970–72: Stallings 1978, 247. For years 1979–89: Haagh 2002b, 119. For years 1990–2012: Dirección del Trabajo 2013.

[a] Data for years 1979 to 1989 include both legal and illegal strikes.

** Data not available.

Beginning with the transition government of President Patricio Aylwin, labor reform negotiations with Concertación governments preserved the institutional arrangements underlying these negative patterns of labor organization and mobilization, and thus perpetuated the negative patterns themselves. The Aylwin government proclaimed as one of its primary objectives the achievement of "growth with equity."[9] In other words, the Concertación would preserve the neoliberal model's emphasis on economic growth, but it would also emphasize the promotion of greater economic and social equality by adopting social and labor policies aimed at improving conditions for Chile's poorest citizens. Reforming the more extreme elements of the military regime's labor code was an essential step in achieving this objective. In contrast, the CPC staunchly defended the status quo. It resisted any attempts to limit employers' ability to modify work contracts granted them by the military regime's 1979 Plan Laboral (Labor Plan). Above all, the CPC steadfastly opposed any reforms that would facilitate the discussion of labor issues beyond the firm level (Haagh 2002b, 95–96).

As the Aylwin government needed the support of the business community to maintain macroeconomic stability and employment levels, it sought to contain confrontation over its proposed reforms. Thus, to limit debate and minimize conflict, the Aylwin government introduced the most important labor reform projects in the Senate, where, given the presence of the designated senators, the Concertación was in the minority. As a result, it succeeded in passing only modest reforms but was able to attribute culpability for the significant concessions it made to its rightist opposition (Barrett 2001, 585). The new law proscribed any matters that "may limit the employer's ability to organize, direct or administer the firm" (González Moya 1991, 52). This provision perpetuated the most important element of the 1979 code (Haagh 2002b, 101). The new labor code's preservation of bargaining groups reinforced employer dominance vis-à-vis labor.

Labor code reforms under President Eduardo Frei did little to rectify these inequities. In attempts to placate the labor movement and counteract its pro-business image, the government submitted a package of substantial labor reforms to Congress in January 1995. The proposal package included reforms to expand collective bargaining, to end the employer's right to replace striking workers, and to adopt flexibility provisions that were less lopsided in favor of business (Frank 2002, 43–45). Taken together, these reforms, if enacted, would have substantially improved protections for Chilean workers. However, the rightist majority in the Senate immediately rejected the reform package while business launched a strident campaign attacking the CUT. In response to what it perceived as the government's half-hearted attempts to pass the reforms, the CUT assumed an increasingly confrontational stance. In the 1996 CUT elections, Socialist vice president Arturo Martínez defied his own party by negotiating with the Communist Party to help elect a Socialist as president and a Communist as vice president, reflecting the growing divide between the government and the labor movement (Barrett 2001, 591–92). The Frei administration's failed reform efforts in 1997 and 1999 did little to repair this divide.

The pattern of labor reform witnessed under the Aylwin and Frei administrations persisted under President Ricardo Lagos. Like its predecessors, the Lagos government proclaimed the importance of significant labor reform early on in its administration and laid out an ambitious reform program, only to significantly scale back its proposals in response to opposition from business associations and employers. During the 1999 presidential campaign, Lagos and his team emphasized their commitment to passage of an ambitious labor reform program that included a substantial increase in collective bargaining rights and the prohibition of employers from replacing striking workers. By July 2000, however, only a few months after its original proclamations, the government had de-emphasized the importance of these reform proposals. With respect to the replacement of striking workers, for example, labor minister Ricardo Solari asserted that though the law allows this practice, it had actually never occurred. This was, as Frank notes, an "astonishing" claim, given that throughout the 1990s the Labor Bureau regularly published reports substantiating and criticizing precisely this kind of employer abuse (2002, 51).

What was ultimately most influential in determining government labor policy was not data documenting employer use of replacement workers during strikes but pressure from business to keep this right intact. On September 7, 2000, in a meeting to discuss major economic issues, representatives from Chile's most influential employer associations asserted to Lagos and his top ministers that the stalled labor reform project was creating uncertainty and jeopardizing reactivation of the economy. The next day, Solari announced that the government would drop from its reform proposal inter-enterprise collective bargaining and the prohibition against replacing striking workers (Frank 2002, 52).

Thus, once again, pressure from the business community had succeeded in forcing the Concertación to dramatically scale back labor reform, despite strong opposition from the CUT. The labor reform law that the Senate passed on September 11, 2001, did take some modest steps toward addressing the inequities between business and labor. However, little progress was made on the labor movement's primary concerns—collective bargaining and the use of replacement workers during strikes.

With respect to the latter issue, the law did not ban the practice of hiring replacement workers during strikes. It merely made the practice more costly for employers by requiring them to pay a bond for each replacement worker to be shared among the strikers.[10] Workers fared no better with respect to the issue of collective bargaining. The law maintained the established practice of allowing firms to decide voluntarily whether to engage in collective bargaining negotiations.[11] The perpetuation of this practice compounded the impact of a number of other factors that undermine workers' capacity to bargain collectively. For example, workers in firms with more than 50% state ownership were barred from collective bargaining. Moreover, unions that operate beyond the plant level, including inter-enterprise and transitory unions created by the 1979 Labor Plan, did not have the right to bargain collectively. As a result of restrictions such as these, only 10 to 12% of the Chilean labor force enjoyed the right to bargain collectively (Frank 2002, 41). Moreover, since collective bargaining was contingent upon the willingness of employers to engage in negotiations, only about 6% of Chilean workers actually participated in collective bargaining, with less than 4% covered by contracts, rather than the weaker conventions (see figure 3.2).

Given these conditions, relations between the government and the CUT continued to be strained. The Lagos administration continued its emphasis on economic growth, macroeconomic stability, and labor flexibility as the proper means for improving conditions for Chilean workers. Meanwhile, the CUT continued to view the government as insufficiently attentive to labor's concerns. As a result, CUT president Martínez was highly critical of the Lagos government. "In matters of labor flexibility,"

Martínez complained, "the government has not listened to the workers or the labor movement. Its [reform] does not provide employment, only precariousness. We feel cheated because in these types of matters the government only listens to entrepreneurs" (*La Tercera* 2003; my translation).

Such acrimony between the government and the labor movement would persist under President Michelle Bachelet. Upon taking office in March 2006, Bachelet generally continued the pattern of labor reform established by her Concertación predecessors. While her government successfully instituted a notable set of labor reforms, these reforms aimed primarily at shoring up individual labor rights without threatening the political economic status quo. They did little to enhance labor's strength as a collective actor. Moreover, the Bachelet government exacerbated the marginalization of organized labor and workers' collective interests in two additional ways.

First, rather than engage with social organizations, it relied on presidential advisory commissions comprised of technocrats to formulate policy. With respect to the issue of labor, this policymaking strategy led to a substantially diminished role for the CUT in setting the labor agenda (Barría Traverso, Araya Moreno, and Drouillas 2012, 2). Second, consistent with its technocratic mode of policymaking, the Bachelet government adopted an ideological understanding of income inequality that discredited "old policies" associated with redistribution of wealth and instead defined the problem in terms of "a technical deficiency in the efficacy of social expenditure, particularly in education" (Carmago 2012, 23–24). Thus, income inequality came to be associated with inequality of opportunities and disassociated from unjust socioeconomic structures (23). In this manner, Bachelet's government perpetuated the pattern of labor reform pursued in preceding Concertación governments and deepened the labor movement's marginalization.

However, as a partial exception to this pattern, the Bachelet government did adopt a number of reforms intended to minimize the negative impact on workers of Chile's flexible labor regime by strengthening worker protections and individual rights. The most significant of these was Law 20,123, the Law on Subcontracting and Transitory Labor, instituted on October 16, 2006 (Ministerio del Trabajo y Previsión Social 2006). The law's primary intent was to provide legal protections for subcontracted and informal sector employees and to thereby incorporate them into the formal sector. In this regard, the law imposes a subsidiary obligation on principal enterprises for the health and safety of subcontracted employees. In other words, if the contracting enterprise fails to provide adequate health and safety protections, aggrieved employee(s) can lodge complaints with the principal enterprise. However, the law limited the force of this obligation in two ways. First, it required principal enterprises to implement a system to protect worker health and safety only when more than 50 employees are involved in a particular task or job (Ministerio del Trabajo y Previsión Social 2006, 4). Second, the law failed to provide meaningful penalties for statutory noncompliance.

The subcontracting law did establish constraints on the use of temporary employees that, if put into effect, could have severely limited subcontracting and strengthened permanent formal sector employment. However, the Chilean Supreme Court's ruling in response to a conflict between the National Copper Company (CODELCO) and the Confederation of Copper Workers (Confederación de Trabajadores del Cobre, CTC) eviscerated this aspect of the law and severely undermined the authority of the Labor Ministry in its efforts to protect vulnerable workers. The aspect of Law 20,123 in question stipulates that if a worker continues to lend services after the term of her/his temporary contract expires, the temporary contract will be transformed into an indefinite one, essentially elevating the employee to permanent, full-time status. In addition, the law states that the duration of a temporary contract can be no more than 180 days (Ministerio del Trabajo y Previsión Social 2006, 6).

The CTC attempted to employ this statutory restriction to challenge CODELCO's heavy reliance on subcontracted workers. When in April 2008 CODELCO rejected the CTC's demands, the subcontracted workers went on strike. The workers ended their strike on May 5, 2008, after intensive efforts by the Interior and Labor Ministries to broker a resolution (*Radio Cooperativa* 2008a). However, CODELCO subsequently mounted a legal challenge to the stipulation in the brokered agreement that required it to hire permanently more than 5,000 subcontracted employees. The Supreme Court's Constitutional Tribunal ruled in CODELCO's favor, asserting that the Labor Ministry's plan to resolve the labor conflict violated the employer's right to *libre contratación* (freely contracted labor), the right of enterprises to develop their activities in accordance with market fluctuations, and the right to property (*Radio Cooperativa* 2008b).

While CPC president Alfredo Ovalle celebrated the Supreme Court's ruling as a "powerful verdict," Camilo Escalona, senator and Socialist Party president, lamented that the Supreme Court's ruling "gives the bloodsuckers a new reason to celebrate because this [ruling] severely weakens the subcontracting law passed by the National Congress. . . . workers of this country will continue to be victims of all types of abuses" (*Radio Cooperativa* 2008c).

The neutralization of this key element of the subcontracting law intensified the labor movement's already high level of dissatisfaction with the Bachelet administration. When the conflict over subcontract employees originally emerged at CODELCO, in 2007, CUT president Martínez warned that the conflict could spread to other sectors of the economy. He called for expanding collective bargaining rights to strengthen labor's negotiating position and criticized the government for its failure to support such an expansion. "More than deception, there is indignation with President Michelle Bachelet," Martínez declared. "She raised hopes but her government has instigated conflict by throwing police at those that protest. . . . [P]reoccupation is with the macroeconomy without concern for social welfare" (*Radio Cooperativa* 2007b; my translation).

Despite such heated criticism from the CUT and despite possessing a majority in Congress, the government refrained from pursuing reforms that would strengthen labor's collective bargaining rights.[12] Instead, to combat the mounting level of labor strife and public frustration with persistent economic inequality in the country, President Bachelet established on August 20, 2007, an advisory council, Trabajo y Equidad (Labor and Equity), whose mission was to develop labor reform policies and proposals in a more "impartial" way (Trabajo y Equidad 2008; *Radio Cooperativa* 2007a). Claims to impartiality notwithstanding, the advisory council's membership was composed primarily of business sector representatives and mainstream economists. Of 48 total members, only 8 representatives were from social organizations, mainly priests and evangelical pastors. Given that the commission was dominated by proponents of structuring labor markets according to neoliberal logic, the CUT perceived it as adverse to its interests and refused to participate (Barría Traverso, Araya Moreno, and Drouillas 2012, 12). As CUT president Martínez explained, "This [Trabajo y Equidad] is pure bureaucracy; we will not participate" (*Radio Cooperativa* 2007a).

Assessing Labor Reform in Post-Transition Chile

As the preceding analysis demonstrates, labor reform under the first Bachelet administration followed a pattern consistent across all four Concertación governments between 1990 and 2010: the adoption of modest reforms, the preservation of business sector prerogatives, and the continued alienation and marginalization of the organized labor movement. While the reforms that Concertación governments enacted during this period were not irrelevant, they did little to address the fundamental causes underlying the severe power and resource inequities between business and labor in contemporary Chile. The perpetuation of bargaining groups continued to undercut the negotiating power of traditional unions. Collective bargaining remained voluntary, and given the antipathy of Chilean business associations and employers to the practice, its steady decline since the transition was to be expected (see figure 3.2). The original strictures of the military regime's Labor Plan that allowed employers to arbitrarily modify work contracts and prohibited workers from negotiating on any matters that might interfere with the employer's right to organize work remained in force. The 2001 reform measure lowering the number of workers necessary to form a union may have actually weakened the labor movement. Since the reform went into effect, the number of unions steadily increased while the average number of workers per union steadily declined (see table 3.1), indicating a diminution of the labor movement's collective strength.

The expansion of the judicial system to more efficiently adjudicate workers' complaints against employers may have ensured that more workers are duly compensated for their dismissal. Nonetheless, employers retained the right to dismiss workers on the open-ended grounds that it is necessary for the efficient functioning of the firm. Moreover, employers retained the right to hire replacement workers during strikes; the new law merely required them to pay a bond for each striking worker that they hire. Given the relatively low level of strike activity since the 1990 transition, it appears that this powerful right wielded by employers has been a significant deterrent against workers engaging in strikes, at least those legally sanctioned (see table 3.4).[13]

Given these circumstances, the labor movement in Chile has been increasingly critical of its presumed center-left political allies. As labor leader Mauricio González Tapia put it, "The Concertación owes a great debt to workers. Over twenty years in power, it failed to enact any significant labor reform, accommodating itself well to the neoliberal system Pinochet left behind."[14] Luis Destefani San Martín, national director of the Banco Estado union, was even more critical in his assessment of post-transition labor reform: "All the labor reform changes that have taken place through the end of the Bachelet government have been cosmetic; they have not been substantial or profound, as we in the labor movement have proposed and wished for."[15]

Has President Bachelet managed to address these criticisms in her second term? A preliminary assessment suggests that her government has made important strides in reversing the gross inequities in labor rights that have persisted since the dictatorship. In April 2017, her government implemented a new labor code, which among other things prohibits the hiring of replacement workers during strikes, ends most restrictions on who can participate in collective bargaining, and ends restrictions on matters that can be negotiated between workers and employers during collective bargaining (Dirección del Trabajo 2017). Reforms such as these have the potential to greatly enhance workers' bargaining power and their ability to reap a more equitable share of Chile's national wealth.

Nonetheless, Bachelet's new labor reforms are not without problems and shortcomings. Political infighting within her Nueva Mayoría coalition, the successor to the Concertación, eviscerated originally potent legislation while legal challenges launched by the right-wing opposition resulted in the Constitutional Tribunal ruling certain components of the legislation unconstitutional. The Bachelet government did not attempt to replace the parts of the legislation ruled unconstitutional since defections within its own governing coalition left it without the necessary votes. The result, according to Siavelis, has been "gaping regulatory holes when it comes to implementing key aspects of the legislation. This has produced the worst of all worlds with respect to labor legislation in Chile: unions weakened, business leaders dissatisfied, and Bachelet's popularity among workers further damaged" (2016).

Only time will tell if these shortcomings in Chile's most recent round of labor reform can be overcome.[16] In the meantime, it is clear that when taken together, the labor market conditions that have prevailed in the post-transition period have produced a high degree of labor flexibility for Chilean employers and an equally high degree of employment insecurity for Chilean workers. Given these conditions, it is not surprising that the exacerbation of income inequality that occurred under the dictatorship has persisted largely unchanged since the democratic transition. Chile remains one of the most unequal societies in the world. The perpetuation of such high levels of inequality and employment insecurity does not result from a lack of flexibility in the Chilean labor market. Rather, Chile's high degree of labor market flexibility has produced exceptionally high levels of inequality and employment insecurity.

These conditions, in turn, are the legacy of the military regime's efforts to privilege business at the expense of labor under authoritarianism and business's success at maintaining such privilege through more than two decades of democracy. The Chilean state has been embedded in a set of relations in which the business community is highly unified and wields enormous influence with elected officials and policymakers. In contrast, labor is fragmented and weak, with levels of unionization only modestly above what they were during the dictatorship. It is no doubt true, as Heckman and Pagés argue, that "groups with political power [read organized labor] promote job security policies to protect their income" (2000, 29). Yet, analysis of the Chilean case suggests that it is equally true that groups interested in protecting their profits and economic power advocate flexible labor policies in the name of economic efficiency and growth. Thus, if there is a general lesson to be drawn from this study it is that the adoption of flexible labor reforms creates winners and losers whose interests are not readily reconcilable. Ever more labor market liberalization cannot bring about growth with equity. Instead, the Chilean case suggests that the appropriate remedy to precarious employment and inequality in the region is the establishment of institutional reforms that strengthen labor's bargaining power relative to capital.

An early version of this chapter appeared as "Labor Market Flexibility, Employment and Inequality: Lessons from Chile" by Paul W. Posner in *New Political Economy* 22, no. 2 (2017): 237–56, available online at www.tandfonline.com.

4

The Impact of Regime Change and Economic Restructuring on Mexico's Labor Relations, 1988–2012

JEAN FRANÇOIS MAYER

In the last hours of an unusually busy fall Sunday, members of the Mexican Union of Electricians (Sindicato Mexicano de Electricistas, SME) were shocked to see their place of employment, the state-owned electrical power distribution company Downtown Light and Power (Luz y Fuerza del Centro, LFC), invaded by members of the federal police and armed forces. That night, workers were forcibly expelled from the premises, and the LFC was permanently shut down. Although officially grounded in an economic logic—the LFC had been generating substantial deficits—this coercive action also appeared to result from the government's will to silence the SME, a highly vocal critic of the federal administration's economic policies. This harsh takeover reproduced the pattern of labor relations characterizing Mexico's authoritarian regime (1929–2000), defined by the state's limited tolerance of union dissidence. However, the dissolution of the LFC and the SME occurred in 2009, well after the country's transition to democracy. This suggests a fair degree of continuity in the practice of Mexico's labor relations from authoritarianism to democracy.

This anecdotal evidence is compounded by the permanence of the Mexican labor legislation. Indeed, enacting substantial labor reform proved challenging for both the Institutional Revolutionary Party (Partido Revolucionario Institucional, PRI), which led Mexico's authoritarian regime continuously from 1929 to 2000, and the National Action Party (Partido Acción Nacional, PAN), which controlled the federal government from the democratic transition of 2000 until December 2012. No less than five distinct proposals to transform Mexico's labor code were introduced to Congress between 1988 and 2012. The first four projects were eventually abandoned. A fairly mild and rather incomplete reform was finally adopted in November 2012, at the very end of President Felipe Calderón's term. Nonetheless, accounts point to the problematic legal reach and applicability of the reform, and to its limited impact (Alcalde 2012). The essence of labor legislation in Mexico thus remained untouched across regime types.

This continuity represents a puzzle, for two main reasons. First, Mexico was among the first countries in the region to embrace market-oriented economic reforms, and it implemented neoliberal policies in a particularly exhaustive fashion from the mid-1980s on. In that context, one would have expected Mexico to flexibilize its labor legislation, especially given that this was a condition imposed by international creditors (including the IMF and the World Bank) assisting Mexico during the crisis of the 1980s. Creditors insisted on the implementation of these measures as an intrinsic part of market reforms in order to favor job creation, reduce informal labor, and generate economic growth (Cook 2007, 34). Yet, Mexican authorities repeatedly shied away from flexibilizing the country's labor code. Second, Mexico's transition to democracy should have led to a congruent democratization of the country's system of labor relations—in particular through the elimination of the labor code's corporatist provisions inherited from the authoritarian period. Nonetheless, it appears that Mexico's democratic transition had little impact on the probability of achieving a comprehensive labor reform, as the labor code remained relatively intact afterwards.

In other words, despite Mexico undergoing a critical shift in economic models as well as a political regime transition—two processes that should have yielded labor legislation reform—neither significant flexibilization of the labor market nor democratization of labor relations occurred during the period under study. This chapter seeks to uncover the principal reasons explaining the high degree of continuity in Mexico's labor relations between 1988 and 2012. The 24 years under analysis roughly comprise the time period during which the neoliberal model was implemented and consolidated. This period also allows for a comparison between the two PRI presidencies preceding Mexico's democratic transition, as well as the two PAN presidencies following it. Thus, this time frame is well suited for the examination of the effects these profound economic and political transformations had on Mexico's labor market and relations.

This chapter is based upon extensive personal interviews with Mexican union leaders and federal politicians, as well as secondary sources and data. Findings indicate that continuity in Mexico's labor relations appears mainly attributable to the specific configuration taken by the country's neoliberal economic model. This configuration generated a structure of incentives for political and labor elites to favor the persistence of non-democratic patterns of labor relations and to leave the country's labor legislation essentially untouched, following Mexico's regime transition in 2000. Hence, Mexico represents an exception among this book's case studies, given that the country did not formally adopt labor flexibilization measures during the period of neoliberal restructuring and regime democratization under analysis. Nevertheless, successive Mexican governments since 1988 selectively implemented Mexico's labor legislation, which de facto allowed for a significant flexibilization of the labor market.

More specifically, the neoliberal economic model in place since the late 1980s was premised upon low labor costs, considerable labor surplus, and a quiescent labor force. Successive federal governments since 1988 utilized various aspects of the corporatist provisions found in Mexico's labor code in order to guarantee these labor market conditions. In particular, it seems that the four federal administrations under analysis preserved the corporatist and clientelistic essence of state-labor relations, in order to maintain "labor peace"—that is, the demobilization of the labor force—and to garner the support of corporatist union leaders for their policy agenda. The existing labor legislation also offered union leaders great advantages and privileges in the governing of their organizations' internal business, which contributed markedly to the consolidation and sustainability of their leadership. Political and labor elites thus proved reluctant to seek the modification of the institutional and structural conditions regulating Mexico's labor environment, from which they derived political as well as socioeconomic benefits. In turn, this contributed to the preservation of the Mexican labor code, despite the opportunities for change that resulted from the country's economic restructuring and its political regime change.

In the following, I first discuss the main elements that have structured state-labor relations in Mexico before the transition to democracy. I then study the evolution of the country's economy and labor relations during the last two authoritarian governments (1988–2000). I subsequently analyze the manner in which the labor context evolved under the post-transitional PAN governments of 2000–2012. I conclude by underlining the grim situation in which Mexican workers find themselves as a result of the continuity in labor dynamics since 2000.

Labor in Mexico: A History of Corporatism and Clientelism

From the late 1920s until 2000, state-labor relations in Mexico were primarily characterized by a strong corporatist system and an elaborate clientelistic network. This corporatist framework did not tie directly peak associations to the state (as it generally did in other countries) but rather to the PRI itself, which in turn controlled the governing apparatus. Indeed, the corporatist system was crafted during the 1930s with the gradual establishment of a formal relationship between the PRI and three groups representing the main segments of society: urban labor, the peasantry, and the "popular sector"—that is, public servants and segments of the urban middle class (Aziz Nassif 1989; Bizberg 1990). The PRI, therefore, played a pivotal intermediary role in this system.

This corporatist relation entailed that the PRI provide participant organizations with various economic privileges and limited access to the political decision-making process, in exchange for their political support during and between elections. The PRI obtained the financial resources necessary for the maintenance and continuity of this arrangement through its control of the state apparatus, which extracted significant revenues from public-owned enterprises and taxes, among other things (García Villanueva and Stoll 1995; Trejo Delabre 1990; Zapata 1998).

Whereas this corporatist framework seemingly aggregated labor organizations, it was also utilized by the PRI to profoundly divide the labor movement in order to better control it (Grayson 1989; Zapata 1995). On the one hand, corporatism opposed "official" unions (i.e., organizations participating in this system, which comprised the majority of Mexico's labor groups) to independent unions (i.e., groups that refused to participate in the corporatist system).[1] Consequently, independent unions were by and large marginalized from the country's policymaking process and received no particular socioeconomic advantages from the state. On the other hand, the PRI also periodically utilized corporatist incentives to pit official union confederations against one another. This was done in order to prevent their unification around themes of common interests, which could have rendered official unions less pliable to the PRI's policy priorities.

Although, in theory, Mexico's labor laws are progressive and pro-labor, they also contain provisions that, in practice, can be utilized by the state to limit union activities, demobilize workers, and curb labor's political and economic influence. PRI administrations therefore utilized various provisions found in Mexico's labor legislations—comprised principally of Constitutional Article 123 and the Federal Labor Law (Ley Federal del Trabajo, LFT)—to consolidate the corporatist system and limit the workers' capacity to organize and mobilize autonomously (Bensusán 1995, 2000; Ortega and Solís de Alba 1999).

In particular, Article 123 effectively denies the right to strike to public servants and bank employees. Also, it created the Boards of Conciliation and Arbitration (Juntas de Conciliación y Arbitraje, JCA) and enabled them, along with the Secretariat of Labor and Social Welfare (Secretaría de Trabajo y Previsión Social, STPS), to adjudicate labor conflicts. Present at both the national and local levels, these Labor Boards include business, labor, and state representatives. State officials preside over the JCA's work, which allows them to set the agenda and shape the decisions reached by the Boards. Bensusán indicates that PRI governments utilized the JCAs to regulate labor relations and limit labor militancy and political participation (Bensusán 2000, 138). As such, the boards often functioned as politicized institutions under the PRI's authoritarian rule.

For its part, the Federal Labor Law gave the Labor Boards and the STPS power to deny legal registration of unions; to refuse the composition or modifications of union executive committees; to prevent unions from entering into collective bargaining; and to reject strike petitions (de la Garza 1998; Santos Azuela 1989). Under the authoritarian regime, these legal provisions allowed PRI governments to thwart the workers' freedoms of association and organization, as well as their right to strike, in order to minimize the likelihood that unions would develop into a counterweight to state power (Samstad 2002). Unions whose discourse or behavior conflicted with the PRI's policy priorities hence often became the targets of overt or covert state repression. PRI federal governments thus implemented the LFT selectively and in accordance with their own policy priorities and political motivations (Patroni 2001, 255–57; Zapata 1995, 95).

This formal corporatist framework was paralleled by an informal clientelistic network, which played an equally important part in shaping state-labor relations under the PRI's rule. Clientelism is typically understood as an informal scheme of interest intermediation involving two parties with unequal degrees of power—that is, a patron and one or several clients—connected through a system of personalized exchanges and bargaining. During the PRI's authoritarian regime, an expansive network of clientelistic ties linked high-ranking government officials to corporatist union leaders, as well as labor leaders, to their organization's rank and file. This system was underpinned by state-derived resources and privileges, channeled by public officials to corporatist union leaders (Cook 1995; Middlebrook 1995; Ortega and Solís de Alba 1999). Corporatist union leaders therefore received benefits such as seats in state and federal congresses, monetary rewards and social privileges, and control over the distribution to their union members of a variety of economic benefits—including access to state-sponsored housing programs and state-subsidized loans and consumption goods.

The PRI also incorporated an Exclusion clause in the LFT to further cement this relation. This provision is present in the great majority of work contracts and makes it mandatory for workers to hold formal affiliation with a union. In the eventuality that workers voluntarily leave or are excluded from their unions, they are fired (LaBotz 1992). Union leaders often utilized this legal stipulation to discourage the emergence of worker groups openly challenging their rule: opponents were often excluded from the union and subsequently lost their job. This proved a powerful argument to discourage efforts by the rank and file to replace corporatist leaders. The Exclusion clause thus allowed corporatist union leaders to control their unions' organization and finances and reap substantial monetary benefits from their position.

In exchange for these favors, co-opted leaders provided their political support, as well as that of their organizations, to the PRI. This support included delivering en masse the vote of their union members at election times and participating in periodic events and demonstrations in support of the party and of the government (Trejo Delabre 1990). For their parts, workers in corporatist unions were offered a variety of socioeconomic benefits. In return, they were expected to support their union leaders and follow their instructions with regard to mobilizing and voting during national and regional elections.

Corporatism formally came to an end in 2000, when the PRI lost the presidency and hence its control over the state's apparatus and resources, which were necessary to the functioning of this interest representation framework (Camp 2014, 177–78). Still, available research indicates that state-labor relations have not been significantly democratized since the transition and that the essence of pre-transition state-labor relations has remained by and large intact (Alcalde 2003; Bensusán and Middlebrook 2012; Cook 2007; Selee and Peschard 2010; Zapata 2006). In fact, even the mild labor reform that took place in November 2012 did not jeopardize the major elements of the corporatist framework found in the LFT, such as the state's right to deny union registration, control the composition of union executive committees, and limit the right to strike (Alcalde 2012). Furthermore, the literature indicates that clientelistic networks linking the government to leaders of official unions effectively adapted to the new political reality, instead of being abolished.

However, this body of research does not clarify the reasons for which the post-transition PAN governments of Vicente Fox (2000–2006) and Felipe Calderón (2006–12) chose to preserve important features of the previous regime's corporatist scheme and clientelistic relations with labor; the extent to, and the form in, which these patterns were perpetuated; and the reactions of unions—and in particular of their leaders—to the new structure of opportunities emerging since the country's democratic transition. In what follows, I seek to fill this gap in the literature.

Economic and Labor Market Transformations under the PRI (1988–2000)

For most of the 1980s, Mexico was immersed in a severe economic crisis. Sluggish growth, rampant inflation, crushing external debt, and severely declining real wages characterized that "Lost Decade" (Middlebrook and Zepeda 2003, 3–54). This predicament resulted from, among other things, the exhaustion of Mexico's import substitution industrialization (ISI) economic development model; its deficient borrowing and investment strategy; as well as a global economic slowdown. A direct outcome of this crisis was the decision by Mexican policymakers to reorient the country's economic model away from the previous state-led scheme and to implement instead a market-based model. This new economic development model—later formalized in the Washington Consensus—was premised upon the liberalization of trade and financial exchanges, the central role of domestic and international private sector investment in the creation of sustained economic growth, as well as the privatizing of state-owned assets (Haggard and Kaufman 1995).

This neoliberal economic model was implemented relatively swiftly in Mexico, owing to the authoritarian nature of the PRI's rule. The party essentially relied on its majority in Congress to impose a neoliberal policy agenda on Mexico. The PRI remained in power despite the economic crises of the 1980s and 1990s by using repression, corruption, co-optation, vote-buying and electoral fraud, as well as playing on the public's fear of economic and political chaos if the PRI were to leave office (Haber et al. 2008, 131–69).

One of the principal objectives of the PRI-engineered neoliberal policy model was to create favorable market conditions in order to increase foreign and domestic investment as well as to enhance Mexico's international competitiveness. The new economic system was deepened by the implementation of the North American Free Trade Agreement (NAFTA). A drawn-out process that began in 1994 and concluded in 2009, the NAFTA sought to create stronger economic ties between Mexico, the United States, and Canada, by removing tariffs and duties on most of the products each of these countries exported to its regional partners. In this context of significantly increased international exchanges and continental economic integration, PRI presidents Carlos Salinas (1988–94) and Ernesto Zedillo (1994–2000) identified the country's labor force as its comparative advantage (Middlebrook 1995, 292–98). The Mexican neoliberal economic model was therefore implemented in such a way as to favor low real salaries as well as a quiescent and productive labor force.

In order to guarantee these conditions, the Salinas and Zedillo administrations utilized extensively the powers conferred upon the state by the Federal Labor Law—especially those provisions allowing the state to control unions and limit their scope of activities (de la Garza 1998). As such, the Salinas and Zedillo administrations allowed the de facto implementation by business owners of labor flexibilization practices such as subcontracting, varying work schedules, and lower firing and hiring costs—and plant-level negotiations as opposed to national-level dealings—to weaken union solidarity and coordination strategies. These federal governments also declared illegal the strikes that took place in economic sectors they deemed strategic; removed uncooperative union leaders and executive committees; and prevented the emergence of independent unions (because of their alleged defiance) by denying them official recognition (Hamilton and Kim 2004). In other words, the implementation of neoliberal reforms in the 1990s was paralleled by an extensive process of de facto labor market flexibilization. In order to achieve this result, the state refrained from implementing various provisions of the labor code, which allowed for—and effectively encouraged—the widespread adoption of flexibilizing practices by employers.

In the end, this restructuring process yielded rather underwhelming macroeconomic results. For the 12-year duration of the PRI governments of Salinas and Zedillo, the data show GDP growth averaging 3.7%, accompanied by moderate inflation of 19.5% on average. Poverty and inequality indicators exhibit on average exceptionally high levels, with a poverty rate of 57.6%, and a Gini coefficient—a widely used measure of inequality—of 50.5% for the period at hand (World Bank Databank 2015).

As for labor market indicators, the minimum salary—widely utilized as a basis for the determination of salaries in formal as well as informal employment settings—decreased markedly between 1988 and 2000, moving from 105 to 60 pesos daily, in constant 2010 pesos (see figure 4.1). Also, the open unemployment rate averaged 3.8% yearly—a rather high rate by Mexican standards—for the same period (see figure 4.2).

Remarkably, rather than generating outrage among organized labor, the implementation of neoliberal policies corresponded with a reduction of the unions' mobilization and organizational capabilities (see figure 4.3). Indeed, the number of national strikes fell during that time period, from a yearly average of 139 under Salinas to 46 during Zedillo's mandate. An average of 53,705 workers per year were involved in national strikes during Salinas's presidency, whereas only 25,529 workers per year struck during the Zedillo administration. By contrast, there were on average 237 strikes per year in the 1983–88 period, with over 95,000 workers involved yearly.

Existing research explains that this demobilization of organized labor is due to the corporatist union leaders' decision to ultimately accept the neoliberal economic policies set forth by the PRI in order to safeguard

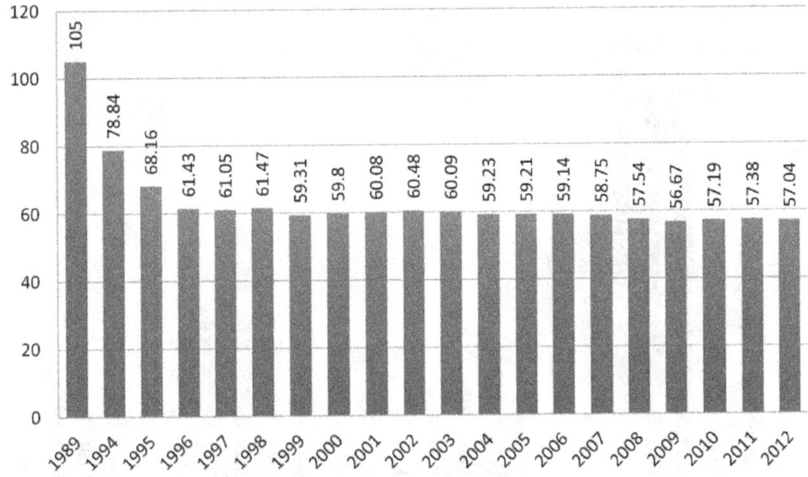

Figure 4.1. Real Minimum Salary, in Constant 2010 Pesos. Source: Secretaría del Trabajo y Previsión Social (STPS) 2015.

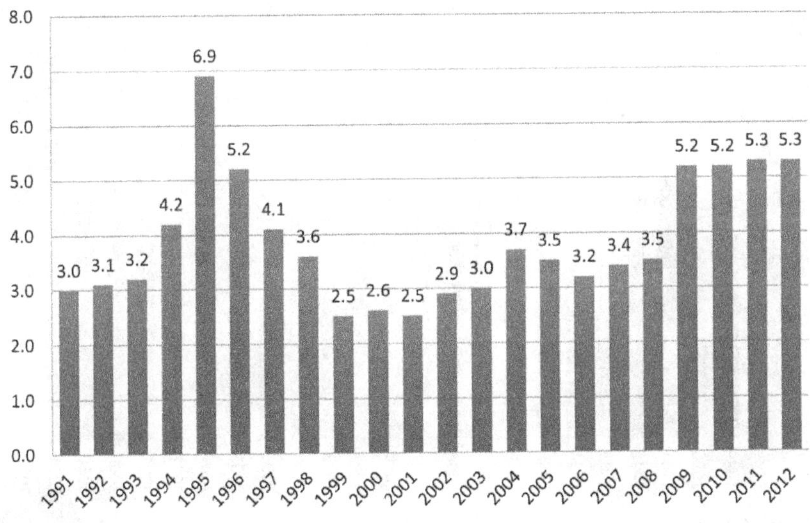

Figure 4.2. Annual Unemployment Rate (in %). Source: World Bank Databank 2015.

their privileged position (de la Garza 1998, 2003; LaBotz 1992; Salas and Zepeda 2003). This decision was in part due to the perspective that the Salinas and Zedillo administrations might utilize the aforementioned LFT provisions to remove "uncooperative" union leaders. But it was also a result of the continued clientelistic ties linking these corporatist leaders to the PRI administrations. Official union leaders did threaten to strike,

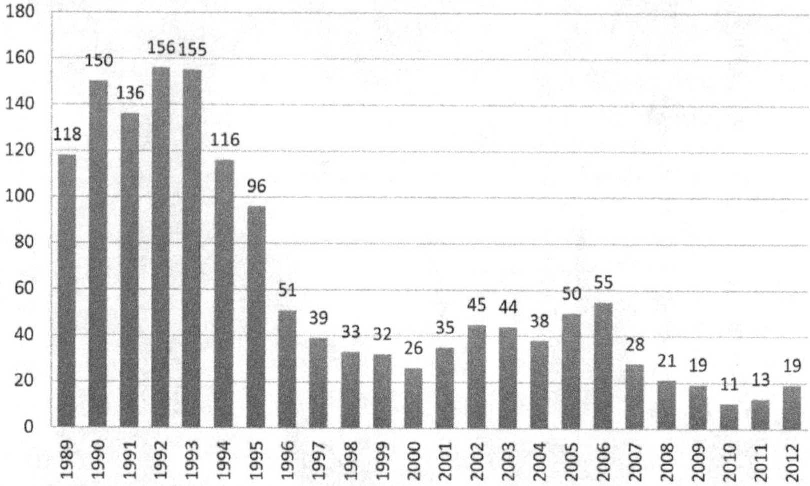

Figure 4.3. Strikes per Year. Source: Secretaría del Trabajo y Previsión Social (STPS) 2015.

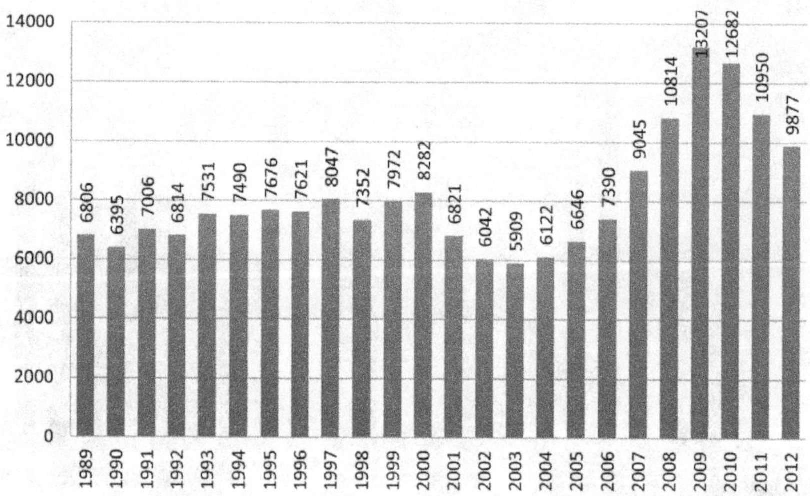

Figure 4.4. Strike Petitions. Source: Secretaría del Trabajo y Previsión Social (STPS) 2015.

flooding the Labor Boards with strike petitions (see figure 4.4). But these actions were mostly designed to show union members that their leaders were attempting to defend the workers' interests.[2] When it came time to announce the numerous concessions they had accepted in the name of their memberships, corporatist leaders explained that the new work contracts were a victory for workers. Corporatist leaders claimed that these contracts guaranteed jobs—which they sometimes, but not always, did—and a few other socioeconomic benefits that these leaders deemed a rarity during a difficult process of economic restructuring. In a context of economic restructuring and job losses, these arguments proved convincing enough for a majority of official union members.

In exchange for their loyalty and the political support of their organizations, corporatist union leaders received support from the PRI governments, under the form of a series of economic payoffs, continued political representation through guaranteed seats in the PRI's delegation in Congress, and the preservation of some access to the decision-making process (Jaime 2004, 41). Also, the PRI did not remove the Exclusion clause from the LFT, thus granting "job security" to corporatist leaders. By supporting electorally the PRI, as well as its governments' policy orientation, corporatist leaders remained precious allies for the Salinas and Zedillo governments (Burgess 2003, 87).

Economic and Labor Market Changes in the Post-Transition Era (2000–2012)

The economic policy priorities of the Fox and Calderón post-transitional presidencies were characterized by strong continuity with those of the Salinas and Zedillo governments. Fox's election completed Mexico's transition to electoral democracy, ushering in a new political era characterized by the implementation of several democratic procedures and the gradual decentralization of power from the federal administration to state governments (Rubio 2004, 18–26). Still, Fox's economic policies closely followed those of Salinas and Zedillo, as he sought to deepen the neoliberal model and conclude Mexico's economic restructuring (Jaime 2004, 58–60). Fox sent successive proposals to Congress to privatize the country's state-owned energy monopolies, as well as to reform Mexico's fiscal scheme, pension systems, and labor market—the latter, through a transformation of the LFT. However, only the Mexican Social Security Institute's (Instituto Mexicano de Seguridad Social, IMSS) relatively small pension system was successfully reformed (Mayer and Marier 2006). Deep divisions between parties in Congress, a lack of political leadership on the part of Fox, and a polarized public opinion were in great part responsible for this limited track record of reforms.

President Felipe Calderón pursued essentially the same economic goals as Fox but was more successful in advancing this policy agenda. Indeed, in 2007, Congress passed a government-backed fiscal reform to improve public spending and tax collection, as well as a major pension restructuring of the Social Security and Social Services Institute for State Workers (Instituto de Seguridad y Servicios Sociales de los Trabajadores del Estado, ISSSTE), which affected most state employees. In 2008, federal legislators adopted a mild reform of the oil sector, allowing for some collaboration between the state-owned monopoly PEMEX and private investors, with regard to distribution and storage. In 2009, Congress passed another fiscal reform, this time increasing the value-added tax (VAT) by 1%. In addition, Calderón's team worked on the privatization of Mexico's electricity monopoly, but after a strategic pause was observed preceding the July 2009 midterm legislative elections, the project was not revived. The Calderón government also reactivated plans to modify the country's labor code, which culminated with a limited reform in the last few days of the president's mandate.

Indicators present a mixed picture of Mexico's economic situation during the Fox and Calderón presidencies. During his electoral campaign, Fox had promised 7% GDP growth per year for the duration of his *sexenio* (a term referring to the six-year duration of the Mexican presidential mandate). By contrast, Mexico only averaged a GDP growth rate of 2.4% per annum during the first PAN administration. Inflation rates gravitated around 4.7% yearly, and showed a tendency toward decline. The Gini coefficient fluctuated, but settled at an average of 49 per year. Poverty rates indicated a tendency to decline, averaging 46.7% yearly (World Bank Databank 2015).

The Calderón years were marked by growth rates fueled in great part by the high prices of oil, but were also affected by the world recession of 2008–9. Therefore, Calderón's presidency averaged a meagre GDP growth of 1.9% yearly. Inflation remained relatively stable at 4.4% yearly. The poverty rate grew from 47.7% in 2008 to 52.3% in 2012—a level not seen in over 12 years. The Gini coefficient diminished slightly, averaging 47.9 (World Bank Databank 2015).

As such, it appears that Mexico was plagued by a continuing inability to generate significant and durable GDP growth rate in the post-transition era. Likewise, unemployment and poverty rates increased noticeably and steadily during that period. By contrast, the country's inflation and Gini statistics point toward some improvement.

Labor market data yield a similarly mixed perspective. In the aggregate, the 2001–12 period is characterized by an annual unemployment rate of 3.9%, which is slightly higher than the average of 3.8% found during the preceding 1988–2000 period (see figure 4.2). The real minimum salary continued to decrease under Fox's and Calderón's presidencies, averaging 58.7 pesos daily, down from 76.9 pesos during the Salinas and Zedillo administrations (see figure 4.1). The average number of strikes per year also continued to fall during the PAN governments, as on average 31.5 strikes took place yearly, versus 92 strikes yearly during the last two PRI presidencies (see figure 4.3). The average number of workers involved in strikes kept diminishing, from 39,617 workers yearly under the PRI governments to 18,090 workers during the PAN administrations. The only exception to this continuity is found in the number of strike petitions, which increased to an average of 8,792 yearly under Fox and Calderón, from 7,416 petitions per year under Salinas and Zedillo (see figure 4.4).

As mentioned above, the post-2000 federal administrations were supportive of the interpretation of the neoliberal model premised upon keeping real salaries low and the workforce quiescent, which was championed by successive PRI presidencies since the late 1980s. In order to assure the maintenance of low salaries, the PAN governments continued the practice of the Salinas and Zedillo administrations to utilize the yearly increase in minimum salary as a ceiling reference for percentage increase in salaries during collective bargaining, as opposed to considering it a floor reference, as it was intended. In that context, it is worth noting that Mexico's real minimum salary—expressed in constant 2010 pesos—effectively declined by 46% from 1989 to 2012, moving from 105 to 57 pesos daily. Although the bulk of this diminution occurred under the Salinas and Zedillo governments, and the minimum salary plateaued during the Fox presidency, it resumed a downward trajectory under Calderón.

But aggregate numbers do not always yield an accurate depiction of the labor market. In this case, the open unemployment rate increased noticeably after the economic crisis of 2008, rising from 3.5% that year to 5.2% in 2009, and to 5.3% by 2012. In previous years, Mexicans who lost their job in the formal economy typically moved to the informal economy and therefore did not register in the unemployment data. In fact, the crisis

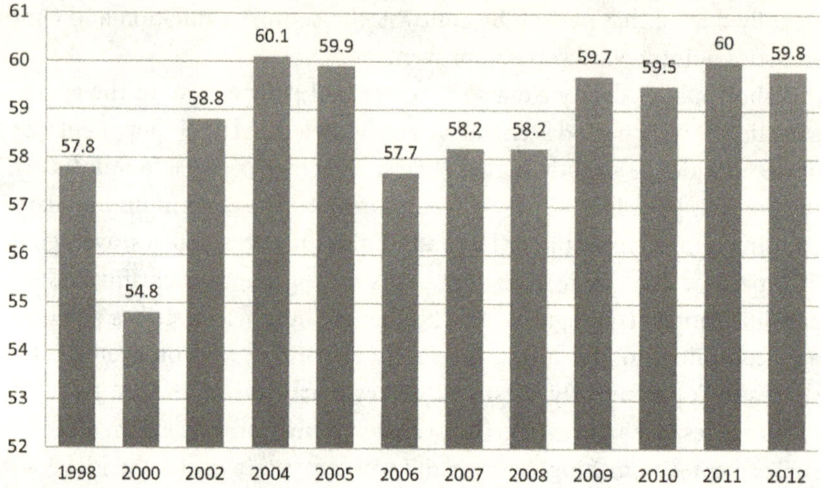

Figure 4.5. Percentage of the Labor Force Employed in the Informal Sector. Source: Instituto Nacional de Estadísticas y Geografía (INEGI) 2018.

of 2008 coincided with an increase in the proportion of the labor force employed in the informal sector (see figure 4.5). But this 1.5% increase in the informal sector labor force between 2008 and 2009 in fact indicates that 800,000 people joined the informal economy, whereas the 1.7% rise in unemployment rate denotes that 900,000 joined the ranks of the unemployed during the same time. Furthermore, this most recent period of increase in informal sector occupation had begun in 2006: on average, over 750,000 people joined the informal economy every year since then.

Thus, the data suggest that the majority of workers who lost their jobs in the formal economy after 2008 did not subsequently join the informal economy. In other words, this suggests that the impact of the 2008 crisis on the labor market has been particularly negative, since the informal economy did not absorb laid-off workers as it previously did. These workers then joined and remained in the ranks of the unemployed and underemployed.

Labor Relations since 2000

At the time Mexico completed its transition to electoral democracy, in 2000, there existed an expectation commonly found among the citizenry and analysts of Mexican politics that the PRI's loss of power as well as the resulting regime change could generate a profound transformation in labor relations. According to this interpretation, the electoral defeat of the PRI could have led official unions to retaliate by disrupting Mexico's production process and destabilizing the political dynamics of the new regime. Indeed, official unions—which comprised the majority of the Mexican labor movement—constituted a central component of the PRI's governing coalition. As such, official union leaderships had traditionally been strongly opposed to regime democratization, among other things, because of the loss of privileges this supposed (Bensusán and Middlebrook 2012; Murillo 2000).

Although the state corporatist framework was formally dismantled when the PRI left the presidency, official unions remained institutionally linked to it. It was therefore reasonable to suppose that these unions would attempt to undermine the new PAN government by staging waves of strikes, work protests, and public demonstrations—as, in fact, had been promised by some official labor leaders before the presidential elections of 2000. This situation was compounded by multiple campaign declarations and promises made by Fox, who indicated his will to reform the labor code and democratize labor relations—going so far as to sign an agreement to that effect with independent unions (Mayer 2006).

Contrary to this expectation, the configuration of labor relations established under the Salinas and Zedillo governments appears to have been preserved after the regime transition. As shown below, the Fox and Calderón governments by and large continued to implement the country's labor legislation—which remained essentially intact under these administrations—in a manner conducive to the defense and promotion of neoliberal economic policy goals. As such, freedoms of association and organization as well as the right to strike remained restricted, and internal union democracy limited. But this continuity in labor relations also resulted from the corporatist union leaders' desire to preserve their personal interests and advantages, which mostly stemmed from selected provisions found in the country's labor legislation and the manner in which it was implemented by the federal administration. The bulk of (by then) corporatist union leaders hence continued to collaborate with the federal government, regardless of the change in party in power. Consequently, labor apathy—typically labeled "labor peace" by successive federal administrations—largely persisted, with a few noticeable exceptions.

Labor Relations under Fox

Initially, Fox exhibited a greater openness than his predecessors to demands stemming from all sectors of the labor movement, and particularly those of the independent unions. He also expressed his commitment to reforming the labor legislation so as to favor labor's autonomy from the state, pluralism in labor interest representation, and greater transparency in the unions' internal processes. Still, Fox rapidly reached an informal modus vivendi with corporatist union leaders that very much resembled the agreement in place between labor and the PRI before 2000. Fox struck this new alliance in the hopes of preserving labor quiescence, as well as getting various reforms and legislation through Congress with the support of official labor representatives—and at times that of their PRI allies (Roman and Velasco Arregui 2006, 97–98). This alliance proved all the more important as time passed, since labor relations became more difficult and Fox's policy agenda faced strong opposition in Congress.

Negotiations surrounding the 2003 labor code reform project were a catalyst for the emergence of this new association between the PAN-led federal government and corporatist unions. Initially advocating a reform that would promote both the democratization of labor relations—such as secret ballots for union votes and establishing a public registry of unions—and labor flexibilization, the Fox government tried to obtain a consensus between representatives of business, corporatist union leaders, and independent union leaders. Discussions rapidly reached an impasse. Independent unions considered labor flexibilization a by-product of the federal government and business representatives' neoliberal policy orientation, which they strongly opposed. Independents thus rejected flexibilization, privileging instead the democratization of labor relations. For their part, corporatist union and business representatives essentially ignored proposals to democratize the labor code, emphasizing the need to flexibilize labor practices so as to further productivity and employment (Mayer 2006).

The Secretariat of Labor eventually chose to sideline independent union representatives, alleging that their staunch rejection of flexibilization derailed negotiation efforts. The Fox administration preferred to collaborate with business and corporatist union representatives in crafting a new reform project, which focused mainly on the flexibilizing of the LFT and paid only lip service to union democracy. But Congress shelved this reform proposal in early 2005, due to resistance from the main opposition party (Party of the Democratic Revolution, PRD) and segments of the PRI—the latter being reluctant to accept a relatively unpopular labor reform in the context of the upcoming 2006 national elections, in which the PRI had much to lose (*MLNA* April 2005).

The alliance between the PAN presidency and corporatist unions was deepened with the 2004 reform of the IMSS's pension system, which sought to significantly limit benefits and increase contributions of the Institute's workers. In this instance, corporatist union leaders and the Fox administration utilized the same rhetoric of social justice and economic responsibility to justify the projected reform. They claimed that the reform was necessary to save Mexico's social security system, and thus it would ultimately benefit the great majority of Mexicans. Corporatist union leaders and the government added that the status quo was unsustainable and favored only a very small minority of workers, while financially burdening the bulk of the population (Mayer and Marier 2006). Although the restructuring penalized unionized workers, IMSS employees were represented by an independent union. Workers affiliated with corporatist unions were therefore not impacted by this reform, and many accepted their leaders' rhetoric. Independent unions strongly opposed the pension reform, but discussions were cut short and the proposal was effectively fast-tracked through Congress by the PAN and its congressional allies.

Hopes of witnessing the establishment of a more open and democratic pattern of labor relations in post-transitional Mexico were dashed by the manner in which negotiations surrounding the failed 2003 labor reform and the 2004 IMSS pension restructuring were conducted. These instances suggested that the PAN administration would not hesitate to jettison its discourse supporting democratic labor relations and labor organizations (such as independent unions) if it felt this could compromise its neoliberal economic priorities. As such, the Fox government showed willingness to ally with corporatist union representatives to further its economic and pro-flexibilization policy agenda. This stance resembled closely the dynamics of state-labor relations that characterized the preceding PRI governments.

This sense of continuity was furthered by the Fox administration's decision to allow the continued widespread utilization of protection contracts, in order to ensure peaceful labor relations.[3] These contracts represented close to 90% of all collective agreements during the Fox *sexenio* and significantly contributed to keeping the labor force demobilized (Bensusán 2007, 20–25). Indeed, workers affected by protection contracts were generally unaware of their existence—and that a company union had usurped the representation of their interests. In that context, when labor issues arose, workers were generally left with little recourse and were therefore unlikely to mobilize, adopt work actions, or go on strike (Otis 2012).

Historically, the so-called white unions that generated these protection contracts were affiliated with official union confederations and operated with the support of the PRI-controlled state. This created a difficult setting for independent labor organizations, which sought to organize and mobilize Mexican workers. By contrast, protection contracts were specifically designed to keep the labor force passive and quiescent. Before the regime transition, workers trying to replace white unions by independent labor organizations were routinely intimidated, repressed, and fired. In the rare occasions when independent unions were successfully created, the Secretariat of Labor and Labor Boards generally refused to officially recognize them (Middlebrook 1995).

The situation changed little under Fox, as protection contracts remained prevalent. Labor Boards continued to obstruct the replacement of white unions by more democratic independent unions and maintained the practice of denying official registration for—or refusing the executive committee composition of—unions they deemed troublesome. Also, the boards allowed employers to continue their utilization of permissive hiring and firing practices that circumvented labor legislation, stalling their examination of unions' and workers' complaints related to that matter (*MLNA* January 2007).

Despite the alliance that had emerged between the Fox government and corporatist unions, labor relations during the first PAN administration became gradually more difficult. This context is illustrated by statistics on strike activities, which steadily increased during Fox's government and reached in 2006 a frequency that, albeit rather modest, had not been seen since 1996 (see figure 4.3). This evolution was paralleled by an intensification of the number of strike petitions in the second half of Fox's mandate (see figure 4.4). Furthermore, the Secretariat of Labor and the Labor Boards reportedly declared illegal an exceptional quantity of strikes during Fox's *sexenio* (*MLNA* April 2006, January 2007).

To be sure, this increasing antagonism in the Mexican labor climate largely involved independent unions. But interestingly, the peak in labor conflicts observed toward the end of Fox's mandate is attributable to two major corporatist unions. These organizations resolved to engage in strike activities following disagreements with their employer and the state's economic orientation, as well as with other corporatist unions (Camp 2014, 160–61). Indeed, these labor organizations, a dissident segment of the National Teachers' Union (Sindicato Nacional de Trabajadores de la Educación, SNTE) (the largest teachers' union in Latin America, with 1.4 million members) active in the state of Oaxaca and the National Union of Miners and Metal Workers (Sindicato Nacional de Trabajadores Mineros y Metalúrgicos, SNTMM) (Mexico's leading mine workers' union) shared a critical position toward state-regulated salary structures, demanding higher pay and better working conditions for their members. But the two unions also denounced the country's economic model and demanded that it be transformed so as to become more worker-friendly. Furthermore, the SNTMM criticized the corporatist unions' organizational framework and denounced the domination of the organization federating most official labor unions (i.e., the Labor Congress) by traditional corporatist leaders.

State and federal authorities interpreted this critical stance as a threat to their economic policy priorities. Moreover, the SNTMM's condemnation of the CT was ill received by the leadership of other corporatist unions, who considered this an attack on their interests and responded by repudiating the striking union and its leader. Also, the Oaxaca teachers rejected directives given by the SNTE's leadership, which advised them to end their work actions (*MLNA* February 2006, January 2007, January 2008). The SNTE had been an integral part of the PRI's corporatist framework, and its secretary general, Elba Esther Gordillo, had become a close ally of President Fox. The dissidents' actions therefore created significant tensions with the SNTE's national executive.

Antagonism degenerated into open confrontation when federal and state authorities engaged in the repression of these unions and their memberships, resorting to police interventions and Labor Board decisions to counter the workers' collective action. As such, the federal Labor Board declared the SNTMM's strike illegal, and the Secretariat of Labor removed Napoleón Gómez Urrutia, the miners' union's secretary general, accusing him of corruption and embezzlement. The federal Labor Board subsequently imposed a new, government-friendly leader on the union. Federal police forces then intervened to forcibly end work-action protests. For their part, the dissident teachers eventually negotiated an improved work contract, but faced ongoing police repression as they tried to continue their independent organizing and mobilization efforts (*MLNA* January 2006, January 2008).

Despite the scale and intensity of the repression, the Fox government faced limited criticisms from the corporatist labor movement. These unions' leadership generally supported the ousting of Gómez Urrutia, because of his harsh critiques of the CT, and approved of the forceful measures taken to impose an end to the miners' strike. A similar logic applied in the case of the dissident Oaxacan teachers, who had allied with supporters from autonomous civil society groups and independent labor organizations and ignored requests for moderation stemming from the SNTE's national leadership. As such, leaders of corporatist unions did not support the striking teachers and called for an end to their work actions.

For their part, independent labor organizations were initially weary of supporting Gómez Urrutia, who in 2001 had taken over the leadership of the SNTMM from his father, a corrupt and violent union leader who embodied the corporatist labor organizations' submission to the PRI's interests. But they eventually allied with the SNTMM in the creation of a "national front." Independent unions also backed the Oaxacan dissident teachers' movement (*MLNA* June 2006). In both cases, independent unions demanded that the government respect freedom of organization—in particular the right for union members to choose their leaders democratically—and the right to strike for labor organizations. Despite the national front's several public statements, marches, and work actions of various forms, their protest had little effect on the unfolding of events.

Labor Relations under Calderón

This antagonism in labor relations was deepened under the presidency of Felipe Calderón. If anything, Calderón grew closer to corporatist unions and adopted a harder line in his relations with defiant labor groups—and in particular those that participated in significant labor conflicts and criticized his administration's economic policies. As such, the Calderón government continued to undermine the resistance efforts of SNTMM members who had remained loyal to their overthrown elected secretary general, rejecting his state-imposed replacement. To that end, the federal government authorized (and in fact supported) the creation of an alternative, pro-business union to divide the miners and disrupt their struggle. Calderón adopted this course of action even though, by 2008, Mexico's Supreme Court had rejected most of the charges brought against Gómez Urrutia and deemed legal the strikes undertaken by the SNTMM in the defense of its members' interests. Likewise, the leader of the Popular Assembly of the Peoples of Oaxaca (Asamblea Popular de los Pueblos de Oaxaca, APPO), an association of grassroots organizations that had supported the Oaxacan striking teachers, was imprisoned shortly after Calderón took power. Police scrutiny and repression successfully demobilized the teachers' movement and its APPO allies (*MLNA* January 2008, January 2009).

But it is the manner in which the Calderón government dealt with the SME, the union representing the bulk of electrical workers active in the Federal District area, which constitutes perhaps the most remarkable illustration of the dynamics of labor relations between 2006 and 2012. The SME was active in a strategic sector of the Mexican economy (electricity distribution) and was considered one of the foremost independent unions in terms of its mobilization level and sociopolitical activities—especially its pro-democracy and anti-neoliberal agenda. From the late 1980s on, the SME vigorously criticized the federal government's efforts at restructuring the country's economy and opposed most facets of the neoliberal model implemented by successive PRI and PAN administrations (Aguilar García 2010, 13).

Although the SME was an outspoken critic of the Mexican federal government, it nevertheless refrained from undertaking any consequential work stoppages since 1987 (*MLNA* March 2008). The union occasionally threatened the government with strike petitions, but, as is the case for most Mexican unions, the threats did not become reality. More importantly, the SME was instrumental in building and participating in large union and popular fronts against the neoliberal policies furthered by the PAN governments. The SME's critical stance became more salient after Calderón's accession to power, as the union helped to create and lead an alliance of labor and social organizations opposed to the federal government's projects to reform and privatize the oil and electrical industries in Mexico (*MLNA* October 2009). As such, the SME became one of the principal and most visible opponents to the Calderón government's reformist agenda and neoliberal policy orientation.

In this context, elections were held in August 2009 for the renewal of the SME's executive team. Incumbent secretary general Martin Esparza Flores was reelected by a slim majority, which led his only rival to place a grievance with the Secretariat of Labor and the federal Labor Board. The Labor Board subsequently rejected the reelection of Esparza Flores and his team, leaving the union without an executive and compromising its ability to organize and mobilize. Esparza Flores and his supporters denounced this action as politically motivated and blamed the federal government for engineering a crisis within the SME (*MLNA* August 2009).

The Calderón government took advantage of this severe internal conflict paralyzing the SME to crack down on LFC, the parastatal agency that employed the great majority of SME members and which suffered from recurring yearly deficits of millions of dollars (*MLNA* August 2009). Pronouncing the LFC insolvent and unsustainable, the federal government declared the agency bankrupt. It simultaneously sent federal police and army troops to take possession of the LFC and expel SME members from the agency's facilities. In the process, the Calderón government fired over 44,000 workers and effectively abolished the SME. The government thus silenced a vocal opponent to its economic policies and a significant actor in the country's labor relation dynamics. Within the labor movement, only independent unions vigorously protested this action. The CT, to which the SME had remained affiliated despite being a leading independent union, the Confederation of Mexican Workers (Confederación de Trabajadores Mexicanos, CTM) (the main union in the CT), and other corporatist unions never denounced the government's decision, preferring to keep silent (*MLNA* October 2009).

President Calderón deepened the relations between the PAN-led federal government and corporatist unions such as the SNTE, the Sole Union of Electrical Workers (Sindicato Único de Trabajadores Electricistas de la República Mexicana, SUTERM) (the other main union representing electrical workers from across the country), the Mexican Oil Workers' Union (Sindicato de Trabajadores Petroleros de la República Mexicana, STPRM), and the Revolutionary Confederation of Workers and Peasants (Confederación Revolucionaria de Obreros y Campesinos, CROC). This alliance was particularly strong and visible in the case of Gordillo, then secretary-general of the SNTE and an ex-PRI leader. After having served as a faithful—if informal—advisor to President Fox, she left the PRI in 2006 and created a political party closely based upon the SNTE, which garnered a few seats in Congress and frequently collaborated with the PAN. Under Gordillo's leadership, the SNTE's executive also joined the government in an alliance to help impose an unpopular reform of Mexico's education system, against the will of a majority of her union's membership (*MLNA* May 2008).

Furthermore, the Calderón administration carried on with the practice of allowing white unions, affiliated with corporatist labor confederations, to sign protection contracts. These still represented as much as 90% of all collective agreements by the end of 2012, continuing to buttress labor peace through preserving the demobilization of workers (*MLNA* August 2009, January 2013). In addition, the Calderón government successfully allied with the National Union of Social Security Workers (Sindicato Nacional de Trabajadores del Seguro Social, SNTSS), co-opting its leader Valdemar Gutiérrez Fragoso, who was elected to the federal Congress under the PAN banner in 2009. Shortly after being elected, Gutiérrez Fragoso officially disaffiliated his union from the UNT, the main independent union confederation of which the SNTSS constituted the principal membership segment.

As such, it appears that President Calderón relied on a selective implementation of the LFT and on recurring formal and informal alliances with corporatist union leaders to further his administration's economic and reformist agenda. Indeed, the federal government resorted to repression and intimidation in its relations with the SNTMM, dissident SNTE members, and the SME, among others, while it favored a conciliatory approach in its dealings with corporatist and white unions, as well as toward protection contracts. Calderón furthermore successfully split the independent union movements, with the breakaway of the SNTSS from the UNT. This action, combined with the elimination of the SME, badly weakened the UNT and contributed to further marginalizing politically the independent union movement at large.

The labor market statistics presented above help to illustrate the harder line adopted by the Calderón government. In particular, the data indicate that the incidence of strikes fell radically from a yearly average of 44.5 under Fox to 18.5 under Calderón (see figure 4.3). The most pronounced dip in this indicator occurred just following the accession of Calderón to the presidency and immediately after the harsh resolution of the Miners and Teachers conflicts, as the number of strikes diminished from 55 in 2006 to 28 in 2007. This decline persisted and was again more pronounced following the clash between the SME and the federal government in 2009, as only 11 strikes were recorded in 2010—an unprecedented low point for this type of event. The number of strikes increased slightly during the last year of Calderón's mandate, but with only 19 official work stoppages recorded, this statistic remains in the historically low range.

There hence appears to be a strong correlation between clashes opposing the federal government and organized labor on the one hand, and a reduction in strike frequency on the other. This is likely explained by the position of weakness in which dissident labor organizations in general, and independent unions in particular, found themselves after the repression of the SNTMM, the Oaxacan teachers, and the SME; by the PAN government's co-optation of the SNTSS; and by the hard-line approach adopted by the Calderón administration in labor relations. This situation was compounded by the generally subdued attitude of corporatist union leaders in their relations with PAN federal governments.

Strike petitions data show a pattern opposite to that of strike occurrences (see figure 4.4). Indeed, strike petitions increased radically under the Calderón government, shifting from a yearly average of 6,488 under Fox to 11,096 under his successor. The data indicate a clear upward tendency as of 2005, as new antagonisms emerged in labor relations. This tendency followed a pattern established during the Salinas and Zedillo presidencies, at a time when organized labor found itself in a position of structural weakness, faced with a federal government determined to reduce its privileges and the cost of labor. Similarly, the frequency of strike petitions increased as the occurrence of actual strikes diminished after 2006, reaching a record high of 13,207 petitions in 2009—the year of the SME conflict and of the record low in actual strikes registered. In other words, it appears that organized labor resorted to similar strategies during the PAN presidencies as it did under the PRI's rule, that is, flooding the federal administration with strike petitions when labor relations became tense, but simultaneously shying away from actual work stoppages and open labor conflicts. It should also be underlined that this occurred in the context of the 2008–9 global economic recession, which worsened the already difficult labor context in Mexico and contributed to rendering workers and union leaders all the more reluctant to strike in order to settle labor conflicts.

Taking Stock of Labor Relations since 1988

During the authoritarian period, the corporatist and clientelistic systems linking most labor organizations to the PRI as well as the selective manner in which successive governments implemented the country's labor legislation, left very little leeway for the labor movement to constitute itself as a truly autonomous and dynamic sociopolitical actor. Despite hopes to the contrary, Mexico's transition to electoral democracy does not appear to have significantly modified the nature of the country's labor relations. PAN presidents Fox and Calderón have broadly followed the previously implemented patterns when dealing with unions, favoring clientelist ties with corporatist union leaders while marginalizing labor organizations that denounced and resisted the federal government's economic policy priorities. Available evidence suggests that this strategy was adopted in order to preserve labor peace—despite the occasional conflicts that punctuated the PAN governments—seen as a necessary condition for the deepening of the neoliberal model.

This context proved especially difficult for independent unions. These organizations and their leaderships were historically more representative of their members' demands and more transparent in their functioning, in comparison with corporatist unions. Also, contrary to corporatist unions, independent labor organizations supported a regime transition to democracy, believing this would also markedly transform the dynamics of labor relations in Mexico. In particular, independent unions had hoped that the transition to democracy would result in their obtaining greater prestige and increased membership, and in the congruent decline of corporatist unions. Instead, the PAN federal governments generally maintained a hard-line approach when dealing with independent unions. In addition to being considered an undesirable interlocutor by the PAN federal administrations, independent unions found themselves the target of repression at the end of the Fox *sexenio* and during Calderón's mandate. As a result, the labor movement has continued a historical trend of relatively low mobilization levels and limited gains in the defense of workers' rights and interests. Confronted with this reality, it appears that Mexican workers have increasingly resisted unionization campaigns, and have chosen to discontinue their union membership (Aguilar García 2010, 2012).

Accordingly, indicators of unionization rates and the labor movement's cohesion show significant variations under the successive PAN governments. Following the democratic transition, a noticeable increase in the unionization rate took place, reaching a peak of 17.5% by 2004, before falling to a rate of 16.3% in 2006—a rate more akin to the numbers seen until 2000. Overall, Fox's *sexenio* averaged a unionization rate of 16.6%, relatively in line with the rates that characterized his immediate predecessors. By contrast, Calderón's mandate was marked by near constant decline in rates of unionization, closing at 13.6%—the lowest recorded rate in decades (Blanchflower 2006, 30; Fairris and Levine 2004, 11). This decline in unionization rates can be attributed in great part to the process of neoliberal economic restructuring that has affected Mexico since the late 1980s and led, among other things, to the privatization of numerous state-owned companies. But the reduction in unionization can also be interpreted as a symptom of the difficult labor relations climate discussed above, which characterized the end of the Fox government and the entirety of the Calderón administration.

Likewise, there is strong evidence of union fragmentation taking place between 1988 and 2012. In particular, the CT lost several of its important member unions, such as the SNTMM and the SME, which left due to irreconcilable divergences or organizational crises. In addition, the CT suffered from deep divisions with regard to its leadership composition, which led the CROC and the Regional Confederation of Mexican Workers (Confederación Regional Obrera Mexicana, CROM)—two longstanding and well-established corporatist industrial unions—to leave this confederation.[4] The Federation of Public Service Workers' Unions (Federación de Sindicatos de Trabajadores al Servicio del Estado, FSTSE) also experienced a scission in 2004, as the SNTE and another twenty unions left that organization to create a new, parallel federation of public servants: the Democratic Federation of Unions of Public Servants (Federación Democrática de Sindicatos de Servidores Públicos, FEDESSP). In addition, following divergences with the PRI, the SNTE together with the SUTERM and the STPRM, created in 2008 a new association of corporatist unions, thus further dividing the corporatist labor movement (*MLNA* January 2008, July 2008, January 2009, January 2010).

Independent unions were not immune to this phenomenon, as the UNT lost roughly a third of its membership when the SNTSS left this confederation in 2010 (Notimex 2010). The FSM, the other independent labor coalition of significance, was essentially destroyed when the SME—its leading member—ceased to represent active workers following the Calderón government's actions of 2009 (*MLNA* January 2010). Both these events left the independent labor movement in a very difficult and vulnerable situation, placing it further on the defensive in its relations with the state, employers, and official unions—against which it competes for attracting new members, among other things.

Another sign of fragmentation is perceptible in the diminishing membership of labor organizations. For instance, the CT's membership fell from two million workers in the early 1990s to 1.25 million in 2000, and to 1.034 million workers in 2008. The CTM saw its membership diminish from 1.1 million in 2000 to 754,286 in 2008. Similarly, the membership of the CROM was reduced from 176,000 in 2000 to 81,000 by the end of the Fox government. For its part, the FSTSE, which also claimed more than two million members in the 1990s, saw its ranks melting to 740,000 workers by 2008—mostly due to the creation of the rival FEDESSP (Aguilar García 2010, 15; Muñoz Ríos 2007). It is more difficult to obtain a precise evaluation of the UNT's membership, given the multitude of minor unions that it congregates. The most plausible available numbers suggest a strong reduction in its membership from 1.3 million workers at the time of its founding in 1997, to roughly 600,000 members by 2010. This reduction is mostly—but not solely—attributable to the SNTSS's departure that year (Robles 2011).

A correlation can be established between the reduction in union density and the increasing union fragmentation on the one hand, and Mexico's economic restructuring as well as its transition to democracy on the other. Indeed, available evidence suggests that corporatist union leaders have been unable but also unwilling to defend the labor rights and socioeconomic interests of their organizations' members during the difficult times that accompanied the implementation of market-based policies in the 1988–2012 period, during which successive administrations sought to liberalize trade, rationalize production, and flexibilize labor (Aguilar García 2010, 2012). When confronted with these challenges, corporatist union leaders primarily strived to safeguard their position of power within the unions, which allowed them to receive multiple political and economic advantages from successive federal governments, regardless of partisan alignment (Selee and Peschard 2010, 20–22). As indicated above, corporatist union leaders thus generally collaborated with successive federal administrations, insuring labor peace and allowing the relatively unimpeded implementation of their economic program. This often occurred to the general detriment of their unions' membership, which suffered reductions in real salaries, de facto flexibilization, deteriorating work conditions, and job losses. In exchange, corporatist union leaders sought (and obtained) the preservation of LFT articles, such as the Exclusion clause, that allowed for the continuation of their political and socioeconomic privileges.

As a way to explain this strategy of corporatist union leaders, PRI deputy Leobardo Soto Martínez, leader of the CTM and ex-president of the House of Deputies' Commission on Labor and Social Welfare (2010–12), commented that "the CTM and the CT seek solutions through dialogue, so there is no need for demonstrating and protesting. Demonstrations and protests is not the way to make agreements and deals. We make many agreements and reach consensus through dialogue with the state and employers."[5] Nonetheless, Soto Martínez indicated that corporatist labor leaders never enjoyed particular privileges and favors in return for their accommodating stance, and that they were thinking primarily of "the good of their members" in choosing this strategy.

By contrast, PAN senator Alfredo Rodríguez y Pacheco, ex-secretary of the federal Senate's Commission on Labor and Social Welfare (2006–12), stated that corporatist union members "are now more aware of what their leaders are doing [and] that they are being taken advantage of. Workers no longer trust and respect their leaders. . . . They have realized that their leaders only look for political positions and seats in Congress, and are not interested in promoting the interests of their members."[6] Reflecting on the subject of union density and fragmentation, Arturo Vega, secretary-general of the Independent Union of Workers at the Metropolitan Autonomous University (Sindicato Independiente de Trabajadores de la UAM, SITUAM) added that, "People no longer believe in the importance of unions. This is a growing situation, especially in Mexico with all the corporatist unions. The latest generation to integrate the labor market has a vision of society that does not include the importance of fighting for obtaining rights. For the new workers, participating in unions is secondary."[7]

When independent union representatives were asked to assess the evolution of labor relations in Mexico during the Fox government, they were unequivocal. Sergio Sánchez, vice-secretary of External Affairs for the SME, stated that "the labor situation under Fox has continued just as it was before [the transition]: strikes are constantly rejected by the Labor

Boards, and the Boards also make it very difficult for independent unions to be officially recognized and to have their executive board approved."[8] Alejandra Barrales, ex–secretary general of the Union of Flight Attendants (Asociación Sindical de Sobrecargos de Aviación, ASSA), explained that "the IMSS reform dealt a blow to the unions, as they could not prevent the reform from taking place. . . . Although independent unions had all of the resources they needed to stop the reform, they lacked the political will to do so."[9] Agustin Rodríguez, leader of the independent Union of Workers of the National Autonomous University of Mexico (Sindicato de Trabajadores de la Universidad Nacional Autónoma de México, STUNAM) concluded that Mexico's labor relations context "did not really change under Fox, although there was initially a bit more political opening. But that's where things ended. This was due to the Fox government's overreliance and overdependence on the most conservative and reactionary sectors of society, the CT and the COPARMEX [the Employers' Confederation of the Mexican Republic (Confederación Patronal de la República Mexicana)], to support his economic program. Fox was effectively a hostage of the CT."[10]

More generally, José Olivera, secretary of Political Affairs for the STUNAM, believed that "the main changes since the arrival of the PAN in government have been: the increase of flexibilization, the larger exercise of corporatism, and more repression against independent unions."[11] Benito Martínez, secretary general of the FAT, one of the oldest independent organizations in Mexico, added that between 2000 and 2012, "the people and institutions in charge of verifying that labor rights are respected did not do their job. Instead of implementing the LFT, they put more obstacles [to it], they attempted to demobilize the working class, and they did not demand that businesses respect the labor law. Independent unions are generally not invited to [state-business-labor] negotiation and bargaining tables. And when we are, it is done in a symbolic manner so that [the government] can say: all unions agreed with the resulting policies. But we actually are not given a voice at all."[12]

Interestingly, this perspective tended to be corroborated by PAN senator Rodríguez y Pacheco, who indicated that, "Independent unions that gained the support of their members legitimately do not have space in the political arena. . . . In the Labor Commissions of both chambers [of the federal Congress], the main unionist leaders are part of the CTM. These leaders gain more personal power, and the union members do not. There is no transparency in how they manage large sums of money. [These labor] leaders do not want to improve the rights of workers."[13]

Conclusion

Despite expectations to the contrary, Mexico's shift to a market-based economic model and transition to democracy yielded neither significant flexibilization of the labor market nor democratization of labor relations. This chapter suggests that this high degree of continuity is mainly attributable to the specific configuration taken by the country's neoliberal economic model. This generated a structure of incentives for political and labor elites to favor the persistence of nondemocratic patterns of labor relations and to leave the country's labor legislation essentially untouched. Therefore, similar to the situation outlined in the chapter on Chile, the legacy of structural adjustment and authoritarianism deeply affected labor relations in Mexico's post-transition period. This institutional and structural context was also significant in determining the changing nature of ties between labor and political parties, as well as in limiting the political influence of the Mexican labor movement after the transition to democracy.

As such, whereas Fox showed an initial openness to inputs from all segments of organized labor, labor relations in Mexico rapidly returned to the status quo pro ante during his mandate and that of his successor. In a nutshell, corporatist union leaders offered to deliver the compliance and passivity of a majority of workers employed in Mexico's formal economy. By contrast, independent labor organizations, which represented only a minority of formal sector workers, strongly challenged the Fox and Calderón governments' neoliberal economic policies. The PAN governments therefore associated with corporatist unions, politically marginalized independent unions, and based their relations with organized labor upon a restrictive interpretation and selective implementation of the LFT.

These characteristics contributed to creating a significant continuity with the labor relation dynamics that prevailed under the PRI's dictatorship. Indeed, the repression of labor organizations carried out under the Calderón government is reminiscent of the beginning of Salinas's presidency, which witnessed the imprisonment of dissident union leaders by federal authorities (Middlebrook 1995, 294). But whereas labor repression under Salinas gradually relaxed as his *sexenio* progressed, it seems to have been sustained under Calderón. Interestingly, this situation prevailed despite several judgments by the Supreme Court, which gradually weakened the regulatory power of the state over labor organizations (*MLNA* June 2011). Hence, the democratization of Mexican politics seems to have had a limited effect on that country's labor relations and the labor market.

The continuity in state-labor relations across regime types and parties in government has had numerous consequences. First, among other things, the quality of Mexico's democracy is severely affected by the limitations of workers' rights and freedoms. Second, divisions between corporatist unions and independent unions are deeper than ever, the latter group considering the former as lackeys of federal authorities while corporatist unions see independent labor organizations as an irritant that should be eliminated. These divisions severely compromise the ability of the labor movement to effectively negotiate with the government and business owners. Third, workers have gradually deserted unions since the transition. This is no doubt a reflection of the lack of representativeness and transparency that characterize corporatist unions' leaderships. But this exodus also affected independent unions, likely as a result of their political marginalization and relative ineffectiveness in defending Mexican workers' rights. Fourth, and finally, organized labor has fragmented, thus reducing the cohesion and diluting the labor movement's political influence. The return of the PRI to the federal presidency in December 2012 has offered very little hope of changing these patterns of labor relations in Mexico.

5

Uncertain Transitions

Labor and the Politics of Reform in Argentina

VIVIANA PATRONI

Workers and their organizations have played a critical role in the modern history of Argentina. Starting with the early activation of its labor movement during the rapid transformation of the country at the turn of the twentieth century, through the midcentury rise of its particular variant of populism heavily immersed in the language of labor, to the undisputable role trade unionism played in defining the nature of political conflict for the remainder of the century, labor has been at the core of politics in Argentina. Workers' centrality as a political force and the high levels of organization unions attained go a long way toward explaining the country's more equitable income distribution when compared to the rest of the region. Notwithstanding these strengths, however, the labor movement in Argentina has also suffered from critical structural weaknesses. These became painfully evident as workers confronted repression, neoliberal reforms, and, most recently, the changing economic and political realities of the twenty-first century.

The broad objective of this chapter is to elucidate what lies at the core of labor's strengths and weaknesses, how these affected its response to the neoliberal reforms introduced during the 1990s by the administration of Carlos Menem—the president for the Peronist party, historically the party of the working class in Argentina—and how political decisions then determined the nature of labor's political engagement in post-neoliberal Argentina.[1] It is with this perspective that I provide an overview of the trajectory of Argentina's dominant working-class organizations, particularly the CGT. During the critical transformation of the country in the 1990s, when Argentina was the stage for a radical neoliberal reform program, the flexibilization of labor markets figured prominently in the government's plans. The Menem administration introduced at that time a number of critical changes to existing labor legislation that, reinforced by economic conditions that also pushed in the direction of informalization and flexibilization, resulted in the undermining of workers' rights.

The commitment to the implementation of this neoliberal reform agenda deeply transformed the Peronist party. I argue that these changes significantly transformed also the nature of the CGT, both as the main organization within the labor movement in Argentina and as a key force within the Peronist party. The 1990s constituted a watershed for the CGT even if its connection to power allowed it to dodge the dismantling of its core organizational rights. One of the most critical expressions of the impact of the decade was the growing political distance that developed between the Peronist party and the CGT. Moreover, while workers encountered a much more propitious context for their demands and labor unions regained considerable strength after 2003, the relationship worsened progressively, particularly after 2010. At the core of the dilemma were the tensions within a Peronist party divided over the role organized labor should play in it. The questioning was made all the more significant in the context of a structurally much weaker CGT and the growing tensions between the conditions for sustained economic growth and the redistributive expectations such growth fostered under the administrations of Néstor and Cristina Kirchner.

While the focus of my analysis is the most powerful organization within the labor movement, the CGT, my premise is that the only way to grasp the political role of this institution in the country, and of the body of legislation that has shaped it, is to examine it in the context of workers' struggles more broadly. The question of how to encompass, direct, and represent these struggles has been decisive for the CGT, both before and after the critical transformation of the 1990s. Its effectiveness in doing so has depended on its ability to overcome the limitations placed on it not only by the state and employers but also, and fundamentally, by other forces within the working class.

The chapter is divided into four main sections. The first section provides a general framework for this discussion, connecting the labor movement in Argentina with the contemporary development of the country. In the second section, I focus on the experience of Argentina's working-class organizations from the return to democracy in 1983 until the end of the Menem administration in 1999. It was with the return to democracy that the transformations initiated during the 1976–83 military dictatorship were finally cemented. In terms of labor markets, changes increasingly acquired the characteristics of what later became popularly known as labor flexibilization. In the third section I explore the particular ways in which the legacies of the 1990s transformed the role labor organizations and the CGT played in unleashing the political events that led to crisis in 2001–2. The fourth section addresses the relationship between the CGT and the three Peronist administrations that ruled the country between 2003 and 2015. While these governments were originally more open to the historical distributional concerns of labor, they were not equally permeable to the CGT's political expectations. The chapter concludes with a reflection on the implications of the transformation of the Peronist party and its relationship with organized labor and some concluding notes about what lies at the core of the transformation of the CGT.

Labor Reform, Labor Power, and the Politics of Transformation in Contemporary Argentina

To account for the political and economic transformation of the country during the critical decade of the 1990s, it is essential to reflect on the complex, often ambiguous but always critical role the CGT has played in the modern history of Argentina. While the growing social dislocation resulting from labor flexibilization was partly due to organized labor's inability, and in some cases even unwillingness, to fend off reforms, it is also the case that despite all of its shortcomings and contradictions, the CGT was central to Argentine workers' previous success in securing levels of protection and welfare that were high by regional standards. What changed in the 1990s? What constellation of factors led to the labor movement's inability to defend its rights?

Inclusion, Exclusion, and the Political Economy of Labor Conflicts

Three factors seem particularly instructive for understanding the CGT's decisive political role in Argentina. First is the peculiarities of Peronism as the hegemonic party of the working class. Argentina's rapid economic transformation over the first decade of the twentieth century had generated by the 1940s a relatively large urban working class, particularly when measured by regional standards. Although considerably well organized, workers had not been successful in overcoming their political and economic exclusion. It was in this context of workers' marginalization as a social group that Juan Perón's appeal as an ally and advocate can best be grasped. For their part, workers offered Perón all the political possibilities of a formidable ally. The political significance of workers in the constitutive period of Peronism can best be appreciated in the very discourse of populism in the country. In particular, workers and their demands for social justice and inclusion came to embody the demands of all those Peronism sought to represent. Moreover, it was the language of workers' demands for their recognition as citizens that provided Peronism with its transformative discourse, and in so doing it also allowed the working class to develop a new political identity that transformed it into a key social and political player. What is more, Peronism provided political coherence to both the working class and its union leadership as newly dignified agents of transformation that withstood the growing challenges they faced over the following decades. For reasons further explored below, the political content of this relationship between Peronism and working-class organizations—if not the working class—was significantly transformed during the 1990s.

A second factor relates to the connection between the organized labor movement and the state. As in the rest of Latin America, and as mentioned in chapter 2, the Argentine state acquired a pivotal role in mediating the conflict between capital and labor. This relationship between state and labor was reinforced through the enactment of labor legislation that secured the CGT monopoly of representation at the national level. In the particular case of Argentina, union power was additionally cemented through the existence of only one industry-wide union with the legal entitlement to negotiate collective agreements (*personería gremial*) and, since 1969, the right to administer health care services (*obras sociales*) for union members. In this administrative capacity they acquired the power to control extensive financial resources. In view of what would happen later in the 1990s, this list should also include the structural power that very low levels of unemployment had provided to unions and that, in practice, allowed them to actually benefit from the privileges formally granted to them in existing legislation.

A third factor accounting for the important role of the CGT lies in the dynamics of the relationship between the dominant union leadership and the labor movement more broadly, which conferred true political value to the position of the former within the Peronist party, or Justicialist Party (Partido Justicialista, PJ) as it is officially known. To be of political significance to both the PJ and the workers it claimed to represent, the CGT leadership needed to be able to neutralize opposition to its claim as the sole legitimate representative of the working class. Overall the CGT met the objective successfully although it was not always an easy task, as challenges to the labor leadership were a constant feature in the country's political landscape.

Despite all their shortcomings, conflicts, contradictions, and increasing bureaucratization, unions, and in particular the CGT, remained vital political forces because they were instrumental in advancing demands most workers considered central. Moreover, they did so as part of the party that represented the political voice of a large segment of the working class. The common identity Peronism conferred to the working class, the privileged position labor legislation granted to unions and, by extension, to the CGT, and the way both of these developments strengthened the clout of the official labor movement among the working class and within the Peronist movement itself, made the CGT a key political player during the period considered the "golden age" of ISI, from the early 1950s to 1975 (Neffa and Panigo 2010, 262). The last decade of ISI in Argentina was characterized not only by sustained growth but also by the steady growth of real income, no doubt a result of the CGT's assertive role in labor conflicts. The proportion of GDP accruing to salaries had reached a peak of almost 50% in 1954, toward the end of the second Peronist government. The share fell to 36.5% in 1959 but recovered thereafter, unevenly at times, reaching roughly 50% again by 1974, with Perón's return to power (Lindenboim, Kennedy, and Graña 2010, 543–44).

In the language of Schneider (2013), there was considerable "complementarity" between labor and the strategy of accumulation employed by capitalists in key economic sectors. Nevertheless, the tensions between them were just as important, and these mounted as the conflict between capital and labor intensified over time, each vying for a larger share of the economic pie. While this conflict in itself did not imperil longer-term economic growth, it did raise the political stakes to the point of inescapable crisis by the mid-1970s. By that time growing social and labor unrest, widespread political violence, high inflation, market shortages, and an unfavorable external situation all combined to create a climate of chaos and crisis. Labor mobilization, at points beyond and against the CGT's control, was a central facet of a broader process of radicalization and polarization in the country, and both changes deeply transformed Peronism itself, as it increasingly encompassed a widely divergent group of political organizations with conflicting political ideologies (Sidicaro 2002, 103). By mid-1975, the CGT was the main source of political support for the increasingly isolated, politically conservative and chaotic administration of Isabel Perón, who had succeeded her husband upon his death in 1974 (137).

The radicalization of the working-class demands was matched by the burgeoning conviction within the traditional right-wing forces in Argentine society that the crisis was the outcome of a mistaken development pattern that had pushed the country to the brink of civil war. This perception of the crisis implied not only a prescription for economic change but also, tragically, a justification among key economic groups for the use of any violence necessary to see it through. In March 1976, the military took power with the stated objective of resolving the crisis, based on the premise that dismantling protectionism and deregulating markets would discipline the labor movement, putting a check once and for all on its political power.[2] What closed this chapter in the history of the country, then, was the installation of a regime of terror that sought to create the conditions for structural economic change by eliminating all those posing a perceived threat or potentially opposed to the reform program.

Organized labor and workers more generally bore the heaviest losses.[3] A combination of "extermination of the base," where dissidence had grown, and "incarceration at the peak" of the mainstream Peronist union leadership was put in place to undermine the possibilities of a labor response to the economic restructuring the military sought to implement (Drake 1996, 157). The CGT was banned, its constituent unions were placed under the control of military-appointed officers, and participation in any form of work action was severely punished. Labor legislation reform sanctioned these changes, in particular Laws 21,621, 21,400, 22,105 (1979) and 21,297, which modified the existing Labor Contract Law of 1974. Notwithstanding the legal and extrajudicial limitations on the freedom of association and the right to organize and strike, unions manifested their opposition to the military regime in various ways, ranging from more spontaneous and localized acts of resistance to the declaration of five general strikes starting as soon as 1979 (Carrera 2013, 120).

Finally, the military oversaw a deep structural change in the economy that substantively transformed the material conditions upon which the industrial working class had, until then, based its power and organization. In many ways, the transformation reflects global changes in the accumulation strategies of capitalism starting in the early 1970s, which preconfigured a new balance of power between workers and employers. What sets Argentina apart, however, was the magnitude of the damage the new policies produced. By 1982, seven years of trade liberalization, capital market deregulation, privatization, and fiscal discipline rendered an economy that was 9% smaller per capita than it had been in 1975 (Smith 1991, 260).

Restructuring inflicted harsh new conditions for the industrial sector, including the loss of about 10% of industrial production between 1974 and 1983 (Basualdo 2010, 136). Manufacturing thus went from 28.2% of total GDP in 1974 to only 22.4% in 1982. The suspension of collective bargaining and the imposition of government-dictated salaries resulted in a 40% drop in real salaries by 1983 compared to 1974 (137). The share of salaries in national income dropped by 17.5% in just the first year after the military takeover. By 1977, it had reached its lowest historical level at less than 30%. Though it later increased, salaries never again represented more than 40% of the national income (Lindenboim, Kennedy, and Graña 2010, 544). These critical changes—both economic restructuring and the drop in the share of income accruing to salaries—evidence a breaking point in the development history of the country and in the power of labor to alter its course, even under democratic rule. At the same time, the increasing weakness of organized labor and the CGT more generally must also be explained in political terms, and the struggles around labor legislation reforms in the 1980s and 1990s offer an exceptional standpoint from which to analyze the process. This is the subject of the next section.

Workers, the CGT, and Post-Dictatorial Argentina

As mentioned in chapter 2, in countries like Argentina and Brazil the return to democracy afforded workers more propitious conditions for their struggles to protect basic rights, but democratization was certainly no panacea. Some of the strongest forces influencing the direction of flexibilization of labor markets—changes in development strategies favoring freer trade, economic deregulation, and a reorientation of state involvement in the economy—became incrementally ubiquitous in post-dictatorial governments. This happened as the heterodox adjustment plans transitional governments implemented to mend the political cleavages the military dictatorship had created faltered. For workers and the CGT in Argentina, the return to constitutional order unfolded in unexpected ways—a preamble to the inauspicious course events were to take in the new democratic period.

First of all, there was a substantial reconfiguration of forces within the labor movement. Military repression had physically eliminated many within the main forces opposed to the CGT leadership. Equally important, some of the more radical political ideals that had nourished the development of these forces became increasingly marginalized as the country returned to democracy. In political terms, both of these changes reinforced the mainstream leadership within the CGT and reduced the capacity of the broader labor movement to be an influential and progressive participant in this transitional period. Indeed, it was mostly nonlabor actors that promoted a debate over the need for labor renewal in the new era of democracy in Argentina. However, there were also major challenges to the capacity of the CGT as a political actor. While the extraordinary repressive measures the military unleashed against the labor movement had not entirely deterred union opposition, unions underwent a substantial political upset when the presidential candidate for the Radical Civic Union (Unión Cívica Radical, UCR), Raúl Alfonsín, implicated them, and through them Peronism itself, in a "military-union pact" designed to cover up human rights abuses. The tide also turned against the Peronist labor movement within the party, as many in it saw the CGT as responsible for the first defeat of Peronism in free and open elections in 1983.

Against this backdrop, President Alfonsín (1983–89) charted the course of the reforms his administration considered essential to safeguard the government at a time of great economic and political uncertainty. It is not at all surprising that one of his first acts of government was to send a proposal to Congress for changes to labor legislation. The stated objectives of Alfonsín's "Law for Union Reorganization" were to both promote the renewal of union leadership with new electoral rules and secure minority representation within the leadership. These changes were calculated as means to displace the CGT's traditional Peronist leadership and thus also neutralize some of the organization's power. In response, notwithstanding the CGT's weakened structural and political position, its leaders accomplished the double feat of unifying contending factions within its own ranks and regaining the support of disapproving Peronist members of Congress who had imputed unionists with the electoral defeat. Though the legislation was approved by the lower chamber of Congress, it was eventually defeated in a vote in the Senate in March 1984 (Buchanan 1995, 136–37; Thompson 1993, 87).

This setback for the government, a win for the Peronist labor leadership, set the tone of their relationship for the rest of Alfonsín's presidential mandate. Not only was the CGT able to reaffirm its political capabilities even at a time of relative structural weakness but also its organizational and political strength acquired new meaning in the context of the various heterodox stabilization plans with which the government attempted to overcome the economic crises it faced. Under these circumstances, and in contrast with the original inclination of the Alfonsín administration, the centralized and tight top-down control the labor leadership exercised within unions was an asset for the government. The strategy of the CGT was to demand the restoration of the legal framework that had ensured precisely its tight control over the union structure, and, as economic conditions became increasingly challenging, the Radical administration saw in that demand a space for negotiation. Following a familiar pattern, the conflict with organized labor was mediated and then tempered by extending some concessions of key importance to its leadership that included, in addition to the labor laws mentioned above, the preservation of unions' right to administer health care funds (Thompson 1993, 88). Thirteen general strikes reminded the government of the critical role the CGT would play in making adjustment policies viable.

Eventually, setting aside its original plans, the government appointed a new minister of labor representing a dissenting faction of the CGT, who supported a set of laws that restored historical labor rights and practices in Argentina.[4] Between 1987–88, the Congress passed legislation protecting sector-wide collective bargaining, historical forms of union organizing in the country, and union control over the administration of health care services (Buchanan 1995, 141–42; Cook 2007, 66; Bisio, Battistini, and Montes Cató 1999, 148–51).

The CGT's show of strength against Alfonsín's labor policy and adjustment plans was quite ineffectual, however, in altering the pattern of economic and social transformation the country had followed. As in the rest of Latin America, and in fact most of the global south, the 1980s were a period of austerity and structural adjustment to the new conditions imposed by the debt crisis. As elsewhere, this period was not kind to workers or other vulnerable sectors in society.[5] In Argentina, the various crises created by restructuring took on increasingly severe connotations as the decade progressed, culminating with the hyperinflationary crises of 1989 and 1990. Overall, the CGT was unable to reduce the negative impact that the economic reforms introduced in the democratic period had on real salaries and income distribution (Thompson 1993, 89).

Similarly, within Peronism itself, the CGT's mobilizing capability was not sufficient to significantly affect the course of the internal transformation under way, which was to have critical implications for organized labor after the election of Carlos Menem in 1989. Nonetheless, while the party's transformation seemed to signal a shift away from the key role organized labor had played until then, Menem carried the party once more to electoral success by mobilizing supporters around some of the same historical principles that had been constitutive of the party's political identity. In this sense, labor appeared to recover the political relevance that was so central to both its own identity and the defense of its key demands. But this proved to be only an ephemeral, and probably the last, moment of consensus within the party.

Menem, Labor Reforms, and Workers: A Harsh End to the Century

If Menem's win in 1989 created expectations that his government would reaffirm and act on the distributional concerns so central to labor and the Peronist party, these vanished quickly in the wake of the incoming administration's early reform plans. Hyperinflation in 1989 and 1990 granted legitimacy to the draconian measures the government presented as a way out of the crisis—measures that would further define and give new impetus to the restructuring policies so long in the making in Argentina. Despite these harsh policy shifts, though, economic volatility continued until the government, under the leadership of a new economy minister, Domingo Cavallo, introduced another stabilization plan in 1991.[6] The central component of the plan was a new Convertibility Law pegging the domestic currency to the U.S. dollar and forcing the Central Bank to limit the country's monetary base to the availability of international reserves.[7] Convertibility finally succeeded in both curbing inflation and pushing forward an ambitious program of economic reforms. Sustaining the convertibility of the peso imposed specific conditions on the restructuring policies the country would pursue in the name of market efficiency, and changes to labor regulations—a demand business had vehemently pressed for since 1989, a time at which the heterodox approach President Alfonsín had followed turned into an economic debacle—became a central area of reform during this Convertibility era in Argentina.

The early period of declining inflation and renewed economic growth was key in cementing the popularity of Menem and the economic plan. However, the package of reforms had a very direct and negative impact on employment conditions, and, as Convertibility's early positive impact on growth gave way to instability and recession, the economy as a whole began to suffer. Between 1991 and the first recession of the period in 1995—related to the "Tequila" crisis—the economy grew on average by 5% per year. However, unemployment trebled during the same period, from 6.9% to over 18.4% by May 1995 (Novick, Lengyel, and Sarabia 2009, 239). While there was some improvement in the following years, in 1998 unemployment began to grow relentlessly, reaching 21.5% by 2002. The deterioration of employment was also evidenced in the growth of underemployment and unregistered employment (see table 5.1). Involuntary underemployment increased from 16.4% in 1995 to 24.3% in 2002. Unregistered employment, as in the rest of Latin America, increased exponentially during the 1990s, from approximately 27% in 1990 to almost 44% in 2003. Though labor market figures at the beginning of the 1990s already reflected the effects of the economically troubled 1980s and the severe crises that afflicted the country between 1989 and 1991, things became consistently worse for workers during the 1990s, reaching the point of disaster early in 2002 and remaining dire until the economy reacted to the new conditions created by the end of Convertibility starting in mid-2003.

Table 5.1. Economically Active Population (EAP) and Main Employment Indicators as % of EAP, 1995–2012

Year	Economically Active Population	Unemployment	Involuntary Underemployment	Unregistered Employment
1995	44.64%	17.54%	16.43%	38.47%
1996	44.66%	18.26%	17.38%	39.76%
1997	45.50%	15.82%	17.04%	42.12%
1998	45.63%	13.69%	17.11%	42.41%
1999	46.14%	15.12%	17.94%	42.68%
2000	45.90%	16.60%	18.84%	42.55%
2001	45.73%	19.87%	20.28%	42.41%
2002	46.22%	24.37%	24.30%	41.65%
2003	46.26%	21.66%	19.93%	43.95%
2004	46.51%	18.39%	17.57%	43.93%
2005	46.31%	15.11%	14.64%	43.37%
2006	46.66%	12.56%	13.20%	41.28%
2007	46.21%	9.90%	11.28%	39.47%
2008	45.87%	8.46%	10.56%	36.68%
2009	46.36%	9.09%	12.23%	35.79%
2010	46.01%	8.33%	10.87%	34.90%
2011	46.35%	7.91%	10.12%	33.95%
2012	46.28%	7.79%	10.31%	34.18%

Source: Felder and Patroni 2016.

Economic restructuring, then, resulted in a very concrete transformation of working conditions. Indeed, in many respects, the labor legislation reform promoted by the government simply institutionalized the new working conditions that structural reforms were imposing on workers de facto (Tissera et al. 2000, 134), but the institutionalization of these working conditions was a key demand of the private sector, and the government took it seriously. Moreover, as the economy faced growing challenges and setbacks, labor reform became increasingly important as a policy target for both the government and employers.

It is in this context of the de facto flexibilization of labor relations that the politics of labor reform unfolded. It was a critical moment for labor and one from which it emerged transformed. Not only was the existing labor legislation considered the culprit for "rigidities" that supposedly crippled the economy's capacity to generate employment, but the power that the CGT and unions had wielded within Peronism also became a matter of dispute.

Although gaining congressional support for new labor legislation took some time, soon after taking office Menem sanctioned a number of decrees that directly affected labor rights. As part of the emergency measures to respond to the grave economic predicaments the country faced, official decrees in 1989 (decrees 1477 and 1478) allowed employers to provide up to 20% of workers' salaries in the form of vouchers exempted from all legal contributions. In 1990, with privatization in mind, the government modified collective agreements in public enterprises to set wage limits, and, through decree 2184/90, restricted the right to strike in services the government declared essential. It was only in 1991 and after the Convertibility Law had also been implemented that the government was able to secure congressional approval for laws modifying core areas of labor legislation, particularly in the sphere of individual rights, though not exclusively so. As discussed below, collective labor rights were a key arena of political negotiations between Menem and the CGT.

After almost two years of negotiations, in 1991 Congress sanctioned the National Employment Law. This law formalized some critical changes leading to the flexibilization of individual employment contracts—changes that became more pervasive with the introduction of further legislation that remained in effect until 1998, when many of these legal changes were reversed. One important area of reform was the establishment of various types of temporary employment contracts, which became the main conduit for the expansion and normalization of precarious employment in the country. While these positions were originally limited by a number of stipulations, when the unemployment crisis worsened in 1995, a new law to promote employment extended the probationary period of contracts to up to six months and expanded the menu of temporary contracts to provide incentive for hiring those belonging to a number of vulnerable groups. The law also instituted a new apprenticeship program for youth between the ages of 14 and 25, relieving employers from any kind of contractual responsibility to the apprentices. Another form of precarious employment for young workers were internships lasting up to four years, which decree 340/92 exempted from the definition of formal employment. Toward the end of the decade, this internship system was further extended as the employment crisis reached its peak (Bonnet 2007, 24–25).

Beyond the flexibility afforded by temporary contracts, another benefit they promised was a reduction in indirect costs for employers—the second key trend in labor legislation reform. Indeed, severance pay was not applicable to short-term workers, and payroll taxes and other social security contributions associated with their employment were also greatly reduced (Cook 2007, 74–75; Marshall 2004, 12). After 1993, these same concessions were extended to longer-term contracts through the deduction of employers' contributions to retirement, the health care system, family allowances, and the employment fund (Marshall 2004, 13).

These trends toward greater flexibility in individual contracts and lower payroll contributions by employers were further reinforced with the sanctioning of a Law for Small and Medium Enterprises in 1995, which allowed firms of up to 40 employees—considered small under the law—to bypass some of the exceptions contemplated in the 1991 National Employment Law. A series of decrees the following year introduced further changes in the rules applying to the negotiation of collective agreements for these firms. In particular, a decree was introduced to eliminate the principle of *ultraactividad*—the ongoing validity of the terms established in the existing collective contract even after its expiration if no new contract exists. This principle had allowed unions to protect historical gains by putting off renegotiating collective agreements, sometimes for a long period of time. In its place, the law established a period of only three months, after which the agreement was considered obsolete.

Another critical reform was the decentralization of collective negotiation, as unions agreed to delegate authority to lower-level union representatives under the condition that the bargaining unit at the plant level was still a member of the industry-wide union and not an independent enterprise union. Thus, at least on paper, the concession did not directly imply a major blow to unions while it provided the means to appease employers' demands for changes to collective bargaining regulations. This had been a particularly thorny issue for unions, since their strength, as has been seen, derives in no small measure from centralized bargaining at the industry or sector level.

Strict control over wage increments was another area of state intervention in the quest for greater labor flexibilization. In line with the intent of the Convertibility Law, decree 1334 in 1991 prohibited indexation clauses in collective agreements. Instead, wage increases in the private sector were only approved on the basis of productivity increases. In practice, this meant that wages stagnated or declined throughout the decade. The minimum monthly wage was set at ARS $200 (in dollar-equivalent pesos) in 1991 and was not modified until 2003. In the public sector, workers not only faced an initial wage freeze but also their salaries were cut back several times starting in 1998 as the fiscal crisis of the state worsened, ending with the final crisis in 2001. After a decade of reforms, real salaries were 23% below their 1986 level and 30% below their 1980 level (Mancebo 1998, 187).

Drafting a New Labor Map: Flexibilization and Collective Rights

The labor reforms the government pursued and, in many cases, imposed, created a climate of crisis, conflict, and uncertainty within the labor movement. Carlos Menem's about-face after his election led to a division in the CGT between those who decided to lend their support to the proposed economic reforms (the "officialist" CGT-San Martín) and those opposing the reforms (the CGT-Azopardo). Beyond their differences, though, both organizations responded similarly, and ultimately equally ineffectively, to early decrees in the area of labor relations and the passing of the 1991 National Employment Law. Concerns about the government's plan to deregulate the union-administered health funds eventually reunited the CGT in 1992. However, their decision to present a common front did not entirely bridge the divisions that now existed between these two main factions.

As previously stated, the health funds constituted a major source of financial power for unions; thus, the threat of losing ground in this area was not taken lightly. As the decade progressed, it became an area of repeated frictions and negotiations between the government and the CGT. This was also the case with the decentralization of collective agreements, a change that threatened to undermine another pillar of Argentina's union power. In a decade in which its political influence was clearly under attack, the CGT bet its survival on the defense of these collective rights (Murillo 2013, 341; Patroni 2001, 271; Tissera et al. 2000, 137). In some cases, unions sought to improve their financial standing by participating in the purchase of privatized public firms and in the newly created private retirement funds and work-related accident insurance schemes. However, the consolidation of this "business unionism" created new distance between the union leadership and its grassroots, including the creation of objective economic interests at odds with historical labor demands (Carrera 2013, 121).

Labor flexibilization via formal legislative reform gained momentum after 1994, when the government, through the intervention of Minister of Labor Armando Caro Figueroa, mediated an agreement between the CGT and the employers represented by the Argentine Industrial Union (Unión Industrial Argentina, UIA) (Etchemendy and Palermo 1998, 571). This Framework Agreement for Employment, Productivity, and Social Equity was intended as a tool through which the government could negotiate the terms of legislation with the representatives of capital and labor in order to submit it to Congress. This was of primary importance for the government, as a substantial part of the progress toward flexibilization had been accomplished through decrees, which generated considerable friction with the CGT. Moreover, by 1994, some of the main tensions in the pattern of economic growth set in motion by the Convertibility plan had begun to be palpable. The growth of unemployment was one key indicator; the other was the growing overvaluation of the peso, which made it imperative to reduce production costs. The former provided the political justification for further flexibilization, as the dogma of the time sustained that more flexible labor markets were the only way economic growth could translate into employment generation.[8] The latter became increasingly urgent, while, at the same time, labor costs turned into the only feasible means of adjustment for the economy. For the rest of the decade, high unemployment and the need to reduce labor costs remained the main source of pressure to expand and formalize labor flexibilization.

As suggested above, a key concern for the CGT in the negotiation of labor code reforms was the preservation of the core legal provisions that had bolstered its institutional power. In this regard, it could claim only a partial victory. While the reform to the Union Health Plan had been delayed for a few years, after Menem's reelection in 1996 the government finally moved forward with its plan to deregulate health provision. While the intention of the government during the first few years had been to open up the area for private competition, the CGT managed to limit changes to workers' ability to choose only among various union-led health care providers. In exchange for this concession, it agreed to make affiliation with the health care program optional (Etchemendy and Palermo 1998, 579–81). The CGT also managed to maintain the principle of a single union per area of activity throughout the period, notwithstanding pressure from both the private sector and the government seeking to promote the emergence of unions at the level of the firm. Nonetheless, in practice, as mentioned above, it agreed to the delegation of negotiations to lower-level bodies in the case of small enterprises. In effect, the decentralization of collective agreements became a reality for workers during the 1990s: the number of collective agreements negotiated at the plant level rose from 18.3% in 1991 to 88.3% in 1998 (Bisio, Battistini, and Montes Cató 1999, 157).

The CGT's defensive position also included a tepid opposition to the economic reforms that were central to the government's overall restructuring plan. As suggested above, this was a problematic strategy, as the transformations that affected workers most directly were the result not only of formal labor reform but also, crucially, of the de facto flexibilization imposed by the discipline of growing unemployment and precariousness. In turn, the shrinking base of formal workers weakened the structural power of unions and set major constraints in articulating a more assertive and effective strategy against the reform program the government implemented. Was there any way the CGT could have presented an effective opposition to the restructuring Menem pushed forward so forcefully? Judging from the global turn in favor of capitalist demands, the answer would appear obvious. It seems even more unlikely if one considers the high approval ratings Menem enjoyed until at least 1997. However, even in this situation, with such limited opportunities, there were options that the CGT did not venture to explore, in particular the mobilization of its grassroots through a coherent program of protests to fend off the implementation of economic policies that in the name of modernization seriously undermined both workers' rights and living standards. This shortcoming is particularly blatant considering the trajectory of Argentina's organized labor movement as a colossal political adversary.

Uncertain Transitions: The End of an Era for the CGT

A number of conditions made the 1990s unique for the CGT. First, as mentioned above, until 1997 Carlos Menem enjoyed very high levels of political support, even as the economic and social costs of his anti-inflationary plan became patently clear. Equally important, support for Menem's policies was also an indication of the overall appeal "market reforms" possessed at that time. During those first years, there was a very strong consensus—called *pensamiento único* (the equivalent of There is No Alternative [TINA] in English) by local critics—which made opposition to such ideas appear highly politically risky, if not absurd.

Second, and despite the first point above, the CGT's failure to confront the government more assertively resulted in deep divisions within the official labor movement. Early on in the decade, as the nature of the program of reforms became more evident, key unions within the public sector split from the CGT to form an alternative labor organization, the Congress of Argentine Workers, which later became the Argentine Workers' Central (Central de Trabajadores de la Argentina, CTA). Founded in 1992, the CTA made critical strides in providing new forms of organization for an increasingly heterogeneous working class. The CTA's thorough critique of corporatist practices at such a critical juncture for workers in Argentina injected new dynamism into the debate over union democracy as well as hope for renewal in the labor movement. The CTA took a leading role both in the wave of protests after the mid-1990s that challenged the neoliberal discourse on prosperity in the country and in broadening the alliances that made these struggles possible.

Similarly, unions under the leadership of Hugo Moyano in the service and transportation sector united to form the Movement of Argentinean Workers (Movimiento de Trabajadores Argentinos, MTA) in 1994. While the MTA remained within the CGT and continued to foster its connections to the Peronist party, it adopted a much more militant stand against some of the policies pursued by the government, particularly when they threatened key corporate prerogatives. Unions within the MTA represented workers in activities that had not been as negatively affected as those in the manufacturing or public sectors, so they confronted the government's policies from a position of relative strength. The MTA's greater structural power and the contentious political program it pursued, including alliances with the CTA and the growing movement of the unemployed, provided Moyano with the legitimacy required not only to withstand the challenges of the decade but also to increase his power after the end of Convertibility.

The CTA's split from the CGT was not the only organizational transformation of the period. As unemployment grew and affected sectors in the economy that had previously been highly organized, such as public enterprises, workers in these sectors found novel ways to mobilize and demonstrate their opposition to the government. Their rapidly growing organization came to encompass the very heterogeneous movement known as *piqueteros*, so named after their common practice of using roadblocks or *piquetes* as a form of protest. The CTA incorporated important segments of this movement into its ranks, though the organizations of the unemployed remained highly segmented and organizationally dispersed (Svampa and Pereyra 2003).[9]

Third, the way the official CGT positioned itself vis-à-vis the government was also mediated by the new scope of labor mobilization after the second half of the decade. Both the MTA and the CTA were central actors in organizing opposition, as were the organizations of the unemployed and other political forces that reached considerable prominence at the time, in particular the Classist and Combative Current (Corriente Clasista Combativa, CCC). Their mobilization increased as economic policies not only failed to sustain economic growth but also transferred most of the cost of the crisis to workers. While not the most consistent voice in the opposition, the official CGT was nonetheless willing to demonstrate its mobilizing power when needed, particularly through calls for general strikes. Between 1993 and the end of the Menem administration in 1998, there were eight general strikes, three of which had the support of the official CGT (Carrera 2013, 122). Overall, though, the militant stand of emerging opposition forces within the labor movement overshadowed the political presence of the official CGT, which for the first time since the return to constitutional rule was relegated to a secondary role within the labor movement.[10]

Rising labor conflicts and the PJ's poor showing in the congressional elections of 1997, which compounded the fear of an electoral defeat in the presidential elections scheduled for 1999, prompted Menem to reconsider his approach toward labor. In particular, the government became more amenable to negotiating a new bill for further labor reform with the CGT, including the dissenting MTA, which was finally approved by Congress in September 1998 (Law 25,013). The new law was a gesture toward the CGT, showing the government's willingness to recognize its organizational interests, in particular the principle of *ultraactividad*, centralized collective bargaining, and the protection of union health care programs from private competition. Equally important for the CGT, the new law formally did away with the temporary contracts created through the labor reforms of 1991 and 1995.

Law 25,013 is usually seen as a "reversal" of the flexibilizing reforms undertaken during the Menem administration, and on paper it did undo a number of earlier reforms. However, the changes did very little to affect the actual conditions in labor markets, as the economy took its final descent into recession during the Convertibility period. The law was also quite ineffective in procuring renewed political support for the government. In October 1999, the Peronist party was unseated in presidential elections by Fernando de la Rúa, the candidate for the Alliance, a coalition of center and center-left forces that included the Radical Party and the Front for a Country in Solidarity (Frente País Solidario, FrePaSo).

The defeat of the Peronist party returned the CGT to a position of open opposition, generating a new set of internal tensions. As the economy continued to deteriorate, the dilemma for the CGT was how to find the grounds for both negotiation and conflict with a non-Peronist administration, a predicament that resulted in 2000 in the formal split of the CGT into two groupings, one under the direction of Adolfo Daer (Official CGT) and the other under Hugo Moyano's leadership (Dissident CGT). Another issue distancing the two factions was differences in how each group adapted to the weakened links that had previously connected the organized labor movement with the Peronist party (Etchemendy and Berins Collier 2007, 369). The connection—so central to the political identity of both—had become more tenuous since the return to democracy and quite strained under Menem's presidency. Adjusting to this change was one of the main political challenges for the CGT at the time and, as discussed below, a critical predicament in the following decade.

Defining its strategy toward the new government was all the more critical for the CGT as President de la Rúa pushed for a new labor law (Law 25,250), passed by Congress in April 2000 amid allegations of bribing senators to secure their vote for the bill. Notwithstanding the political crisis this generated, the new labor law introduced changes that the Peronist labor leadership had previously considered absolutely nonnegotiable. Indeed, the new law sanctioned the decentralization of collective bargaining and the end of *ultraactividad*. Moreover, and after a decade of struggles over the regulations governing union health care plans, the Alliance government introduced a decree allowing competition in the provision of health care services to include private firms. The CGT's two factions united to call for a general strike—along with other labor associations—as early as June 2000. A general strike in December of the same year constituted another major show of force against the government. These general strikes added to the period's high levels of labor mobilization, creating a mounting political crisis for the government. As the recession continued unabated, now combined with a growing external crisis and increasing pressure from the IMF, the government saw its repertoire of economic and political alternatives narrow at an alarming pace.

By the end of 2001, following a year of additional economic setbacks and growing labor mobilization, the government's alternatives had run their course. There were six general strikes that year, with the participation of the main labor forces at the time—CGT-Moyano, CTA, CCC, and CGT-Daer (the latter of which participated in four of them). The same four main forces called for a general strike and day of protest on December 13th, which ultimately triggered the massive uprising that toppled the de la Rúa government a week later. The protest marked the highest point in what had been a growing process of labor mobilization dating back to the middle of the previous decade. In addition to the labor organizations, the movement of the unemployed was a key actor accompanying the general strikes. It was also a moment of high levels of working-class unity and participation (Carrera 2013, 122–23).

The mass uprising of December 19 and 20 and the weeks that followed were a demonstration of the various and heterogeneous experiences of dissatisfaction that existed in Argentina and the rather broad range of demands against both the government and the orientation economic policy had taken since the 1990s. Demonstrators in Argentina demanded not only the resignation of de la Rúa; their cry of "out with them all" also reflected a general sense that Argentina's crisis was the responsibility of a much broader spectrum of politicians, all of whom had been complicit in the transformation of the country with devastating social consequences. The first demand, to oust Fernando de la Rúa, was achieved within a few days. The second, though, would take a very different turn.

Post-Convertibility and the Labor Movement

The collapse of the Alliance government opened the door once again for a return to Peronism. It was a difficult transition, marked by an economic crisis bordering on meltdown and very high levels of political instability. Notwithstanding these critical circumstances, the worst manifestations of both the economic and political crises were overcome relatively quickly. Recovery was particularly swift when it came to the economy, which responded positively to government intervention to control some key economic variables. Political unrest proved more difficult to tackle, but the call for elections and the victory of Néstor Kirchner (2003–7)—the candidate for the Front for Victory (Frente para la Victoria, FpV), one of the three tickets running for the Peronist party—set the stage for a significant change in both economic policy and political order. In many respects, along with the subsequent terms of Cristina Fernández (2007–15), the period starting in 2003 marks a departure from the neoliberal policies followed in the 1990s.

Nonetheless, there were also important continuities, in particular the reliance on primary commodities exports as a key source of economic dynamism. Both presidents professed political values in line with other governments in the Latin American turn to the left: critical of neoliberalism, the deterioration of democratic practices, the role of IFIs in determining policy, and the heavy social costs pro-market reforms had inflicted on the country. With nationalist convictions and committed to developing stronger links to other Latin American countries, they aligned their governments with some of the principles and values associated with the left-wing currents of Peronism, particularly those of the "Peronist Youth," the common designation for left-wing Peronism. Much of the party, and significant segments within the CGT, never shared these political views, either in the past or the present. In the 2003 elections, in fact, the CGT had given its support to the other contending candidates for the Peronist party.

The crisis of employment and poverty the government confronted in 2003 made intervention in these areas a priority while offering the incoming government the opportunity to forge new political alliances. Moreover, the high levels of mobilization of the groups most affected by these problems created another major incentive to act quickly (Felder and Patroni 2012, 277). The creation of more encompassing social protection programs and measures geared toward increasing real wages were key pieces in the antipoverty initiatives of the government. Starting in 2002, wage increases were promoted through presidential decrees that sought to offset the disastrous impact of the sharp devaluations after the end of Convertibility (Orovitz Sanmartino 2010). Since 2003, there was also a significant reactivation of collective bargaining. The more active intervention of unions in salary negotiations cemented the rise in real wages among organized workers, but it continued to be government-mandated minimum wage increments that addressed the major decline in real wages of more vulnerable workers in the formal economy.

Rising wages and declining poverty levels combined with the unfolding of an export boom and the new economic opportunities for domestic production created by devaluation to fuel a period of rapid economic growth (8.8% on average between 2003 and 2007).[11] Economic growth, in turn, enabled the sustained growth of employment and wages, although for workers as a whole, real wages did not surpass the level reached during the early Convertibility period even by as late as 2012.[12] Between 2002 and 2008, during the period of highest economic growth, the unemployment rate fell from 24.4% to around 8.5%. Most important, as opposed to what happened during the 1990s when the majority of jobs created were informal, between 2003 and 2008, 85% of new jobs satisfied all legal requirements in terms of social protection (Panigo and Neffa 2009, 14).[13] All in all, though, these positive trends did not suffice to bring the levels of informality and unregistered work back to historical levels (see table 5.1).[14] In short, while formal employment, the mainstay of traditional unionism in Argentina, increased substantially, structural change since the 1980s produced a segmentation in labor markets in ways that economic growth alone could not overcome. The most revealing shortcoming in how the CGT positioned itself at this critical time was connected precisely to its incapacity to respond either organizationally or politically to this challenge.

Bringing Together a Governing Alliance

To the extent that there was a shift in Argentina after 2003, it was only possible because the consensus around neoliberalism collapsed under the weight of unprecedented levels of social mobilization (Felder and Patroni 2012). By the same token, widespread discontent and high levels of social mobilization limited the choices available to the new government. This was a particularly pressing problem for Néstor Kirchner, as his own bases of support were rather weak and unstable. He had won the elections with only 22% of the vote as the candidate for one of the factions of the now deeply fractured Peronist party. Hence, while Peronism represented a force with a long-established political apparatus, Kirchner's faction did not have a strong basis of support either within or outside the party. Seeking new alliances to extend the government's basis of support was therefore an urgent task (Etchemendy and Garay 2011; Murillo 2013).

Although the CTA and many of its leaders had closer political ties to Néstor Kirchner, it was the CGT—reunited since 2004 and under the exclusive leadership of Hugo Moyano since 2005—that became vital for the implementation of Kirchner's political and economic strategy. Moyano's control over the CGT at the time made the institution a considerably less problematic ally for Kirchner, since the labor leader had been a vocal opponent of Carlos Menem's policies. Nonetheless, it took more than a year for the new alliance with the CGT to be worked out. As Kirchner realized, the circumstances were ripe for the reactivation of labor conflicts, as indeed happened as soon as economic recovery became evident in 2003. In a moment of considerable political and economic uncertainty, the CGT appeared to be well positioned to contain these conflicts and to control the pace of salary increments.

However, the CGT was not always successful in accomplishing these objectives. Not only did labor conflicts sometimes escape the CGT's control in the early years of economic reactivation but also, as had happened recurrently in the past, many of these conflicts specifically challenged the organization's bureaucratic practices (Scolnik 2014, 243). Although it was not always on the CGT's agenda to accommodate all of Kirchner's expectations, the activation of collective bargaining under the CGT's control proved an effective means for containing wage increases within the bounds the government considered viable. In doing so, the CGT also proved essential for smoothing the relationship with employers—another fundamental target for the government.

The growth of formal employment and the presence of a government much more open to the demands of the labor movement combined to create very different conditions from those that had beset unions for almost three decades. Between 2003 and 2010, union membership increased by 53%, and as a result, the proportion of all salaried workers who were unionized—the country's union density—increased from 19% to 24% (Palomino 2011, 26–27). The government's good will toward the CGT was expressed in a new labor law reform that rolled back some of the flexibilizing regulations established during the 1990s. In particular, the sanctioning of the Employment Organization Law (Law 25877, *Ley de Ordenamiento Laboral*) did away with many of the flexibilizing measures implemented in the 1990s, and, key for the CGT, the new law brought back the principle of *ultraactividad* and the primacy of sector-wide negotiations as opposed to firm-level agreements. As discussed above, these principles provided the CGT with substantial organizational power (Etchemendy and Garay 2011, 294; Marticorena 2015). Moreover, with the resolution of the financial troubles affecting the workers' health system, unions once again secured the resources that had been so important in the past in cementing their power.

Besides organized labor, other key sectors Néstor Kirchner sought to include in an alliance were the highly mobilized organizations representing the unemployed and other marginalized groups. To those more amenable to a closer relationship with the government, Kirchner offered new opportunities to influence policy in the key area of social assistance. After 2005, political connections with these sectors widened to include both their appointment of *piquetero* representatives to government offices and the participation in electoral lists as national and provincial deputies. There were obvious benefits in attempting to capture these groups politically, as they were not only highly mobilized but also they articulated some grievances that the general public considered legitimate (Felder and Patroni 2012). At the same time, and probably not without benefits for Kirchner, participation with the government further divided the *piquetero* movement.

Eventually, the growth of employment addressed many issues for a sizeable portion of this sector, and, consequently, its political prevalence dissipated. To those not benefitting directly from economic reactivation, the government extended a number of social programs. The original program President Eduardo Duhalde had introduced in January 2002 to respond to the employment crisis (the Program for Unemployed Heads of Family [Programa Jefes y Jefas de Hogares Desocupados, PJJHD]), later expanded under Néstor Kirchner early in his presidency, was replaced with a number of smaller programs delivered by the Ministry of Labor and the Ministry of Social Development.

Kirchner's success in capturing sectors of the unemployed and the reestablishment of the CGT as the government's main political interlocutor in the area of labor relations cut short the CTA's expectations with respect to its prospects in the post-Convertibility period. The promising beginnings of its relationship with Kirchner regarding the possibility of a recognition of its long-standing claim to be legally entitled to represent unions and federations gave way to the reassurance the government extended to the CGT that its monopoly of representation would not be challenged. Later, in 2008, the Supreme Court declared unconstitutional a regulation in the Labor Code that prohibited anyone outside of the union with official union status (*personería gremial*) from running as a plant delegate. This represented once again a challenge to the CGT's monopoly of representation. However, the government never promoted the changes to the labor law that would have made it possible to make the decision operational, and neither the CTA nor the unions it represents were granted such official union status.

The changing political landscape was equally problematic for the CTA, as its own contingent of organizations representing the unemployed also developed close ties with the government, disputing some of the principles at the core of the labor Central regarding autonomy from political parties and government. More generally, these events also meant the end of a process many observers had hoped could lead to a renewal of the labor movement in Argentina. Torn after years of disagreement over the best way to position itself with respect to the political turn of post-Convertibility governments and its own internal differences, in 2010 the CTA divided into a government-allied Workers' CTA under the leadership of Hugo Yasky and an opposition Autonomous CTA directed by Pablo Micheli.

The president's approach to building support was rewarded with very successful midterm congressional elections in 2005—an outcome that also consolidated his power within the party and put him in a most advantageous position to seek reelection. However, it was his wife, Senator Cristina Fernández de Kirchner, who ran for the position in 2007. Her election as president coincided with a moment of peak economic buoyancy, but also with the global economy on the verge of its most serious crisis since the 1930s. Moreover, the problems the new government was about to face were not only economic.

First, in 2008, the government proposed a new export tax on foodstuffs, particularly soybeans and sunflowers. The country's main landowner associations responded to the government initiative with a nationwide protest that garnered a great deal of support. Ultimately, the government failed to obtain both congressional approval for its plan and a way to overcome the negative political consequences emanating from the conflict. Second, as the export tax conflict unfolded, the country was

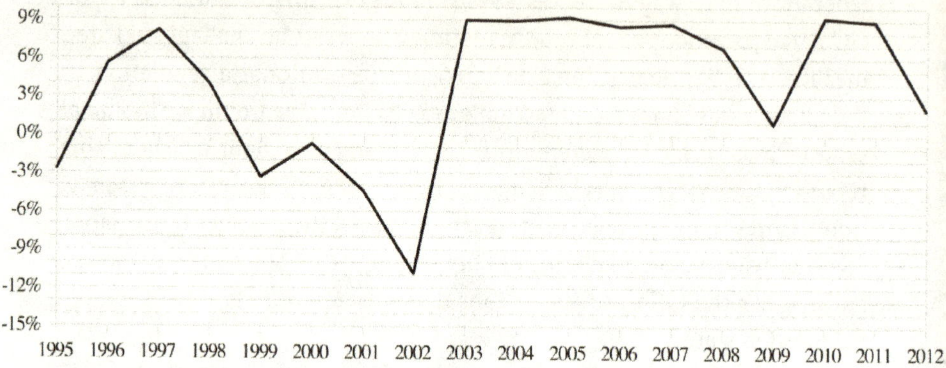

Figure 5.1. Annual Variation of GDP in Constant Prices, 1995–2012. Source: Felder and Patroni 2016.

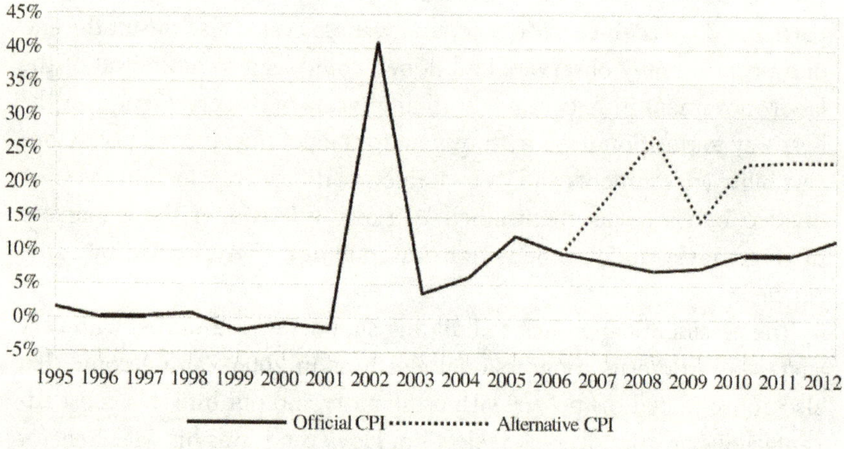

Figure 5.2. Annual Variation in Consumer Price Index, 1995–2012. Source: Felder and Patroni 2016.

also experiencing considerable economic turmoil as a result of the world recession of 2008–9. Economic recovery was quick—according to official statistics the rate of growth had reached a robust 9.2% by 2010—but by 2012 it was down again to only 0.9% (see figure 5.1). Since then, growth has not been promising (3% in 2013 and 0.2% in 2014) (ECLAC 2014a). Growing financial uncertainty and declining export revenues complicated the economic forecast for the country. To make things worse, inflation, a growing concern dating back to the previous decade, also began to accelerate, as indicated in figure 5.2.

A third challenge faced by Fernández's government was its relationship with the CGT. The CGT was an important ally to the government during this very turbulent time, providing key political support during the conflict with agricultural producers. However, the original period of political alignment between the CGT and the government, tense and feeble as it might have been, gave way to a much more uncertain and confrontational period after Néstor Kirchner's death in 2010, and particularly after Cristina Fernández's reelection in 2011.

Shifting Alliances: Fernández de Kirchner and the CGT

A number of factors, then, combined to create a widening gap between the strategic interests of the government and the CGT, prompting Hugo Moyano in 2011 to describe the provincial Peronist party as an "empty shell, lacking in Peronism." While self-interested, this statement did point to the critical transformation of the PJ since the 1980s. Moyano's resignation from the party was the culmination of a number of public clashes with the president, most significantly over the configuration of electoral lists, and, after her reelection, over the introduction of important changes to labor policies, coinciding with a "fine-tuning" of economic objectives.

First, the configuration of electoral lists returned to the pattern established in the 1990s, displacing the more historical practices whereby one-third of the candidates for the legislature were chosen from the ranks of unions, and union leaders were selected for key party positions (Schipani 2012). This was a very strategic conflict for the CGT, because as many of its leaders saw it, Moyano key among them, it had been precisely the CGT's organic connection to the Peronist party that had buttressed its claims to legitimacy. Second, the tensions around political representation were all the more critical as the economy was entering into a new stage with mounting contradictions, where a cap on salary increments appeared an irresistible choice. To confront the pressure the economic downturn imposed, labor policy was redirected to limit salary increases to increments in productivity, heighten the Ministry of Labor's control over wage negotiations, and reduce the number of beneficiaries in family allowance provisions. In short, the original proposition of "economic growth with social inclusion" was, by the beginning of the second decade of the new century, an increasingly evasive goal.

Inflation was another key area of tension. It had been a problem since the middle of the previous decade, but starting in 2010 it became a source of constant conflict with organized labor (see figure 5.2). While the actual inflation rate is the subject of considerable debate, there is little doubt it surpassed most regional measures, reaching figures between 25 and 30% on average, and probably as much as 38% in 2014. Avoiding devaluation, although impossible in 2014, was a central policy for controlling inflation, but putting the lid on salary negotiations also became essential. This resulted in the erosion of real salaries, which compounded disagreements with the CGT and CTA over the imposition of a new income tax system that, for the first time, forced workers to pay taxes on salaries above a minimum. Equally contentious were the introduction of a new law on workplace accidents, a proposed law to force companies to share their profits with workers, and initiatives by the government to displace union health care plans in favor of a more centralized system.

As in the past, the shift in government policy toward labor and debates about the best way to respond to it deeply divided the CGT. In 2012, Hugo Moyano broke away from the CGT to reorganize the CGT-Azopardo, a strong voice of opposition to the Fernández administration. The official CGT—under the direction of the leader of the Metal Workers Union, Antonio Caló—remained closely connected to the government and much more open to accepting a secondary role in the party. Nonetheless, this "official" CGT was critical of the government's new approach to workers' demands and did not hesitate to voice its opposition, sometimes in very strong terms. Prior to this major division, in the midst of the conflict over the agricultural export tax, the leader of restaurant workers, Luis Barrionuevo, also split from the main organization, creating the Blue-and-White CGT, which would become an occasional ally to Moyano.

Hugo Moyano had fought the president assertively in defense of the principle of labor representation within the party—a principle the Peronist party had historically promoted. However, two factors worked against him. One was that by 2011, it was clear that Cristina Fernández did not see her political future as a function of support from organized labor. The other was the perception, strengthened with the resounding 54% of votes the FpV obtained in the 2011 presidential election, that the electoral support of the union rank and file was not at stake. Indeed, workers—including a large segment of those marginalized from labor markets—were and have remained Peronists, and at this point in time they widely supported the particular version of Peronism the Kirchners offered through the FpV.

To counteract the mounting political opposition to her government, Fernández sought to strengthen her alliance with sectors beyond the traditional Peronist bases of support and formal workers' unions. One such sector consisted of those who remained marginal to the benefits emerging from rising employment. The government had reached out to these groups and the organizations that represented them from the very beginning, through an extensive body of social policy. Later in the decade, the social protection architecture was extended to provide access to key universal entitlements, such as child allowances and pensions (which until then had been limited to the formally employed), and new labor legislation was passed providing protection to workers in private homes (Murillo 2013, 344). Although it is not clear where these sectors would have deposited their political support in the absence of these material incentives, it could be argued that the government's objective was not only to retain their support but also to mobilize them as major actors in the governing alliance. Others, much more disapprovingly, have explained the government's extension of rights and social protection as new expressions of long-standing and recurrent clientelism (Mazzuca 2013, 120–21).

The other sectors that became key in Fernández's new coalition were a range of political organizations, some of which emerged under the direct tutelage of the state. In this last group, La Cámpora—an organization representing mostly students and youth, which grew rapidly after 2011—figures most prominently. In contrast to her approach to organized labor, Cristina Fernández promoted the participation of these nonunion allies in both appointed and elected political positions, at all levels of government, and beyond traditional areas of social development.

The government's search for autonomy from unionism and the displacement of the CGT from the party were not without political consequences. In particular, economic difficulties after 2012 and the policies through which the government responded to them fueled growing labor opposition, starting with the first general strike called by Moyano and the Autonomous CTA by the end of that year. More important, the change in approach to unionism also speaks of the profound transformation of the Peronist party and politics in Argentina more broadly and, significantly, the marginal position of organized labor in both.

Conclusion: Democracy, not Corporatism?

As the discussion in this chapter shows, although the CGT suffered serious setbacks during the 1990s, it managed to retain the pillars of its organizational power almost intact: a single union per sector of economic activity authorized to negotiate collective agreements and financial control over the provision of health care services for its members. Armed with strong organizational power, after 2004 the CGT was in a much better position to reassert its role as the most powerful organization of the working class. Yet, at the same time, Carlos Menem's neoliberal reforms—reforms the CGT failed to oppose vigorously—had decimated the ranks of many unions, and the working class it claimed to represent had become much more heterogeneous and segmented (Etchemendy and Berins Collier 2007). Nonetheless, official unions were able to reassert their authority over their rank and file, and the CGT in general was seen by employers' associations as an effective interlocutor in wage negotiations. The confluence of corporatist interests at this juncture, though, could only be as solid as a fractured Peronist party and a CGT with a much-reduced membership and representativeness within a substantially more heterogeneous working class. Labor's expectations to regain its political clout within the party did not measure up against its diminished economic relevance in determining the viability of economic plans. The breakdown in relations between Fernández and Moyano was the outcome of the clash between these two realities.

After its considerable revival in the first decade of the century, the organized labor movement confronted the less auspicious conditions under Fernández without much imagination or success. The political challenges the period presented for working-class organizations can be appreciated in the divisions that by 2012 the labor movement in Argentina confronted: the CGT was split in three, and the CTA in two. The Autonomous CTA continued to represent a more progressive alternative of unionism but without the potential it acquired during the 1990s to both challenge orthodox unionism and move forward with alternative forms of grassroots organizing.[15] Eventually, Moyano offered his tacit support to the right-wing coalition that defeated Fernández's candidate in the runoff election in November 2015. More importantly, in this second round the FpV only lost by 3% of the vote, proof in my view that most workers still support some variant of Peronism, regardless of the political standing of their leaders. However, the legacy of 12 years of "progressive" politics in Argentina appears to be a substantial deficit in the promotion of more democratic and representative forms of unionism or the search through a pluralistic consultative process for labor institutions that strengthen the capacity of labor to defend and advance its rights.

The victory of Cambiemos (Let's Change), the conservative coalition that brought Mauricio Macri to the presidency in December 2015, provided the CGT with renewed incentives to seek internal unity and also new alliances, both critical to increasing its political capital in ways that could strengthen its position within the Peronist party. In July 2016 the CGT reunited under the direction of a triumvirate representing the three fractions into which it had been divided. Notwithstanding the far-reaching negative implication of Macri's economic measures on workers, especially the fall of both real wages and levels of employment, unity did not presage an open and active opposition to the new government.

Thus, while in 2016 the CGT participated in a number of protests and mobilizations, it only called for its first general strike against the economic policies of the government in early April 2017, and this after months of pressure to do so. The action came after the two CTAs had called for a national strike[16] and day of action on March 30, an event that closed out a month of mobilizations and protests in the country. Part of the reluctance to confront the government more forcefully might be related to its internal divisions, but it is equally likely it is a strategy connected to the CGT's well-rehearsed historical practices of its organizational power residing not only in mobilizing working class discontent but also in stifling it.

With the same overall objective of finding the most effective way of positioning itself vis-à-vis both the new government as well as the Peronist party, the CGT has very actively nurtured new alliances with the very significant body of organizations representing informal workers. This has been most clearly the case with the Confederation of Workers of the Popular Economy (Confederación de Trabajadores de la Economía Popular, CTEP), created in 2011 by a highly mobilized and politically diverse group of movements representing nonwaged workers.[17] Some of these organizations have been close to the government of Fernández, some have strong connections to the Catholic church, while still others have a trajectory within the radical left (Felder and Patroni 2017). The strategy, even when it might not count with the fervent approval of all the CGT's leadership, seems to represent a substantial change for the organization, though not without its perils. On the one hand, the large and growing informal sector is an obvious site from which to strengthen the labor movement. On the other hand, while the CGT has some representation among informal workers, the strategy implies pursuing a coalition with organizations it does not control.

The challenges that lie ahead in seeking union renewal under the newly elected conservative government might make painfully evident the democratic deficit that imperils the labor movement—a reality that limits the possibilities of strengthening the labor movement not only in terms of numbers but also in regard to its effectiveness. Ultimately, what is at stake is the rebuilding of the legitimacy of a labor movement that, while not without organizational resources, has for too long avoided vital questions about transparency in its practices and democracy in its decision making.

Figures 5.1, 5.2, and table 5.1 were first published as figures 2, 4, and table 1 in "Precarious Work in Recession and Growth: A New Structural Feature of Labor Markets in Argentina?" in the *Review of Radical Political Economics* in 2016, DOI: 10.1177/0486613416635053.

6

The Limits of Labor Legislation Reforms

Rigidity, Growth, and Employment in Brazil, 1995–2010

JEAN FRANÇOIS MAYER

The literature addressing market dynamics typically assumes that reforming labor legislation has a direct impact on economic performance, the configuration of labor markets, and the strength of labor organizations. One prevalent school of thought within this literature advocates flexibilizing labor laws in order to create economic prosperity, enhance labor productivity, increase formal sector employment, and successfully fight poverty and socioeconomic inequality.

In this chapter, I test the explanatory power of this approach by analyzing the case of Brazil between 1995 and 2010. In particular, I seek to find out whether changes in the configuration of labor legislation can be linked to the above-mentioned transformations in market and socioeconomic indicators. I propose to verify these claims through a single-case historical analysis, using both quantitative (socioeconomic measures) and qualitative (survey-based) data. Brazil appears to be a well-suited case study for this purpose given that it (1) has one of Latin America's highest levels of union density, (2) exhibits one of the highest rates of socioeconomic inequality in the world, and (3) is characterized by an informal economic sector that has constituted over 40% of its gross domestic product during the past 20 years and has traditionally absorbed a very significant percentage of its workforce (ECLAC 2013, 2014b).

Perhaps most importantly for this chapter's purpose, Brazil has also been subject to a variation of labor market policy approaches taken by successive federal governments. Indeed, the government of Fernando Henrique Cardoso (1995–2002) adopted a policy orientation that appeared largely based upon the approach outlined above: it considered "rigid" labor legislation to be the principal cause of Brazil's poor labor market conditions and problematic economic performance. As such, the country's Consolidation of Labor Laws (Consolidação das Leis do Trabalho, CLT) was particularly blamed for low economic growth; a lack of job creation in the formal economy, which resulted in significant informality in the labor market; persistent poverty; and the *custo Brasil* (i.e., the cost of doing business in Brazil, which is an estimated 35% higher than in countries with flexible labor legislation). Cardoso's administration therefore deemed reforming Brazil's labor code a key element in solving this predicament.

By contrast, the government of ex-unionist Luiz Inácio Lula da Silva (2003–10) adopted a policy position that was overall friendlier to organized labor's interests. His administration's efforts to modify Brazil's labor code by and large attempted to strengthen the labor movement's interest representation structure and its collective bargaining position. Lula's government especially sought to remove corporatist constraints on labor organization and collective action. Lula's administration also adopted other pro-labor measures, such as markedly increasing the country's minimum wage. This effectively contradicted the labor policy orientation of the previous administration.

The Cardoso government altered the country's labor code by flexibilizing the labor market and altering the structure of labor interest representation. Nevertheless, this chapter finds that these reforms appear to have had limited success in stimulating economic growth, generating formal sector jobs, and reducing poverty and inequality. By contrast, the available data indicate that Brazil's economy grew more rapidly between 2003 and 2010 than it did in the preceding 20 years. During that same eight-year period, the country also moved away from informality and reduced unemployment, poverty, and inequality. These positive outcomes occurred even though the Lula government did not seek to flexibilize labor rights and was largely unsuccessful in its efforts to abolish corporatist restrictions.

As such, this chapter suggests that transformations in Brazil's labor market and socioeconomic performance since the mid-1990s do not correlate well with shifts in the country's labor legislation. These findings tend to contradict the claims of those who advocate labor law reform and echo those of the other case studies in this book. It appears instead that transformations in international economic contexts, changes in successive federal governments' policy orientations, and, to a lesser extent, the strategic behavior of the country's main socioeconomic actors hold greater explanatory value in the Brazilian case. These results are also generally congruent with claims found in a body of scholarship often associated with neo-structuralism.

In the following pages, I first look at the literature on labor law reform. Subsequently, I outline the origin and composition of the Brazilian corporatist framework, as it is often blamed for being the main source of labor rigidity. I then present the principal labor reforms and policies adopted under the Cardoso and Lula periods, followed by an analysis of their impact on the country's economy and labor market. For both presidencies, I also go beyond labor legislation reforms and present alternative explanations to shifts in economic and market indicators during the time under study. I conclude that the key to understanding the evolution of the labor market and labor organization in Brazil entails going beyond a narrow focus on labor code reforms. My analysis advocates a consequent reorientation of the literature's analytical focus on this matter.

Labor Legislation Reform in the Literature

The structural adjustment programs (SAPs) adopted in Latin America starting in the mid-1980s aimed at stabilizing and revitalizing the region's ailing economies. In particular, they sought to further economic deregulation, reduce state spending, liberalize trade and financial transactions, and privatize state-owned enterprises. The overarching goal of these market-oriented reforms—later known as the Washington Consensus—was to revive growth and favor formal sector employment by moving away from state intervention in economic dynamics.

As shown in chapter 2 and discussed in the chapter on Chile, legislation favoring greater flexibility of the labor market represented an intrinsic part of these stabilizing and restructuring reforms. In fact, labor law reform often constituted one of the conditions attached to the loans granted by international financial institutions—such as the IMF, the World Bank, and the Inter-American Development Bank—to Latin American countries in economic difficulties. But although conditionalities aimed at privatization, austerity, and market opening were widely implemented in Latin America during the 1980s and 1990s, labor law reform was not (Sabatini and Farnsworth 2006, 51–53). This can be attributed to several factors, not least of which is the political resistance of civil society. Workers organizations, in particular, were opposed to these reforms and intently pressured governments seeking to implement them. In the context of the more open, newly democratized Latin American political regimes of the 1980s and 1990s, union opposition to labor reform proved consequential.

An important body of literature thus emerged in the 1990s and the first decade of the twenty-first century, insisting on the importance of, among other things, reforming labor legislation in order to "complete" the economic restructuring process undertaken in the region and enable it to reap the above-mentioned intended benefits (Dömeland and Gill 2002, 1–3). In line with the tenets of the Washington Consensus, this literature depicts Latin American labor laws as being too rigid, thus preventing demand-driven shifts in wages, employment, and the nature of contracted work. In turn, these characteristics are alleged to generate market distortions and economic inefficiencies (Lora and Pagés 1997, 14, 30, 33).

Indeed, this body of literature, first and foremost, considers that the labor legislation of most Latin American countries discourages the creation of jobs in the formal sector because of its emphasis on job security and protection. This is believed to significantly increase labor costs and make them more uncertain, thus reducing employment opportunities (Edwards and Lustig 1997, 20–21; Gill and Montenegro 2002, 221; Heckman and Pagés 2000, 5, 14; Heckman and Pagés 2004, 6; IADB 1997, 47). Second, it argues that countries with flexible labor legislation grow more rapidly and more significantly, exhibit higher levels of productivity and competitiveness, and receive more investment than countries with rigid labor laws (Cox Edwards 1997, 129, 148; Heckman and Pagés 2004, 75; IADB 1997, 55, 60; Sabatini and Farnsworth 2006, 62).

Third, and finally, this literature contends that rigid labor legislation ultimately serves to protect the interests, income, and jobs of older, male, relatively wealthy formal sector workers. By contrast, most other categories of workers (i.e., the young, women, the unskilled, the marginal, the temporary, and the self-employed—particularly in rural areas) see their income depressed and their possibilities of employment in the formal sector reduced by labor rigidity (Heckman and Pagés 2000, 5; Heckman and Pagés 2004, 6; IADB 1998, 139–40). In particular, this body of work claims that binding minimum-wage policies have a distortionary impact on income distribution, favoring wealthier workers in the formal sector of the economy to the detriment of poorer workers in the informal sector (Maloney and Nuñez 2004, 17–18; Cox Edwards 2007, 8, 29). This literature hence sees rigid labor codes as a source of social injustice, growing socioeconomic inequality, and persistent poverty.

For this body of work, the solution to these ills stems from labor law reform, given its conviction that "regulations matter and the choice of labor market institutions matters" (Heckman and Pagés 2004, 75). In particular, this literature advocates the establishment of labor legislation reforms "that change the mechanisms of labor protection and regulation so that these may maximize the protection granted to workers at a minimum cost in terms of efficiency" (Lora and Pagés 1997, 33; my translation). As a summary of this literature's emphasis on the need to implement flexibility, Sabatini and Farnsworth insist that "the keystone of [economic] reform has to be the updating of outmoded labor codes, especially insofar as these make the cost of dismissing workers unreasonably and destructively high" (2006, 62).

In order to enhance formal sector employment, growth, and competitiveness; further prosperity and greater social justice; and reduce socioeconomic inequalities, this literature argues that job security and payroll taxes must be reduced and that wages and working conditions must be decided through negotiations between employers and workers without being hampered by state intervention or a restrictive labor code (Cox Edwards 2007, 28; Kugler and Kugler 2009, 235). According to Marques and Pagés, "The state will need to change its role, and center its action in the active promotion and protection of freedom of organization and bargaining" and thus refrain from intervening directly in labor negotiations (1998, 1).

As suggested in chapter 2, another body of literature, generally referred to as neo-structuralism, offers an alternative perspective on the region's socioeconomic challenges. Briefly put, neo-structuralism posits that shifts in international economic dynamics play a key role in explaining changes in domestic market conditions, particularly in the context of globalization (Leiva 2006, 341; Stallings 1992, 43, 82–83). This perspective argues that the neoliberal restructuring and trade liberalization of Latin American economies in the 1990s have made them more dependent on world market fluctuations and more vulnerable to international economic shocks. Furthermore, neo-structuralists blame SAPs for increases in income inequality, poverty, and social conflicts (Saad-Filho and Mollo 2002, 109). Neo-structuralist literature also insists that changes in governmental policy priorities help to explain transformations in labor markets, as well as in economic and social indicators. The pro-business labor policies that accompanied SAPs in many Latin American countries are therefore believed to have contributed to sluggish growth and increases in precarious employment, informality, and low-paying jobs (Kay and Gwynne 2000, 147–49, 153).

Neo-structuralists thus advocate selective integration into the world economy and carefully crafted economic policy, emphasizing—among other things—state (re)investment in social programs and enhanced regulations of market conditions, such as real improvements to minimum wages (Ramirez 1993, 17). The influence of neo-structuralist policies explains transformations in the Brazilian labor market between 1995 and 2010.

The Corporatist Foundations of State-Labor Relations in Brazil

Brazil's labor code, the CLT, was established in 1943 under the Getúlio Vargas government. It sought to aggregate and streamline the disparate labor laws that existed at that time mainly by providing legal tools that could be used by the state in order to regulate labor relations (Boito 1991; French 2004, 14). As such, the CLT created a state corporatist structure of interest intermediation that remained largely intact until the constitutional reform of 1988 (Levine 1999, 144). This allowed the state to play a central role in determining Brazilian labor relations. The literature identifies at least three pillars in Brazil's corporatist system: representation hierarchy and *unicidade sindical* (exclusive unionizing), *imposto sindical* (union tax), and labor courts and the Ministry of Labor.

The first pillar, the *unicidade sindical*, was implemented in order to divide labor organizations, thus limiting labor's strength in collective agreement negotiations and preventing the emergence of a strongly organized and autonomous labor movement that could challenge the state. As such, unions were generally organized along *município* (county) lines and prohibited from having direct ties with other unions in the same *município* or from representing a similar trade in other *municípios* within the same state (Alexander 2003, 70; Skidmore 2010, 118). Furthermore, each union could only represent one line of occupation in each *município*—though each was compensated with a monopoly over representation within that particular *município*. Even though state federations and national confederations contained many unions from the same economic categories, the CLT did not allow the labor movement to create peak associations to represent the general interests of workers from different occupational backgrounds (Erickson 1977, 32–33; Power and Doctor 2004, 222–23; Riethof 2004, 47). With this hierarchical system of interest intermediation in place, labor organizations rarely went beyond promoting and defending the narrow concerns of their respective trades.

The second pillar, the *imposto sindical*, is a mandatory union tax that is equivalent to a day's salary for a worker. The Ministry of Labor is responsible for collecting the *imposto sindical* and also injects additional state funds in the *imposto*. The ministry then redistributes these funds to labor organizations (Alexander 2003, 69–70). This provision of the CLT granted the Ministry of Labor a significant amount of discretionary power. In particular, it allowed the ministry to financially reward labor organizations that were considered more loyal to the state's policy orientation and interests and punish those that were not. In fact, Buchanan explains that the *imposto sindical* was, "In practice, . . . used as an instrument of patronage" (1995, 171). Since the state-controlled *imposto sindical* represented the principal source of income for unions, significant pressure was exercised on union leaders to comply with state directives in exchange for this financial support. In return for their quiescence, union leaders were also given control over the manner in which the *imposto sindical* was spent (French 1992, 5; Mericle 1977, 325; Power and Doctor 2004, 223).

The third pillar, the Ministry of Labor and the labor courts, played a crucial role in labor relations given their mandate to interpret and implement the various aspects of the CLT. In addition to collecting and redistributing the *imposto sindical*, the Ministry of Labor approved or denied the creation of new unions and the election of the executive committees of established unions. This allowed ministry officials to reject leadership candidates they deemed inappropriate in favor of more compliant ones

(Drake 1996, 77; Skidmore 2010, 118). Effectively, this meant that the Ministry of Labor held the power to threaten and, when needed, punish the more unruly elements of organized labor.

For their part, the state-controlled tripartite labor courts arbitrated labor conflicts between workers and employers, regulated contract negotiations, and validated the legality of strikes (Cardoso 1999, 31).[1] Essentially nonexistent under Vargas's Estado Nôvo (New State) government (1937–45), the right to strike was selectively and scarcely granted to workers by labor courts from 1946 until 1985 (Weffort 1989, 335). This system hence made it difficult for labor organizations to mobilize their memberships or to hold legal strikes. In addition, legal provisions existed that granted the state the power to intervene in other aspects of labor relations. Such was the case of the Wage Adjustment Law, created in 1965 for the purpose of "determining the minimum rate of increase for all wages in the economy," which was utilized by successive governments as an "instrument of wage control [that] inhibited collective bargaining" and eroded real wages (Arbache 2001, 5–6).

Notwithstanding its restrictive corporatist elements, the CLT also guaranteed a significant number of privileges and degree of protection for workers in the formal sector: (1) no termination without "just cause," (2) unemployment insurance, (3) a reduced working week, (4) a minimum wage, (5) a guaranteed right to create unions and conduct contract negotiations, (6) a right to salubrious working conditions, and (7) a ban on child labor. In this respect, the CLT represented a remarkably progressive and all-encompassing labor code, perhaps only rivaled by the Mexican Federal Labor Law of 1929. Nevertheless, between 1943 and 1985 Brazilian labor relations were mostly characterized by a lack of implementation and selective interpretation of these pro-worker provisions by state authorities (French 2004, 41–42). During this period, the state more often than not infringed rather than supported the workers' rights set out in the CLT.

The 1988 Constitution introduced a marked liberalization of labor relations in Brazil, which was generally perceived as favorable to organized labor (Cook 2007, 70). Among other things, the Constitution formally endorsed freedom of organization (thus the Ministry of Labor could no longer deny registration to unions, except in special cases), guaranteed the right to strike for all workers (including public sector employees), and obligated unions and employers to bargain collectively and directly without interference from the labor courts.

Hence, the 1988 Constitution effectively abolished some of the elements comprising the three pillars of the Vargas-era corporatist framework. Nonetheless, several fundamental corporatist provisions (mirrored in the CLT) remained intact—for instance, *unicidade sindical*, *imposto sindical*, and the clauses preventing the official recognition and legalization of peak national labor organizations (which would be able to aggregate unions horizontally and directly represent them in collective bargaining). Furthermore, the labor courts were to still serve as arbiters of labor conflicts and had the power to decide on matters related to collective agreements (Boito 1994, 16; CLT 2014, Title IV). In addition, none of the aforementioned transformations removed the state's capacity to selectively implement CLT provisions, thus leaving it in a position to favor restrictive elements over progressive ones, as was often the case under successive regimes from 1943 onward. It is this legal framework that the Cardoso and Lula administrations sought to reform.

Labor Market Flexibilization under the Cardoso Government (1995–2002)

Labor Reforms and Their Impact

Neoliberal restructuring measures were implemented later in Brazil than in most other countries of South America. Neoliberal measures were for the most part not adopted during the military government, but rather in the post-transition period. In Brazil, this restructuring began in earnest with the implementation of the Plano Real (Real Plan) in 1994. This comparative lag is due to several reasons. First, organized labor—and especially the New Unionism movement led by CUT—carried out successful resistance efforts to neoliberal reforms between 1985 and 1994. During that period, New Unionism enjoyed great prestige due to its significant role in bringing about Brazil's transition to democracy. Its high level of legitimacy, as well as its ability to efficiently organize and mobilize its considerable membership, afforded the labor movement and its allies in Congress sufficient political influence to derail these restructuring attempts. Second, Brazil's first post-transitional government was reluctant

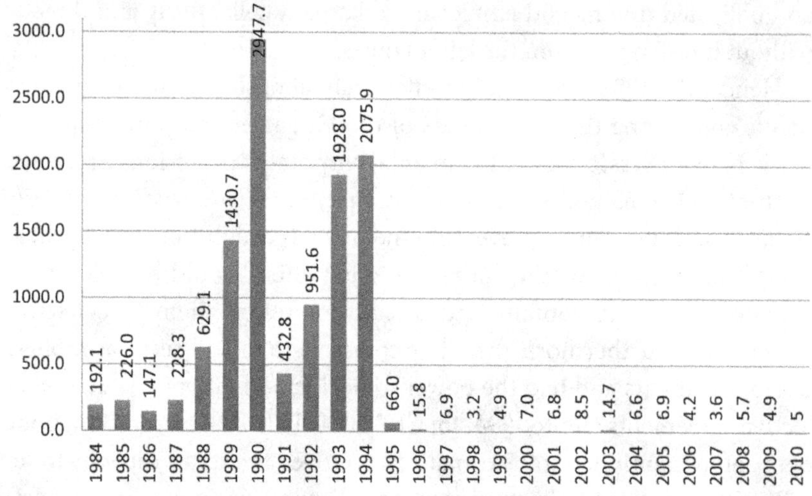

Figure 6.1. Annual Variation in Consumer Prices (Inflation Rate), 1984–2010. Source: World Bank Databank 2013.

to implement restructuring measures, given that the country's economy (in particular, its GDP growth rate and unemployment level) appeared to fare relatively well overall—until the emergence of hyperinflation in the late 1980s. In that context, the government had no taste for implementing restructuring measures that promised to be socially painful and politically costly. A third main reason, pro-flexibilization forces—and, in particular, the business sector—were still divided and disorganized in the post-transition period and were therefore unable to generate a coherent platform in favor of restructuring and flexibilization measures.[2]

At the time of his election Fernando Henrique Cardoso was perhaps best known in Brazil for being the originator of the Real Plan, which successfully tackled Brazil's hyperinflation, dramatically reducing it from 2,075.9% in 1994 to 66% in 1995 and to 15.8% in 1996 (see figure 6.1).[3] Cardoso's center-right government was intent on continuing the market-based economic policies that underpinned the Plano Real in order to restructure Brazil's economy (Cheibub Figueiredo 2007). This orientation had a significant impact on the labor market and labor relations during Cardoso's two consecutive mandates (Cardoso 2004, 12–13).

To be sure, Cardoso made it clear from the very beginning of his presidency that he considered flexibilizing labor conditions and reforming the structure of labor organization away from corporatism as priorities for his government (Cook 2007, 83–84). He believed that such transformations

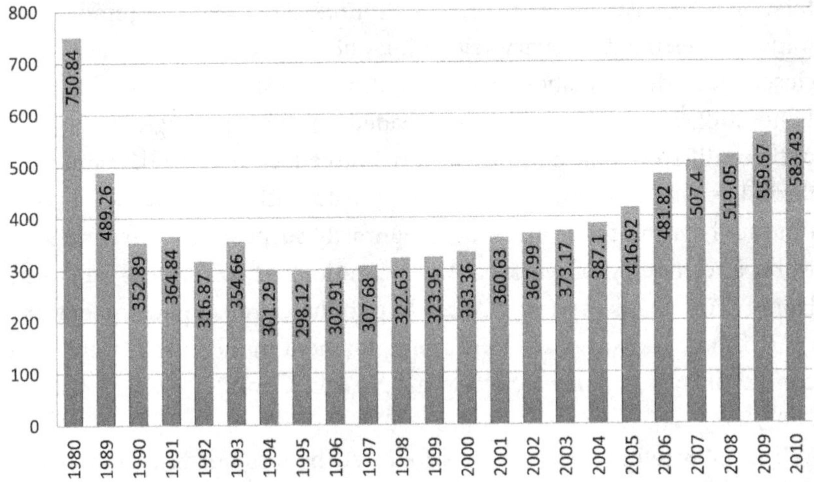

Figure 6.2. Variations in Real Minimum Salary (in Constant 2011 Real), 1980–2010. Source: DIEESE 2014.

were consistent with the Plano Real and would help to complement economic stabilization by giving preference to growth and employment. This conviction was reflected in Cardoso's minimum wage policy orientation, which emphasized restraint in order to lower labor costs and promote greater international competitiveness. As a result, Cardoso's government was characterized by a very modest increase of real minimum wages (see figure 6.2).

With regard to flexibilization, this perspective corresponded closely to that of international financial institutions and Brazil's main business associations, which had been very supportive of Cardoso's candidacy—particularly given that his main opponent was Lula da Silva, whom they considered an untrustworthy radical socialist (Lisbôa Romão 2006, 146). These organizations posited that "flexibilization measures such as flexibilization of contracts and reduction of social costs would be essential prerequisites to diminishing the cost of labor, incentivizing hiring, formalizing the labor market, and fighting unemployment in order to consolidate the inflationary controls and reactivate the economy" (Galvão 2003, 226; my translation).

The Cardoso administration pursued a de jure approach to flexibilization, as was the case in Chile and Argentina. Cardoso's government therefore pushed Congress to pass several modifications to the Brazilian labor regulatory framework that were designed to flexibilize the labor market.

First, the Wage Adjustment Law was eliminated in 1995. This removed an important element of salary regulation and allowed wages to vary more closely according to labor market conditions (Estevão and de Carvalho Filho 2012, 5). Cardoso also spearheaded a reform package (comprised of three different bills and which came into effect in 1998) that aimed to flexibilize work contracts by allowing greater latitude in hiring of part-time staff, easing procedures for temporarily suspending or terminating work, and modifying work contract durations as well as the Banco de Horas (Time Bank) system.[4] According to the Cardoso government, the goal of these measures was to spur employment in the formal sector in a context of lagging domestic economic growth (Cook 2007, 90–91; Galvão 2003, 235).

The 1998 reform package was followed by another implemented in early 2000. Although originally broader in scope and reach, it ended up mostly restructuring the operations of the labor justice system (Dal Morin 2011, 156–16). The principal objective of the reforms was to enhance the efficiency of the labor courts' administration of justice, which was then characterized by their onerous nature and a staggering backlog of pending cases. This legal restructuring redistributed responsibilities for settling minor work-related disputes to bilateral worker-employer commissions and removed the potential for state interference into these matters. The Cardoso government hence sought to introduce a market-based bargaining process to Brazilian labor relations and thus reduce the role of the state as arbiter. Although this approach intended to destroy parts of the aforementioned third pillar of corporatism (i.e., the dominant role played by labor courts in labor relations), it should be noted that the state retained the ability to ultimately regulate labor conflicts. The reform of 2000 also arguably sought to reduce the influence of labor organizations on these legal procedures by making individual workers—as opposed to their unions—shoulder the burden of these processes.

The literature does not agree on the extent to which these reforms flexibilized the labor market in Brazil. For instance, Mazali and Divino argue that there is evidence of aggregate real wage rigidity since the implementation of the Plano Real in 1994 (2010, 294, 303). Indeed, the Plano Real contained anti-inflationary provisions that, by law, sought to effectively limit salary fluctuations. These authors echo Arbache and de Negri's (2004) finding that "the Brazilian wage structure is rigid and insensitive to the economic cycle" during the period under consideration.

Nevertheless, Estevão and de Carvalho Filho partially contradict these conclusions, arguing that wages have become more flexible since 1999 due to the abolition of the Wage Adjustment Law, greater sensitivity to fluctuations in unemployment, and the gradual opening of the Brazilian market to international trade (2012, 17).

In fact, Estevão and de Carvalho Filho find that labor market flexibility noticeably increased after 1999, following the passing of legislation that made hiring and firing practices easier, simplified requirements for temporary work creation, and varied work assignments (5, 17). The authors indicate that this greater flexibilization may be attributable to the Cardoso government's reform of labor legislation, greater openness of the Brazilian economy to the international market since the early 1990s, and the introduction of a more credible monetary framework, which would have contributed to lowering the expectations of organized labor concerning prospective increases in nominal wages.

Given that Estevão and de Carvalho Filho's work focuses on more than one dimension of flexibility by utilizing more comprehensive and disaggregated data that cover a longer period of time, their analysis of the Brazilian labor market's fundamental characteristics seems more accurate and reliable. Therefore, the principal components of the Brazilian labor market appear to have been flexibilized as a result of, among other things, the legislative reforms carried out under the Cardoso government. Salaries were perhaps less affected by these measures owing in particular to the legacy of the Plano Real's anti-inflationary elements. Nevertheless, wages were somewhat flexibilized by the cumulative effect of SAPs (including labor reform) that have been implemented since the early 1990s, as the country has become more open to international trade and foreign capital investment.

According to the aforementioned theoretical perspective advocating labor code flexibilizing, one should expect to see positive changes in indicators of economic growth, labor productivity, formal sector employment, and poverty and socioeconomic inequality levels during Cardoso's presidency. However, the changes to Brazil's labor legislation did not seem to have a noticeable positive impact on the country's economy, labor market, or poverty and socioeconomic inequality measures. In fact, GDP growth averaged a humble 2.5% for Cardoso's first mandate—a rate that fell to 2.1% during the years 1999–2002, following the introduction of the main elements of Cardoso's labor reform packages (see figure 6.3).

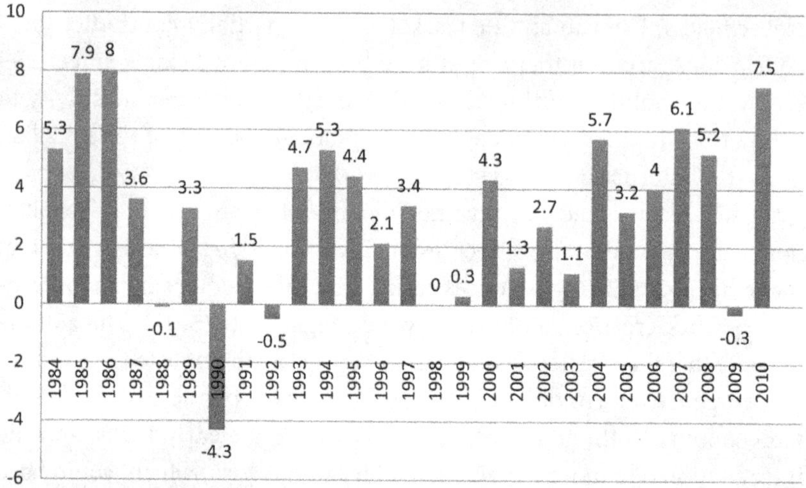

Figure 6.3. Annual GDP Growth Rate, 1984–2010. Source: World Bank Databank 2013.

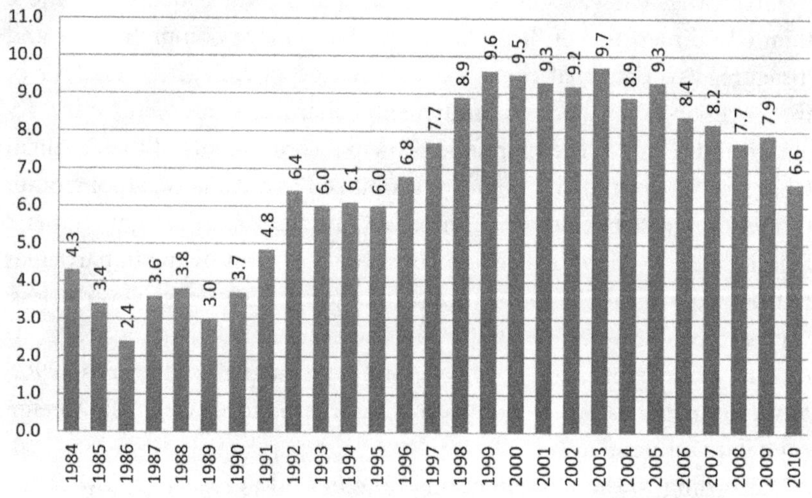

Figure 6.4. Annual Unemployment Rate, 1984–2010. Source: IPEA 2014; ILO 2014.

Inflation averaged 14.9% for the entirety of the Cardoso government—a remarkable achievement given the astronomical levels of the preceding 10 years (see figure 6.1).

Overall, the labor market also did not react to these reforms in the anticipated manner either. In fact, open unemployment climbed, averaging 7.4% yearly between 1995 and 1998, and 9.3% for the period between 1999 and 2002 (see figure 6.4). Similarly, the proportion of the labor force

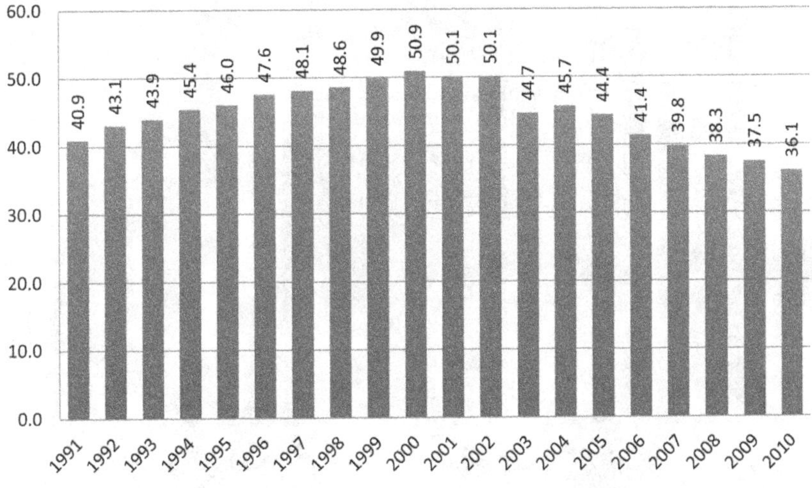

Figure 6.5. Variation in Size of the Labor Force Employed in the Informal Sector, 1991–2010. Source: IPEA 2014.

employed in the informal sector rose steadily, averaging 47.6% annually between 1995 and 1998, and 50.3% between 1999 and 2002 (see figure 6.5). Nonetheless, labor costs, one of the principal measures of the overall level of Brazil's economic competitiveness, exhibited a declining curve. As such, labor costs averaged 105 index points for 1995–98, and roughly 98 index points for the 1999–2002 period (Banco Central do Brasil 2015). This suggests that the international economic competitiveness of labor-intensive firms based in Brazil increased during the Cardoso years.

Finally, poverty and inequality rates showed no real improvement under the Cardoso administrations. Poverty averaged 34.8% between 1995 and 1998, slightly increasing to 35% between 1999 and 2002 (see figure 6.6). Inequality rates, calculated with the Gini coefficient, averaged a staggering 60 during Cardoso's first mandate, falling slightly to 59.3 during his second mandate (see figure 6.7).

Supporters of flexibilization policies often argue that time is needed before one can evaluate the impact of legislation reforms on the labor market and the principal socioeconomic indicators (Cox Edwards 1997, 132). The principal labor law reforms under Cardoso were adopted in 1995, 1998, and early 2000—the heart of these measures being the 1995 and 1998 reforms. Thus, these reforms had ample time to yield results before the end of Cardoso's second term (in 2002). However, the evidence suggests that lengthening the analysis's time horizon by a year or even

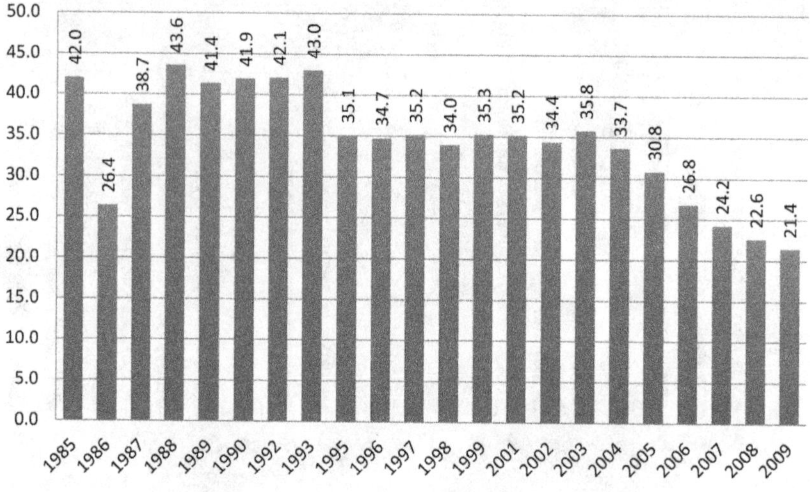

Figure 6.6. Poverty Rate, 1985–2009. Source: IPEA 2014.

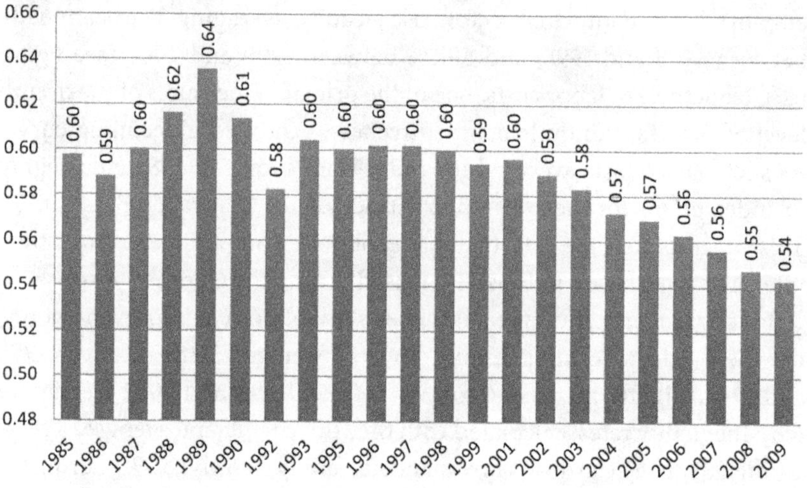

Figure 6.7. Gini Index of Socioeconomic Inequality, 1985–2009. Source: IPEA 2014.

two will not produce results that differ significantly from those presented above. Furthermore, including the year 2004 would represent an analytical stretch given that the Lula government's social and wage policy orientation, which diverged significantly from those of Cardoso, were already having a noticeable impact by that point. Moreover, the international economic context changed in 2004 as demand for Brazil's main exports increased—the only significant difference in indicators from previous years, which helps to explain the strong GDP growth rate that year.

Interpreting the Results

These findings suggest that flexibilizing measures did not have the positive socioeconomic impact anticipated by the Cardoso government, international financial institutions, or pro-flexibilization proponents. In fact, these measures seem to have had the opposite effect, as their implementation correlates with a worsening of employment figures and declining formal sector employment. Other factors appear to have influenced the labor market under Cardoso—namely, the larger international economic context in which Brazil found itself during that period, the government's policy orientation, and the strategies employed by Brazilian business and labor. I briefly explore these factors below.

Brazil had to navigate a difficult international economic environment in the late 1990s. The successive Asian (1997) and Russian (1998) crises precipitated a speculative run on the real, which resulted in a rapid depletion of the country's foreign reserves and severe capital flight. In order to constrain the recession that subsequently affected Brazil, Cardoso's team increased interest rates and let the real float freely—hence creating a significant devaluation. In addition, the Cardoso administration accepted an emergency loan from the IMF, World Bank, and U.S. government, which required the federal government to increase taxes and cut expenditures in order to generate a budget surplus (Baer 2014, 146–48). Although these measures stabilized inflation in Brazil, they also contributed to increasing unemployment and low rates of economic growth during Cardoso's second mandate. This situation was compounded by the 2001 crisis in Argentina, one of Brazil's main trading partners, which affected negatively the Brazilian export sector.

With regard to the federal government's policy orientation, the Cardoso administration adopted a clear position on what it considered the appropriate shape for the labor market and the direction in which it should evolve. This positioning deeply impacted the labor market and labor relations in Brazil. Indeed, Cook writes that "Cardoso . . . indicated early on that he was willing to take a hard line with the unions" in order to, among other things, introduce flexibilization measures in labor legislation and in the practice of labor relations (2007, 83).

This policy stance was demonstrated in the early stages of Cardoso's mandate, as *petroleiros* (oil workers) decided to strike in May 1995 to resist the privatization of the state-owned oil company Petrobras. After a standoff lasting a few weeks, and marked by the Cardoso administration's refusal to negotiate, the federal government ended the strike by sending in the army to take control of the oil fields and installations occupied by workers (Lisbôa Romão 2006, 407). Strike activities were significant in 1995 and 1996, seeking in particular, to resist privatizations, but the unsuccessful *petroleiros* strike established the standard for the unyielding position taken by Cardoso's administration in its dealings with organized labor. In fact, union leader Marcello Rodrigues de Azevedo of the CUT claimed that "Cardoso had very antagonistic relations with unions, and criminalized labor relations. For instance, when Cardoso partially privatized Petrobras, his goal was also to destroy the union [in place]."[5]

As such, the arrival of Cardoso as the country's president considerably transformed the political opportunity structure of organized labor and business groups. The more-mobilized segments of the workers movement found themselves confronted with an assertive and often antagonistic president who was intent on implementing economic and labor reforms detrimental to their members' interests. The government's policy position dealt a severe blow to the labor movement's confidence and willingness to engage in contentious political activities and labor relations. Mindful of the costs of striking and potentially losing jobs in a context characterized by low growth rates and unprecedented high levels of open unemployment and informal employment, the labor movement adopted a "defensive" stance that emphasized the safeguarding of employment (Boito 1998, 79–84; Carneiro Araujo and Veras de Oliveira 2011, Riethof 2004, 39–40). As a result, union density dropped to record levels during the Cardoso government, with an eight-year average of 16.4% and a low of 15.9% in 1998 (see figure 6.8). Organized labor was therefore not in a position to resist or derail the flexibilizing policies adopted by the federal government. The demobilization of unions also created a propitious environment for the government's labor reforms to yield their intended results. As such, it is doubtful that the apparent failure of flexibilizing policies to redynamize the Brazilian economy can be attributed to organized labor's actions.

As regards Brazilian employers, it appears that they had already developed strategies to de facto circumvent the CLT's provisions on hiring and firing before they were reformed in the late 1990s. According to Galvão

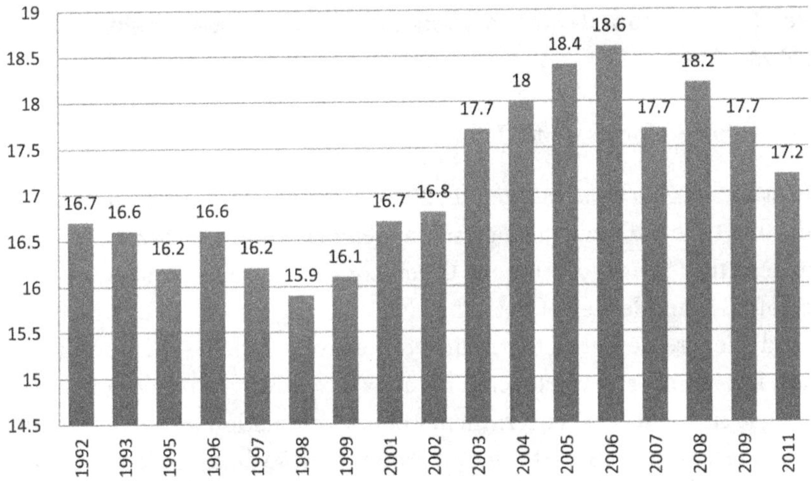

Figure 6.8. Union Density, 1992–2011. Source: Pichler 2011; IBGE 2012.

(2003, 238–39), the emergence of these tactics was made possible, first, by the political climate resulting from the Cardoso government's support for flexibilizing reforms and hardline attitude toward labor organizations and, second, by workers' reluctance to engage in work action during an economic recession. Given that context, the more flexible procedures afforded by changes to the labor code did not have much impact on the business decisions of employers.

In the end, labor legislation reforms under Cardoso do not appear to have had the positive effect on the economy or labor market assumed by advocates of flexibilization. This is particularly remarkable since the hard line adopted by the Cardoso administration in its dealings with organized labor, as well as the strategic choices of labor organizations and the business sector (i.e., the acquiescence of the unions and the tendency of businesses to circumvent "rigid" CLT provisions), should have bolstered the effects of the labor code reforms. My findings show that this did not happen and thus contradict the assumptions of the pro-flexibilization literature. Furthermore, the changing international economic context seemed to significantly contribute to the labor market's negative performance.

Reinforcing Labor Representation during Lula's Government (2003–2010)

Pro-Labor Reforms under Lula

Lula da Silva became president in 2003 after watershed elections that, for the first time in Brazil's history, saw a member of the lower classes chosen to head the federal government. Given Lula's background as a high-profile cofounder and leader of both the CUT and the PT—both of which had until then represented the main political opposition—many Brazilian and foreign observers expected his arrival to power to result in a drastic change in the federal government's policy orientation. Several domestic and international business interest groups went so far as to claim that economic chaos would strike Brazil if Lula were elected president, predicting widespread nationalizations and the replacement of the market-oriented economic model in place by a socialist system (Kliass 2011, 19).

Those fears proved unfounded. In fact, the Lula government adopted an economic stance that was defined by strong continuity with the model developed by his predecessor. For example, he maintained high interest rates to control inflation, favored a positive trade balance to generate surplus, and limited public spending. Lula went so far as to insist on raising the state's primary surplus above the 3.75% of GDP threshold set by the IMF to 4.25% (Baer 2014, 156). In the end, Brazil fared better economically under Lula than it had done during the 20 years prior to his election.

Lula's main goal was clear: he wanted to reassure Brazil's domestic and international partners about his intentions and ability to "responsibly" govern the country (i.e., to not radically diverge from the path established by Cardoso) and thus preserve investment inflows and economic stability. For instance, his first major act as president was to reform the public pension system, which had been attempted by the Cardoso administration only to be blocked in Congress—in no small part due to the opposition of Lula and the PT themselves (Marques and Mendes 2004, 7; Nakoa Nakahodo and Savoia 2008, 49–50). Lula therefore appeared to be a good student of the Cardoso model, intent on replicating its successes but also seeking to avoid its shortcomings, particularly with regard to inflation control and economic growth. These efforts seemingly convinced foreign and domestic entrepreneurs and investors as, among other things, Brazil received more foreign direct investment during Lula's second term in office than ever before (ECLAC 2013).

Still, there were considerable variations between the Cardoso and Lula presidencies with regard to the manner in which they reconciled their economic agendas with their social policy priorities, as well as in their relations with the labor force. These differences emerged early in Lula's presidency, but became particularly salient from the moment the 2008–9 global economic crisis hit Brazil. These disparities stemmed from the varying perspectives taken by these two governments on the desirability of involving the state in socioeconomic matters. In general, Cardoso advocated a (limited) withdrawal of the state from the economy and social affairs, whereas Lula supported a more active role for the state.

Indeed, from the beginning of his government, Lula implemented the Fome Zero (Zero Hunger) food distribution program and the Bolsa Familia (Family Allowance) conditional cash transfer program. These social programs aimed at eradicating poverty and reducing socioeconomic inequalities. *Bolsa Familia* has been instrumental in helping upward of 50 million people out of poverty since its implementation and is considered one of the best-performing conditional cash transfer programs in the world (Veras Soares, Perez Ribas, and Guerreiro Osório 2010, 186–87). Despite the fact that the Lula government's tight fiscal and monetary policies did not allow for budgets that could achieve the goals originally set by these programs, they were still successful in ameliorating the socioeconomic conditions of their beneficiaries.

Another area of difference between the Lula and Cardoso administrations stems from their positions on labor market reform. Cardoso supported a pro-flexibilization perspective, whereas Lula was generally sympathetic to organized labor's interests; this was reflected in the several instances of labor law reform pursued by the Lula administration. Arguably the most notable pro-labor measure adopted by the Lula government was the significant increase of the real minimum wage to a rate unmatched in Brazil's contemporary history (see figure 6.2).

Although this labor policy orientation contrasted with that of the Cardoso administration, it should be noted that Lula did not abolish or reverse the flexibilization policies adopted under Cardoso. In fact, these provisions continued untouched for the most part. Furthermore, although the Lula administration sought to modify the existing political opportunity structures within the labor market in favor of organized labor, the president took great care to establish conciliatory policies favoring the business and financial communities, thus preserving their entrenched privileges (Hunter 2014, 33). In doing so, Lula aimed to secure the political neutrality of the economic elites and their continued support for the economic policy orientation adopted under Cardoso. He apparently succeeded in this endeavor.

Several amendments and reforms of Brazil's labor code and Constitution (those articles pertaining to labor relations and the labor market) were proposed between 2003 and 2010 (Galvão 2008). Contrary to what had been the case under Cardoso, the proposals set forth by Lula's government did not primarily seek to deregulate and flexibilize labor relations. Rather, they intended to transform the organizational structure of labor, thus strengthening its collective bargaining position and enhancing labor rights. Lula's government especially targeted the removal of corporatist constraints on labor organization and collective action. For the most part, however, the Brazilian Congress did not pass these reforms—the one notable exception being the 2008 Constitutional reform that recognized the official and legal existence of labor centrals and validated their role as representatives of workers' interests. This reform hence ended the proscription of the horizontal integration of workers organizations that had been in place since the first Vargas government (1930–45) and thus potentially increased the political and socioeconomic influence of workers' organizations.

Indeed, this reform made it legal for labor central representatives to not only be present throughout collective agreement negotiations involving their affiliated unions but also to speak directly with employers' representatives during these discussions (CLT 2014). Before 2008, labor centrals could informally organize and mobilize their affiliates, but they could not intervene directly in negotiation processes or claim a share of the *imposto sindical*. This was the case for the CUT and Força Sindical (Union Strength)—two peak labor associations that emerged in 1983 and 1991, respectively. In legal terms, labor centrals such as these did not "exist" and therefore did not officially constitute a valid interlocutor for the federal government or business organizations. The 2008 constitutional amendment altered the rapport of strength in Brazil's labor relations. From then on, individual unions—particularly smaller ones—could be accompanied during negotiations by central representatives, who would then be in a position to support their members by offering their expertise as well as the weight of their respective central's considerable membership. In other words, workers would conceivably find themselves in a more credible position when negotiating with private and state employers.

Given the Lula government's stance on labor policy, and given that no significant new provisions designed to flexibilize the labor market were adopted between 2003 and 2010, advocates of the flexibilization approach would expect little difference between the socioeconomic situation that prevailed under Cardoso and that under Lula. This would particularly be the case given that the above-mentioned limited elasticity in Brazil's real wages seemed to endure during the Lula government. In their disaggregated analysis of labor flexibility, Pereira da Silva and Monsueto consider this significant degree of wage rigidity to be an acceptable indicator of the general lack of flexibility of the Brazilian labor market during the Lula government (2012, 13). Furthermore, Brazil's competitiveness reportedly declined during the 2003–10 period—arguably a factor of steady and significant increases in real minimum wages (Canuto, Cavallari, and Reis 2013, 7). Scholars advocating labor law flexibilization would consequently expect the main economic and labor market indicators to perform poorly.

By contrast, economic and social indicators paint an overall positive picture of the Lula years. Although the GDP growth rate fluctuated wildly toward the end of Lula's mandate (due to the 2008–9 global economic crisis), his presidency was nevertheless characterized by substantial average annual growth of 4.1%, which is almost twice that managed during the Cardoso administration (see figure 6.3). Meanwhile, annual variation in consumer prices averaged a reasonable 6.5% (see figure 6.1). The Lula government also maintained a high budget surplus and continued to build the state's reserves, increasing them by 83% between 2002 and 2010. In 2005 Brazil finished repaying its IMF loan and subsequently became a donor to the fund—a gesture of great symbolic importance aimed at confirming Brazil's new status as an emerging economic power (Baer 2014, 199).

The available data also suggest that despite the absence of encompassing reforms seeking to deregulate and flexibilize labor relations during Lula's presidency, the Brazilian labor market evolved significantly and positively. The unemployment rate declined markedly under Lula from a historical peak of 9.7% in 2003 to 6.6% in 2010 (its lowest level in 15 years), for an average yearly rate of 8.3% (see figure 6.4). Equally remarkable is the reduction in the proportion of the Brazilian labor force active in the informal economy, which decreased steadily from 44.7% in 2003 to 36.1% in 2010 (see figure 6.5). The real minimum wage also improved notably under Lula, increasing by almost 60% over eight years from BRL 373.17 to BRL 583.43 in constant 2011 real (see figure 6.2). This increase is particularly impressive when compared to the very modest rate at which the real wage had grown since 1992 and when keeping in mind that the real value of the minimum wage had actually significantly regressed between 1980 and 1992. Perhaps most striking was that poverty fell drastically under Lula, from 35.8% in 2003 to 21.4% in 2009 (see figure 6.6). The wealth gap was also reduced, with the Gini inequality index dropping from 58 in 2003 to 54 in 2010—its lowest level in over three decades (see figure 6.7).

Interpreting the Results

The fact that the Lula government oversaw increased growth, decreasing unemployment, a reduced informal sector, and reduced poverty and inequality without adopting or enhancing significant flexibilizing measures calls into question the claims made in the pro-flexibility literature. As was the case with the Cardoso government, it appears there were factors other than the labor law reforms highlighted in the pro-flexibility literature that had a considerable influence on the Brazilian economy and labor market.

To be sure, the larger international economic context in which Brazil found itself during the Lula government was much more favorable (at least until the last half of 2008) than that during the Cardoso government. The 2003–10 period was indeed characterized by a marked growth in commodity prices in the international market. This context combined with the devaluation of the real that took place at the end of the Cardoso administration bolstered Brazilian exports (of mostly unfinished and primary products) and generated significant economic growth (Baer 2014, 175). The 2008–9 international financial crisis undeniably affected the performance of economic and labor market indicators. This is illustrated by, among other things, the Brazilian economy's lack of growth in 2009. The crisis can also be faulted for the slight increase in unemployment as well as the recrudescence of strikes that same year. Remarkably, however, the labor force continued its migration toward the formal sector during that time. Overall, then, the international situation lent itself to a more positive economic performance under Lula than it did under Cardoso.

The main economic actors—labor and business—adopted a relatively passive stance during the Lula government. Placated by Lula's continuation of most of Cardoso's economic policies—which were generally favorable to their interests—entrepreneurs remained acquiescent on the whole (Hunter 2014, 33). Organized labor, presented with the historical opportunity of having one of their own leading the country, displayed a counterintuitive tendency toward demobilization and passivity. However, when they did mobilize, labor organizations were generally supportive of the government and its policy orientation (de Oliveira 2006, 11; Galvão 2008; Garcia 2008, 230). Beyond their relative passivity, which ensured a form of "labor peace," neither actor seems to have had a significant influence on the evolution of the labor market in Brazil during the period at hand.

By contrast, the government's policy orientation toward poverty alleviation and the real minimum wage appears to have had an important effect on Brazil's labor market and economy. The substantial growth in the value of the real minimum wage under Lula is often considered one of the main factors behind the reduction of the poverty rate in Brazil. The increase in the minimum wage, as well as the introduction of social programs such as *Bolsa Familia*, was likewise credited for providing lower-class families with disposable income, which, among other things, allowed them to consume more (ILO 2011).

This socioeconomic context was also singled out as chiefly responsible for Brazil's resilience in the face of the 2008–9 global financial crisis (ILO 2011; Kliass 2011, 20; Morais and Saad-Filho 2011, 516–19). Ricardo Berzoini—the former minister of labor and of social security, the former PT president, and the former leader of the Union of Bank Employees—claims that "Brazil survived [that] crisis" because of the social nets created during the Lula government and because people from the lower and middle classes spent their newfound disposable income, as requested by Lula, so that neither they nor the country would "be harmed by the crisis."[6] Taken together, it appears that conditional cash transfer programs such as *Bolsa Familia*, real minimum wage increases, tax breaks, and fiscal stimuli adopted under Lula significantly contributed to labor market formalization, poverty reduction, and the shrinking of the lower classes and the subsequent growth of the so-called new middle class (ECLAC 2013).

Generally attributed to the Lula government's policy orientation and to the country's positive economic performance during that period, the reduction in the proportion of informal sector workers represents a major shift in the configuration of the labor market in Brazil (De Andrade Baltar et al. 2010, 8). Among other things, this helped reduce the economic uncertainty faced by thousands of workers, who could now contribute and gain access to state-funded social programs. This transformation was accompanied by the 2007 governmental reform that expanded the public pension system and extended social security benefits to informal (and especially rural) workers (Ansell 2011, 26). This permitted men 60 years of age or older and women 55 years of age or older, who had been mostly active in the informal sector, to receive a minimal pension funded by the state.

On the whole, then, it seems that the Brazilian labor market experienced significant changes under Lula's presidency. But these transformations do not appear to be attributable to a deregulation and flexibilization of Brazilian labor legislation. As shown above, the Lula administration did not adopt any significant flexibilizing reforms. Also, the 2008 reform recognizing peak associations does not seem to have had an impact on economic or labor market indicators. Instead, it appears that the generally favorable international context and the government's policy stance on poverty alleviation programs and minimum wage adjustment had a much stronger effect on the labor market.

Conclusion

Overall, this chapter's findings are at odds with the expectations of a dominant strand of the literature dealing with labor market dynamics, which posits that labor code reform in the direction of increased flexibility is key to generating (1) increased formal sector employment, (2) rapid and sustained growth, (3) increased investment, and (4) a concurrent improvement in the socioeconomic situation. In fact, my analysis suggests that the Cardoso regime's flexibilization of Brazilian labor legislation corresponded with (1) increased formal sector unemployment, (2) a growing informal sector, (3) weak and unsteady growth, and (4) no amelioration of poverty or socioeconomic inequality.

By contrast, the Lula administration did not further flexibilize Brazil's labor legislation, and the labor market arguably became somewhat more rigid due to repeated increases in binding minimum salary legislation. Nevertheless, the Lula government oversaw (1) increased formal sector employment, (2) an important reduction in the size of the informal sector, (3) significant and fairly sustained growth, (4) record high levels of foreign direct investment, and (5) a marked reduction in poverty and inequality levels.

Given this context, I contend that other factors had a greater impact on economic and labor market performance in Brazil between 1995 and 2010. The health of the international market and the federal government's policy orientation are two elements that appear to have been more influential in shaping Brazil's economy and labor market. These findings align well with some of the claims set forth in the neo-structuralist literature discussed above (Kay and Gwynne 2000; Leiva 2006; Saad-Filho and Mollo 2002; Stallings 1992). This chapter's results therefore call for a reorientation of the analytical focus of labor market literature—and a revalorization of shifts in international economic conditions and governmental policy orientation as central explanatory factors of evolving labor market conditions.

An early version of this chapter appeared as "The Limits of Labor Legislation Reforms: Rigidity, Growth, and Employment in Brazil" by Jean François Mayer in *Journal of Politics in Latin America* 8, no. 1 (2016): 95–127.

7

Laboring under Chávez

Populism for the Twenty-First Century

PAUL W. POSNER

With the 1980s debt crisis, neoliberalism emerged as Latin America's dominant mode of development. However, neoliberalism's failure to deliver economic growth and improved employment opportunities for the masses led to a re-evaluation of neoliberal policies and a shift in the political fortunes of the Latin American left. Capitalizing on popular discontent with the prevailing development model, left-wing governments declared their intent to modify or, in the most extreme cases, altogether abandon neoliberalism. Among left-wing governments that have challenged neoliberalism, Venezuela's self-proclaimed socialist regime established under former president Hugo Chávez has been the most prominent.

In rhetoric if not in practice, Chávez's Venezuela eschewed neoliberalism in favor of development focused on the promotion of popular participation and social welfare (Buxton 2011; Ellner 2011). Therefore, in contrast to cases such as Chile and Mexico, which, as detailed in chapters 3 and 4, respectively, have undergone substantial economic liberalization and labor flexibilization, labor reform under the Chávez regime promised greater protection for workers from market forces and the development of a strong, autonomous labor movement capable of advocating effectively for workers' rights and interests. However, this essay argues that such potential was not realized under Chávez and will not likely be realized under his chosen successor, Nicolás Maduro.

Indeed, while in rhetoric the regime vehemently rejected neoliberalism, in practice it promoted de facto flexibilized labor relations through the creation of workers' cooperatives, which serve as sources of subcontracted labor, particularly for state-owned industries. In addition to exploiting vulnerable workers in cooperatives, evidence indicates that the Chávez regime employed divisive institutional practices that fragment and weaken organized labor, impeded the labor movement's autonomy, contravened essential labor rights such as free union elections, collective bargaining, and the right to strike, and engaged in reprisals against unions and workers it perceived as threats. These key features of labor organization in contemporary Venezuela indicate a pronounced contradiction between the Chávez regime's avowed commitment to socialist principles of worker solidarity and equality and its political economy in practice.

The regime's divisive and repressive treatment of the labor movement was facilitated by its reliance on support from unorganized workers, particularly from the substantial informal sector, and its attendant capacity to minimize support from organized labor. As such, the Chávez regime manifests a shift from the populism practiced under the Punto Fijo regime, based on industrialization and the incorporation of organized labor, to what Sebastián Mazzuca (2013) calls rentier populism. Under rentier populism, so-called radical leftist regimes—in Bolivia, Ecuador, and, most prominently, Venezuela—have been able to gain and maintain state control by cultivating support among informal and unemployed workers.[1] Mazzuca emphasizes the importance of the distribution of social welfare benefits financed with rents generated from commodities exports, which allows rentier populists to cultivate support among "informals" and to minimize or eschew support from organized labor (Mazzuca 2013, 110, 112). To this reliance on the distribution of rents should be added the rentier populist's pursuit of charismatic linkage with previously unorganized segments of civil society. On the basis of this mode of linkage, the personalist ruler presents himself as uniquely qualified to comprehend, promote, and protect the will of the people while followers find meaning in their direct identification with the charismatic leader rather than a coherent set of principles or programmatic policies (Hawkins, Rosas, and Johnson 2011, 189).

Through politically targeted distribution of social welfare resources, promotion of the charismatic leader's radical populist vision, and top-down mobilization of previously unorganized segments of civil society, rentier populists are able to build majoritarian mass movements in support of their personalistic rule. Reliance on plebiscitarian support from the largely unorganized popular masses contributes, in turn, to an unconstrained mode of governance, in which the separation of powers is all but nonexistent, and the president dominates the decision-making process. The Chávez regime's adherence to this mode of governance is well documented (Corrales and Penfold-Becerra 2007; Kornblith 2013; López Maya 2011; McCoy 2010; Rodríguez 2008).

Thus, the concept of rentier populism—twenty-first-century populism, if you will—goes a long way toward explaining why Venezuela's so-called radical leftist regime chose to subvert the influence of organized labor. The regime's efforts to undermine labor coupled with its politically targeted distribution of social welfare benefits appear designed to maintain its grip on power rather than to advance a programmatic leftist agenda empowering the marginalized masses. Accordingly, this analysis challenges the "radical leftist" characterization of the Chávez regime and suggests that similar skepticism should be applied to other so-called radical leftist regimes for the same reasons. As such, it suggests the need to more clearly define and distinguish between leftism and populism in Latin America and to develop a more nuanced understanding of their interrelationship and respective impacts on democracy.

The analysis substantiating this argument proceeds as follows. Section one develops a conceptual framework to distinguish between populism and leftism. Section two provides a historical analysis of the rise of the Punto Fijo regime and the labor model associated with it. Subsequently, it details the collapse of Punto Fijo and the emergence of the Chávez regime. Section three chronicles the Chávez's regime's attempts to control and fragment the labor movement through institutional means, while section four examines how its distribution of material resources through workers' cooperatives and missions impedes worker autonomy. Section five evaluates judicial constraints, intimidation, and repression against workers, labor leaders, and unions under the Chávez regime. Finally, the concluding section discusses the implications of the chapter's findings for the quality of Venezuelan democracy, and more broadly, for understanding populism, socialism, and the left in Latin America.

Distinguishing between Populism and Leftism

The notion that the Chávez regime's labor policy should be viewed through the lens of populism rather than socialism is by no means universally accepted among scholars of Latin American politics. Indeed, the relationship between populism and socialism, or leftism more broadly, has been much debated in the literature. Some analysts tend to conflate populism and socialism (or leftism) (Castañeda 2006; Castañeda and Morales 2008; Weyland, Madrid, and Hunter 2010; Weyland 2013) while others argue against conflating the two. For example, Cameron and Hershberg assert that conflating socialism and populism serves to delegitimize radical left alternatives in favor of what may be an "illusory social democracy" (2010, 9–10). Similarly, French understands the division of the Latin American left into populist and social democratic categories as an attempt to delegitimize socioeconomic alternatives that challenge the prevailing neoliberal orthodoxy (2009, 352). Levitsky and Roberts (2011) also reject the conflation of populism and leftism, on grounds that it blurs the lines between two distinct phenomena: leftism, a programmatic orientation focused on promoting redistribution, social equality, and the autonomy and political participation of underprivileged groups, and populism, a top-down mode of political mobilization of mass constituencies by personalistic leaders against established elites on behalf of "the people" (6). From this perspective, the ideological or programmatic content of populism is open and can be left, right, or heterodox (March 2007, 65).

This analysis accepts the basic premise of Levitsky and Roberts's argument. It thus views leftism as a programmatic political project promoting redistribution and social equality and populism as a top-down mode of political mobilization. However, it goes further, arguing that leftism and populism are not only distinct but also in tension with one another. If as Levitsky and Roberts suggest, the left "seeks to enhance the participation of underprivileged groups and erode hierarchical forms of domination that marginalize popular sectors" (2011, 5), this project is fundamentally at odds with populism's top-down mode of political mobilization. Whatever rhetoric they may espouse, populist leaders seek to concentrate and maintain political, economic, and social power in their hands, a disposition antagonistic to eroding "hierarchical forms of domination" (ibid.).

From this perspective, it is fitting to consider not only the extent to which left-wing populist regimes compromise liberal democracy, as many of their critics do, but also to evaluate the extent to which they impede the realization of fundamental leftist goals. In particular, do left-wing populist regimes, whether labeled "contestatory," "radical," or "plebiscitary," "enhance the participation of underprivileged groups and erode hierarchical forms of domination that marginalize popular sectors" (ibid.)? In seeking to address these questions, this analysis follows Roberts (1996, 2007b) and Weyland (2001, 2003), defining populism as a top-down strategy of political mobilization, in which a personalistic leader pursues or exerts state power in opposition to elite groups, through generally unmediated or uninstitutionalized support from largely unorganized, mass followers. In contrast to the perspective of Ellner (2008, 2011), Buxton (2011), and Smilde (2011), among others, this analysis views populist rule as antithetical to a participatory form of democracy that promotes the autonomy and interests of historically marginalized segments of society, whether in Venezuela or elsewhere. It assumes that the largely unmediated, plebiscitarian relationship between the populist leader and *el pueblo* leaves citizens with little capacity to check executive power or to articulate, protect, and promote their interests.

Examination of the Venezuelan case lends support to this assumption while also revealing important ways in which the Chávez regime's populism differs from that of classical populists such as Argentina's Juan Perón or Mexico's Lázaro Cárdenas. Unlike classical populist regimes, the Chávez regime did not close the nation's market to foreign competition nor promote industrialization through increased investment (Corrales 2010, 43). Rather, it pursued a hybrid form of statism, coupling expanded state control over the economy with global market pressure and employment flexibility for workers. Moreover, in order to avoid constraints on its exercise of power, the Chávez regime diverged from classical populism by eschewing reliance on support from organized labor. Instead, consistent with Mazzuca's notion of rentier populism (2013), it sought to build its political base among the unorganized masses.

The Chávez regime's populist project was facilitated by labor market changes—substantially increased informality and a related decline in unionization—precipitated by economic crisis and the adoption of neoliberal reforms under Punto Fijo. Between 1982 and 1998 the percentage of the labor force affiliated with unions declined from 26 to 14%, a 47% drop. Meanwhile, the percentage of labor in the informal sector increased from approximately 32% in the late 1970s to over 50% by 1999 (Hawkins 2010a, 100–101; Orlando 2001, 3). These significant labor market changes help to explain the regime's antagonism toward organized labor and its pursuit of the urban informal sector as its primary base of support.[2]

To generate and maintain mass political support, the regime coupled Chávez's charismatic appeal with top-down control of popular organizations. This top-down control of popular organizations was, in turn, facilitated by the politically targeted distribution of material benefits to subaltern groups, financed with expanded state oil revenues. In other words, while the regime promoted a high level of mass mobilization, it did so in a manner that enhanced its control over the previously unorganized masses and facilitated favorable electoral outcomes. Collier and Handlin label this pattern of mass control "Extensive Partisan Neocorporatism, to capture what appears to be a broad scope, a high degree of politicization, and state dependence" (2009, 324). Other scholars have similarly noted the regime's top-down control of mass organizations, their attendant lack of autonomy, and high degree of politicization and partisanship, coupled with the continued prevalence of clientelism (García-Gaudilla 2011; Goldfrank 2011; Hawkins and Hansen 2006; Hawkins 2010b; Stokes et al. 2013). In this regard, scholars have observed substantial tension between popular organizations' pursuit of autonomy and the regime's efforts at cooptation (Fernandes 2011; García-Gaudilla 2011; Goldfrank 2011; López Maya and Lander 2011; Schiller 2011). The Chávez regime's charismatic linkage to the masses, and the related politicization and partisanship of mass organizations, is reflected in the "importance of affect for Chávez in all forms of Bolivarian organizations whether the participatory initiatives or the missions" (Hawkins 2010b, 51; see also Hawkins and Hansen 2006 and Hawkins, Rosas, and Johnson 2011). Additionally, scholars have observed the regime's politically targeted distribution of material rewards as an effective means of gaining and maintaining electoral support (Collier and Handlin 2009; Handlin 2016; Hawkins, Rosas, and Johnson 2011; Stokes et al. 2013).[3]

Thus, the Chávez regime supplanted the Punto Fijo regime's populism with its own form of populist domination, characterized by top-down mass mobilization of previously unorganized segments of society and the fragmentation and repression of organized labor. Analysis of labor policy under the Punto Fijo regime serves to substantiate this comparison.

Labor and the Rise and Fall of Punto Fijo

The Punto Fijo regime emerged in the wake of the collapse of General Marcos Pérez Jiménez's dictatorship on January 23, 1958. The democratic regime that replaced the dictatorship was founded upon a set of fundamental accords or pacts among political parties—Democratic Action (Acción Democrática, AD, center left), Democratic Republican Union (Unión Republicana Democrática, URD, centrist), and Independent Electoral Political Organization Committee (Comité de Organización Política Electoral Independiente, COPEI, center right)—that wished to protect the new regime from threats from both the right and the left.[4] These pacts subordinated labor to government control. For example, the 1958 Pacto de Avenimiento Obrero-Patronal (Worker-Management Agreement), signed by leftist as well as AD and COPEI labor elites, committed labor to promoting democratic stability by agreeing to seek conciliation of conflicts with management. The labor code reinforced the labor movement's conciliation by giving the Labor Ministry the right of union recognition. The government could deny uncooperative unions legal recognition, making labor organizations vulnerable to the partisan interests of the party in power. Moreover, the labor code seriously compromised labor's right to strike. Workers could not strike legally until they had attempted conciliation and arbitration. Since the government controlled and often delayed the arbitration process and could portray any strike as a betrayal of Venezuelan democracy, strike activity under Punto Fijo was highly constrained (Davis and Coleman 1989, 253–54).

The labor movement's substantial dependence upon state resources further constrained its autonomy. The Workers' Confederation of Venezuela (Confederación de Trabajadores de Venezuela, CTV), the then dominant labor federation established by and closely aligned with AD, received funds from government at all levels, including nearly every ministry of the federal government, the national legislature, governors, and municipalities. AD increased the CTV's indebtedness through a political bargain, in which it provided CTV leaders with party posts, input to party policy, and access to public office through placement on AD electoral lists. In exchange, CTV leaders were expected to deliver support for Venezuelan democracy in general and political support to the AD in particular (Burgess 2004, 124, 126).

These arrangements worked well for AD and the CTV—and for the Punto Fijo regime more broadly—as long as oil revenues and government distribution of the material benefits that they generated were sufficient to placate workers. However, when AD responded to economic crisis with neoliberal reforms, the party-union alliance, and ultimately the Punto Fijo regime, began to unravel. Tensions between the government and organized labor reached their peak under the second AD administration of Carlos Andrés Pérez (1989–93). While campaigning for a second presidential term, Pérez portrayed himself as a traditional populist who would revitalize Venezuela's statist economy. However, once in office he announced the adoption of austerity measures and a structural adjustment agreement with the IMF that called for freezing wages and public employment, easing of price controls, and other neoliberal measures.

Pérez's Gran Viraje—or turnabout in economic and social policy—caused a severe decline in employment and wages and represented a betrayal of core principles upon which the interventionist state and democratic regime were founded. His actions provoked substantial public backlash and forced AD leaders of the CTV to adopt a more adversarial posture vis-à-vis the government. Matters came to a head on February 27, 1989, when rioting and looting broke out in Caracas and 22 other cities over microbus price increases, the so-called Caracazo. Pérez responded by calling in the military to recover the looted property, precipitating an estimated 1,000 deaths. Pérez's mishandling of economic crisis and social protest prompted efforts to oust him from office. While the 1992 military coup attempt (in which Chávez participated) failed, social protest against President Pérez escalated dramatically, and the Supreme Court indicted him for misuse of funds. Finally, in May 1993, AD senators voted along with the opposition to expel Pérez from office (Burgess 2004, 131, 139).

If party leaders hoped that Pérez's expulsion from the presidency would prevent the toxicity afflicting the political system from spreading, they would be disappointed. The public had lost faith not only in Pérez but also in the major parties of the Punto Fijo regime. The split of Rafael Caldera from COPEI, the party he helped found nearly 50 years earlier, was implicit recognition of this new political reality. In attempts to maintain CTV hegemony over the labor movement in this new environment, AD leaders within the labor federation attempted to distance it from all political parties. However, their efforts were too little too late.

President Caldera took two steps that would seal the Punto Fijo regime's fate. First, he sought national reconciliation by freeing Chávez and other imprisoned officers who took part in the coup attempt against Pérez. And second, by the end of his term he had adopted economic policies that were much the same as those that led to Pérez's downfall. The adoption of these neoliberal economic policies led to further deterioration of living standards among the middle and working classes, outraging the public. As labor market conditions deteriorated, informal sector employment grew and unionization levels declined, substantially weakening the labor movement and enabling Chávez to build a winning base of support among the unorganized masses.

Electoral Control and Institutional Fragmentation of the Labor Movement

During the 1998 presidential campaign, Chávez capitalized on the public's extreme disenchantment with the vestiges of the Punto Fijo regime by engaging in harsh antiparty rhetoric and ridiculing the labor leadership linked to AD and COPEI as a "trade-union mafia" (Ellner 2005, 54). After his election, Chávez called for the "demolition" of the CTV (Burgess 2004, 158). Chávez's contempt for dominant party elites and established labor leaders was presaged by a document his group authored while in prison after the 1992 attempted coup, which lamented that in practice "no separation of powers exists in Venezuela, since the political parties, deliberately violating their function as intermediaries between society and the state, conspire to usurp popular sovereignty and allow the [national] executive to assume all state power" (quoted in Ellner 2011, 425).

Ironically, the Chávez regime was no less aggressive than its predecessor in attempting to usurp popular sovereignty and, in particular, to dominate the labor movement. The substantial decline in the AD and other traditional parties since the 1990s has significantly diminished their capacity to control the leadership of the CTV through the inducements of state resources or public office.[5] In fact, Burgess observes, "too close an association with AD has become a liability in the context of public disenchantment with parties and Chávez's concentration of power" (2004, 157). Yet the decline of traditional party control over the CTV and its efforts to democratize internally through fundamental reforms of its governing statutes failed to mitigate the Chávez regime's antagonism toward organized labor (Burgess 2004, 158–59).

Instead, the Chávez regime utilized similar, if not more extreme, methods as those used by the AD under Punto Fijo to control the labor movement. In contravention of international labor standards, the regime interfered in union elections and denied unions that do not receive state approval of election results the right to bargain collectively. Reinforcing the negative impact of these policies on labor movement autonomy, the Chávez regime promoted and negotiated with new, pro-government unions that are exempt from electoral restrictions when first formed. This strategy has weakened established unions associated with the CTV and further fragmented the labor movement by creating strong incentives for workers to abandon established labor organizations to join new organizations controlled by the government. The regime compounded the fragmentation of the labor movement by pursuing policies that inhibit the efficacy and autonomy of labor organizations challenging the CTV, including those nominally controlled by the government and committed to the Bolivarian Revolution.

The regime justified the institutional reforms that facilitated the employ of these types of strategies against the Venezuelan labor movement in terms of the need to enable workers to remove entrenched and corrupt labor leaders from power. Workers widely perceived that the CTV's support of neoliberal labor reforms and privatization in the 1990s indicated that the labor organization put the interests of business and political elites above the economic interests of the rank and file (Murillo 2000). Moreover, in the eyes of many, the roots of this problem lay in the undue influence of the dominant political parties within labor organizations and their lack of regular, transparent elections (Ellner 1993; Ellner and Tinker Salas 2007). These features of Venezuelan labor organization reflected a compromise of the principle of freedom of association among workers' organizations as articulated in Article 3 of ILO Convention 87. According to this convention, "Workers' and employers' organizations shall have the right to draw up their constitutions and rules, to elect their representatives in full freedom, to organize their administration and activities and to formulate their programs" (ILO Convention 87). In order to address the discrepancy between this principle of freedom of association and the manner in which Venezuelan labor organizations operated in practice, the Chávez regime proposed a referendum whose passage would require the removal of all trade union leaders from office and their replacement within 180 days (Burgess 2004, 159; Human Rights Watch 2008, 154).

The ILO objected to the referendum because of its proposed indiscriminate suspension of union leaders from office, its proscription of reelection of labor officials, and because it would allow undue government intervention by requiring all union elections be supervised and certified by a government entity established for this purpose (Human Rights Watch 2008, 154; ILO Venezuela). Despite ILO objections, the government held the referendum, which passed on December 3, 2000. Subsequent to its passage, the Chávez regime used oversight of union elections through the National Electoral Council (Consejo Nacional Electoral, CNE) to undermine the influence of the CTV within the labor movement and to favor a new labor confederation sympathetic to Chávez, the National Workers' Union (Unión Nacional de Trabajadores, UNT, Venezuela). The following examples illustrate how the regime utilized its control over union elections to effectively exploit divisions within the labor movement to weaken labor unity and autonomy and to impede collective bargaining.

Manipulation of the Union Electoral Process

In response to the referendum passed in 2000 governing union elections, the CTV held state-supervised elections on October 25, 2001. Although the AD candidate, Carlos Ortega, won the election for president, other candidates and their supporters alleged fraud and demanded a new election. The Supreme Court denied their request, indicating no action could be taken until the CNE's review of the election was complete. The CNE finally voided the CTV election in January 2005, more than three years after workers had cast their votes.

In the interim, the government refused to recognize or negotiate with the CTV executive committee. In so doing, the Chávez regime violated ILO Convention 87 (Freedom of Association and Protection of the Right to Organize), according to which "complaints brought before labor courts by administrative authority challenging the results of trade union elections should not—pending the final outcome of the judicial proceedings—have the effect of suspending the validity of such elections" (ILO 2004, 126). In addition, the government violated Venezuelan law by refusing to call national tripartite discussions to review its proposed minimum wage increases with the CTV, at the time the most representative national labor organization according to CNE statistics.

Rather than negotiate with the CTV, the Ministry of Labor arbitrarily decreed a minimum wage increase in April 2002, without consulting the CTV or any other labor representatives (Human Rights Watch 2008, 156). This action was a clear example of the government bypassing institutionalized forms of labor mediation in favor of more direct links between Chávez and the masses, thereby undermining the relevance and influence of established labor organizations. Moreover, the government's sidelining of the CTV gave workers strong incentives to abandon it in favor of the pro-government UNT, which was established in March 2003.

The Chávez government's handling of the CTV election is but the most prominent example of its manipulation of electoral rules to exclude established unions from collective bargaining negotiations. In contravention of ILO Conventions 87 and 98 (right to organize and collective bargaining, respectively), it used alleged delays in union elections as justification for not negotiating with established unions, instead negotiating with unions that are not representative but which it controlled (ILO 2004, 127). As new entities, these pro-government unions are initially exempt from electoral requirements. Two additional examples illustrate this pattern of bias and manipulation by the regime. The first deals with public health workers and the second with nutrition workers.

The Single National Union of Public, Professional, Technical, and Administrative Employees of the Ministry of Health and Social Development (Sindicato Único Nacional de Empleados Públicos, Profesionales, Técnicos, Administrativos del Ministerio de Salud y Desarollo Social, SUNEP-SAS) is affiliated with the CTV and is Venezuela's oldest and largest public health union. Historically, it had administered the collective bargaining contract for the public health sector. However, in 2004 the government denied workers belonging to SUNEP-SAS the right to bargain collectively because the CNE had delayed certifying the union's election results for 17 months. While SUNEP-SAS awaited CNE certification of its election results, the government banned it from participating in collective negotiations and instead negotiated a collective agreement with a newly formed pro-government federation that had never held leadership elections, the National Federation of Regional, Sectoral and Allied Trade Unions of

Health Workers (Federación Nacional de Sindicatos Regionales, Sectoriales y Conexos de Trabajadores de la Salud, FENASINTRASALUD), affiliated with the UNT (Human Rights Watch 2008, 162).

In July 2005 the Ministry of Labor rejected SUNEP-SAS's request dating from 2002 to begin contract negotiations. Similarly, in August 2005 the Ministry of Health denied it the right to represent public health workers in sector-wide contract discussions. While the SUNEP-SAS claimed to represent the majority of workers in the public health sector, the Ministry of Health ignored the legal requirement to verify that it negotiate with the entity representing the majority of workers in the sector and pursued negotiations with FENASINTRASALUD. The Ministry of Health and FENASINTRASALUD concluded negotiations on May 12, 2006, one day after the CNE certified the 2004 SUNEP-SAS elections. Thus, the SUNEP-SAS was precluded from participating in the collective bargaining contract negotiations. Its problems were compounded by a Venezuelan law that prohibits labor organizations that have not participated in sector-wide negotiations from submitting claims on behalf of workers covered by the contract. On the basis of this law, the National Labor Inspectorate blocked SUNEP-SAS from representing worker demands and complaints even after the CNE had certified its election results. To add insult to injury, the Ministry of Health denied SUNEP-SAS officials the right to work leave, thereby restricting their capacity to organize union activities (Human Rights Watch 2008, 163).

The Chávez government employed similar tactics when dealing with the Nutrition Workers' Union, the Single National Union of Public Employees of the National Institute for Nutrition (Sindicato Único Nacional de Empleados del Instituto Nacional de Nutrición, SUNEP-INN), the only union representing nutrition workers. In December 2004 SUNEP-INN requested to hold elections. However, due to disagreements over membership rolls, the CNE did not approve and certify its elections until November 2006, almost two years later. In August 2005, while in the midst of wrangling with the CNE over its elections, the SUNEP-INN requested permission to participate in contract discussions for the health sector. These were the same discussions involving the Ministry of Health and FENASINTRASALUD from which SUNEP-SAS had been excluded.

In response to SUNEP-INN's request, the Ministry of Labor determined that because SUNEP-INN had not held elections it was not entitled to participate in the bargaining discussions but rather was only allowed to complete basic administrative functions. Furthermore, the Ministry of Health denied SUNEP-INN funds for union activities established under the public health contract primarily on the basis that SUNEP-INN had not participated in the contract talks and therefore was not party to the agreement. These decisions by the Chávez government clearly impeded SUNEP-INN's ability to engage in organizational activities necessary to promote and defend its members' interests (Human Rights Watch 2008, 165).

Fragmentation of Labor Organization

The preceding example illustrates the Chávez regime's strategy of shifting influence away from the opposition CTV to the pro-government UNT. However, it would be incorrect to conclude that with the adoption of this strategy the regime facilitated the UNT's autonomy and efficacy. Rather, it sought to utilize both the UNT and the more recently created Socialist Workers' Central (Central Socialista de Trabajadores, CST) to control and fragment the incipient labor movement. As a result, the labor movement is now divided between those groups or factions that support working-class autonomy and those that accept the labor movement's subordination to the vanguard PSUV and the state. In this fashion, the Chávez regime effectively impeded the labor movement's ability to represent workers' interests or to challenge its hegemony. A brief analysis of the events leading to the creation of the UNT and CST and their subsequent interrelationship illustrates this point.

In its early years, the Chávez regime demonstrated little interest in supplanting the CTV with alternative labor organizations. Instead, it focused its efforts on undermining the CTV through institutional means, such as the referendum to replace union leaders noted above. However, as the CTV demonstrated its ability to withstand the regime's attacks and became more aggressive in its opposition, Chávez shifted from trying to subvert the CTV through institutional reforms to trying to weaken it by creating rival labor entities. The passage of 49 decree laws in November 2001 marked the beginning of this increasingly antagonistic relationship between the regime and the labor movement.

The radical nature of the decree laws, which involved land reform and increased government control over the Venezuelan state oil company (Petróleos de Venezuela, S.A., PDVSA), galvanized labor union and private sector opposition, leading to a series of demonstrations in 2001 and early 2002 (McCoy 2004, 289). These protests culminated in the march on the presidential palace on April 11, 2002, which precipitated the outbreak of violence between the opposition and Chávez supporters and resulted in nearly two dozen deaths (Ellner 2008, 115). In response to accusations that Chávez had ordered the military to repress the people, dissident generals deposed the president. However, the military restored him to power within forty-eight hours (ibid.).

With the failure of the protests to oust Chávez, the opposition attempted to use economic pressure to force the president from power. Thus, in December 2002, the CTV joined forces with the Federation of Chambers of Commerce and Production (Federación de Cámaras y Asociaciónes de Comercio y Producción, FEDECAMARAS), the PDVSA leadership, and opposition parties to declare an indefinite general strike. While the eight-week general strike did significant damage to the economy, ultimately the government was able to keep PDVSA operating with help from retirees, lower level employees, and experts from other oil exporting countries (Hellinger 2009, 463). Thus, the strike petered out, having failed to achieve its objective of ousting Chávez.

After the 2002–3 petroleum strike, the Chávez regime became more active in trying to control the labor movement. The UNT was created in 2003 for this purpose. Yet, from its inception the UNT was marked by internal divisions that continue to plague the labor movement and which the regime continues to promote and exploit. These internal divisions result from fundamental differences between factions that advocate autonomy for the labor movement (*autonomistas*) and those that support labor's subordination to the will of the PSUV and the state (Leninistas) (López Sánchez 2012, 155).[6] These differences came to a head at the UNT's Second Congress in May 2006, when a minority faction strongly supported by the Chávez government, the Bolivarian Socialist Workers' Force (Fuerza Socialista Bolivariana de Trabajadores, FSBT), abandoned the UNT and advocated the formation of another Bolivarian central, the CST. The CST was founded in April 2008, but has had little impact since that time (López Sánchez 2012, 155; Olivera 2008).

The fate of the UNT has been only marginally better. Though it was formed in 2003, the UNT still does not possess its own headquarters or finances and lacks legitimacy and stability, reflected in (and exacerbated by) its failure to carry out internal elections.[7] The Chávez regime's contradictory treatment of the UNT compounds its instability. For example, the regime recognized the UNT when forming delegations that represent Venezuela before the ILO. Yet in the context of the labor ministry, state enterprises, official communications, and the PSUV, the regime treated the UNT as almost an opposition force, "assuming a pro-employer and anti-union policy in the majority of cases" (Lopéz Sánchez 2012, 175; my translation).

Thus, as the preceding examples illustrate, the Chávez regime engaged in actions and institutionalized labor reforms that have exacerbated fragmentation within the labor movement, impeded union autonomy and collective bargaining, and otherwise vitiated unions as means of interest mediation for workers. In addition, the Chávez regime promoted forms of labor relations through worker cooperatives and missions that make workers highly vulnerable to market forces and highly dependent on politicized government handouts.

Worker Cooperatives and Missions

Labor cooperatives are small groups of workers (with a minimum membership of five) who form an association to share business costs and profits. Since the autocratic government of Juan Vicente Gómez (1908–35) promulgated the first laws governing cooperatives in 1910, governments have varied in their efforts to promote these groups. However, beyond the differences among these various efforts to promote cooperatives, one can identify a constant pattern: those who have controlled the state have promoted cooperatives for their political purposes rather than cultivating them in response to organic demands emanating from civil society (Fernández 2008, 176). In this regard, the Chávez regime was no different than its predecessors. What differed under this regime is the magnitude of its efforts to promote cooperatives and the importance it assigned them in terms of promoting economic development and a new model of labor relations.

The Chávez regime viewed the promotion of cooperatives as part of an effort to supplant the Venezuelan economy's capitalist logic with one focused on the fulfillment of human needs (Piñeiro 2009, 310). At the same time, it promoted cooperatives as part of an explicit effort to avoid the shortcomings of "vertical socialism" associated with the former Soviet Union (Ellner 2008, 186). In practice, however, the cooperatives facilitate top-down, centralized government control and reinforce participating workers' economic precariousness and exclusion from the benefits, protections, and security of formal sector employment. Thus, from the standpoint of labor conditions, cooperatives manifest some of the worst elements of both populist and neoliberal political economies. As is typical of populist regimes, cooperatives rely upon clientelist distribution of state resources for their establishment and preservation. And as is characteristic of neoliberal regimes, cooperatives are subjected to de facto labor flexibilization and precarious employment through their dependence on subcontracts and their lack of legal protections and rights afforded formal sector workers.

These problems stem in part from the legal classification under which cooperative workers fall. Instead of considering cooperative workers as dependent or salaried workers, the state classifies them as self-employed "associates." As such, they are not covered by Venezuelan labor law relevant to "workers," which means that they receive no social security coverage and have no legal protections against unjust dismissal, making them vulnerable to reprisals if they attempt to engage in collective bargaining or strikes (Hernández Alvarez and Romero Milano 2008, 403; Human Rights Watch 2008, 189). Their small size and the precariousness of their employment contracts further impede the collective action of cooperatives. While Venezuelan law requires a minimum of 20 employees to form an enterprise-level union, over 80% of cooperatives have fewer than 10 associates. Cooperative members lack job stability; they typically work on short-term contracts and operate at multiple companies simultaneously. Consequently, their ability to organize collectively and to articulate and effectively press demands at any one work site is severely compromised (Human Rights Watch 2008, 192).

Rather than taking steps to ameliorate these negative features of cooperatives, companies, particularly in the public sector, exploit them to weaken or supplant unions. By replacing permanent employees with cooperative employees, companies such as the state oil, electric, and telephone companies are able to replace workers who possess collective bargaining rights with workers who do not. Opposition labor leaders saw this tactic as part of the regime's overarching policy of labor flexibilization. As Froilán Barrios, executive secretary of the CTV explained: "Chávez pursues a policy of labor flexibilization designed to undermine workers' organizational and social force. Cooperatives have been utilized as part of that strategy, to separate workers from labor relations, it is used above all in state enterprises . . . but it does not generate stable employment. Workers are subcontracted, outside the collective contract and outside of unions."[8]

The UNT's Juan Gómez echoes this critique: "To have a worker in a contract relation with a cooperative is very different from the condition of a worker inside an institution with a collective contract, covered by the Organic Labor Law. The cooperatives are submitted to the logic and culture of capital . . . the state has thus seen the cooperatives as a means to economize, to reduce costs."[9] The state's control of thousands of franchises through its ownership of key industries and commercial operations facilitates this practice. Thus the state has become an entrepreneur in the services sector, where precarious employment and employees' lack of knowledge of labor rights are the norm (Hernández Alvarez and Romero Milano 2008, 421).

Perhaps nowhere is the linkage between state ownership and the promotion of labor flexibility and precarious employment more evident than in the state-owned oil industry, PDVSA. According to the Federation of Oil Workers (Federación de Trabajadores Petroleros, FEDEPETROL) the dominant labor union in the oil sector, PDVSA has contracted 283 cooperatives that fulfill functions typically performed by its permanent, unionized workers. The members of these cooperatives are not covered by the oil workers collective bargaining agreement, nor do they enjoy social security protection. Furthermore, according to accusations by CTV leaders, workers under the Rotating Employment Plan are contracted for periods of only three months (Hernández Alvarez and Romero Milano 2008, 421).

Significant negative repercussions for workers result from these types of practices. The reduction in unionized employees weakens the labor movement. At the same time, cooperative workers, many of whom were former permanent employees in the companies for which they now work, are highly vulnerable to reprisals if they seek to agitate for better working conditions or wages. Companies can legally fire cooperative workers who engage in these practices or simply choose not to rehire them when their contracts expire. These conditions make cooperative workers vulnerable to both economic and political pressure exerted by employers. Indeed, contracts extended to cooperatives in the state sector can be wielded by bureaucrats as a form of patronage. Thus, cooperatives are burdened with the worst features of both statist and market development models. Cooperative workers confront employment insecurity dictated by short-term employment contracts and the volatility of demand. And, at least in the public sector, they are at the mercy of government officials who have the power to extend or withhold offers of employment on the basis of political criteria.

While the Chávez regime promoted cooperatives as means for cultivating worker autonomy and solidarity that will eventually lead to a new model of socialism, government policy and public finance, not grassroots demand, stimulated the significant upsurge in their numbers in recent years. And as Piñeiro notes, "a significant number of new cooperatives partly avoid markets through contracts with state institutions that secure them some of their inputs and buyers for some of their products. . . . this creates a dependency on bureaucracies that are far from efficient, transparent or reliable" (2009, 336). In this context, it is not surprising that many of the new associations are nothing more than *cooperativas de maletín* (briefcase cooperatives), which have single owners and hire wage labor for less than six months at a time, a practice permitted by the Law of Cooperative Associations (Ellner 2008, 187). These owners become, in essence, clients of the state who can take advantage of privileges and subsidies the government offers to promote cooperatives, including state financial aid, special programs for raising collateral, exemption from paying value-added and income taxes, and preferential treatment in bidding for state contracts (ibid.). These benefits enable the owners of briefcase cooperatives to exploit vulnerable workers through short-term contracts that do not grant the social security benefits or labor rights workers in the economy's formal sector enjoy. Such policies further indicate how the Chávez regime's policies promote de facto labor flexibilization, precarious employment, and clientelism.

The lack of government oversight of cooperatives further indicates their clientelist character. Ellner notes that mass numbers of state-financed cooperatives have failed due to "improvisation" or misuse of government funds, which has led to the loss of tens of hundreds of millions of dollars (2008, 130). He suggests that these problems result from the failure of the Ministry of Popular Power for the Community Economy (Ministerio del Poder Popular para la Economía Comunal, MPPEC) to implement sufficient regulatory oversight over the cooperatives. While mechanisms have now been created to monitor cooperatives, Ellner found no cases in which cooperative members were penalized for failing to meet their legal obligations (ibid.). If, as this analysis asserts, the regime's objective is to cultivate economic dependency and political loyalty rather than to generate self-sustaining autonomous employment, then the failure to adequately regulate worker cooperatives and their use of public funds appears perfectly logical.

The Chávez regime's social welfare programs, the so-called missions, reinforce the top-down control evident in the worker cooperatives. As with worker cooperatives, participation in the missions does not provide for social security coverage, the right to collective bargaining, or union organization. Nonetheless, the government counts the beneficiaries of assistance through the missions as employed, though, like many persons involved in worker cooperatives, they contribute little to economic productivity (Hernández Alvarez and Romero Milano 2008, 403). Therefore, while the regime uses the missions and the worker cooperatives to project the illusion that its policies reduce unemployment, these programs, in fact, do little to generate self-sustaining employment or to increase national productivity. The missions do provide needed social welfare resources to the poor and disadvantaged in Venezuela. At the same time, however, they serve as means of political and economic control over marginalized workers that the regime can exploit to its advantage.

The origins of the missions reflect this intent. The regime designed and adopted the missions in 2003 in response to growing political pressure from a mobilized opposition manifested in the 2002 coup and 2004 recall referendum (Penfold-Becerra 2007, 79). In the wake of the 2002–3 oil strike, Chávez's popularity reached an all-time low, 31% (Stokes et al. 2013, 282–83). Penfold-Becerra argues that, in response to Chávez's declining popularity, the missions served two political purposes for the regime: to "buy votes" and to build loyalty among the poor by distributing oil rents directly to them (2007, 79). There is evidence that Chávez perpetuated the clientelism prevalent under Punto Fijo, with about 10–12% of voters indicating in surveys from 2004 onward that they received benefits in exchange for votes (Stokes et al. 2013, 43). However, evidence suggests that benefits from social welfare programs, including the missions, have not been distributed in direct exchange for votes. Rather, the Chávez regime distributed social welfare resources, including resources from mission programs such as the Misión Robinson (adult literacy) and the Misión Ribas (high school equivalency), in a politically targeted manner, intended to build loyalty among followers and to attract swing voters.

The Comando Maisanta was a primary means to accomplish these objectives and integral to the Chávez regime's campaign against the 2004 recall. Evidence indicates that the government utilized the organizational structure of the Comando Maisanta, which descended from Chávez as national command chief to local electoral battle units, to distribute social welfare benefits in a manner that supported its electoral objectives. The Maisanta database, which the government compiled from information from recall petitions signed against Chávez and certain opposition deputies, contained data on the ideological orientation and turnout histories of more than 12 million individuals, all registered voters who as of July 10, 2004, were eligible to vote in the August 15 referendum. The government distributed the data to local party activists via a software program with a user-friendly interface. Database entries included an individual's address, voting center location, access to government-sponsored social programs, whether or not she or he signed a recall petition against Chávez (coded as "opposition" voter), signed a petition against opposition deputies (coded as "patriot"), or signed no recall (Stokes et al. 2013, 44). The data facilitated the regime's politically targeted distribution of social welfare resources.

Field research conducted by Stokes et al. in 2007 indicates that after the failed recall vote, the Chávez regime continued its politically targeted distribution of social welfare resources through mission programs such as Misión Robinson and Misión Ribas. Stokes et al. observe that the distribution of scholarships in these programs was not closely tied to attendance or scholastic achievement; "instead, they served mainly as cash transfers to recipients" (2013, 46). Similarly, Hawkins, Rosas, and Johnson observe that support for Chávez strongly predicted the distribution of benefits for these educational missions: "the municipal level of electoral support for Chávez in 2000 was an excellent predictor of the number of scholarships distributed through these programs" (2011, 202). Additionally, they found evidence that electoral concerns rather than parish-level poverty determine the allocation of government subsidized food stores nationwide: "parishes that delivered more support for Chávez in 2000 were much more likely to receive a store through the Mercal program" (203). These findings reflect a general pattern in the distribution of targeted social welfare benefits: voters loyal to Chávez had a significantly higher probability of participating in targeted social programs than swing voters or opposition voters, while swing voters had a substantially higher probability of receiving targeted benefits than opposition voters (Stokes et al. 2013, 48–50; see also Handlin 2016).

Thus, creation of the missions allowed the Chávez regime to build support among poor voters previously excluded from politics and state economic assistance. This new constituency of poor voters has become a key element in its social coalition and strengthened its political support (Penfold-Becerra 2007, 65). Accordingly, missions—like worker cooperatives—reproduce inferior labor conditions and reinforced the Chávez regime's top-down control of Venezuelan society, particularly of its most disadvantaged citizens.

Restriction of Labor Rights and Repression of Labor Leaders

In conjunction with its efforts to control unorganized, nonunionized workers through missions and worker cooperatives, the Chávez regime employed institutional, extra-institutional, and juridical means to control the organized labor movement. These went well beyond its efforts to control union elections as described above. The most egregious of these efforts involve the failure to honor collective contracts and to support collective contract negotiations, the severe circumscription of the right to strike and the right to engage in union activities, punitive legal measures against labor leaders and workers who engage in strike or boycott activity, and the failure to investigate or bring to justice those who have engaged in assassination of workers and union leaders.

As noted earlier, the regime used its ability to interfere in union elections through the CNE as a means of favoring minority unions that it could more easily control at the expense of more representative unions. The Ministry of Popular Power for Labor and Social Security (Ministerio del Poder Popular para el Trabajo y la Seguridad Social, MINPPTRAS) reinforced the impact of this practice by negotiating collective contracts with minority unions, which violates the Organic Labor Law stipulation to negotiate with those unions with the largest membership (PROVEA 2012, 135). In other cases, however, the government simply failed to negotiate collective contracts. As a result, collective contracts declined since 2004. For example, in 2004 there were 834 collective contracts in force.

By comparison, between 2005 and 2011, the annual average number of collective contracts was 518 (ibid.).

While interpretations vary, labor leaders of diverse ideological stripes attributed responsibility for the decline in collective contracts to the government. According to Marcela Máspero, leader of the UNT, the lack of collective contraction is a problem throughout the country and is attributable to the government's "technobureaucracy." Orlando Chirino, leader of the Trotskyist movement United Revolutionary Autonomous Class Current (Corriente Clasista, Unitaria, Revolucionaria y Autónoma, C-CURA), puts it more bluntly: "This government's claim that it has discussed . . . collective contracts is a gigantic lie. Public employees have gone seven years without discussing their contract framework and contracts for basic enterprises have been expired for between two and five years" (136).

Union leaders and workers who attempted to compel the regime to negotiate collective contracts or to honor those contracts in force confronted severe judicial actions and punitive measures to restrict their activity, particularly with regard to the right to strike. Indeed, through the adoption of various penal code measures the regime increasingly criminalized the right to strike. In this regard, the Organization of American States' Inter-American Commission on Human Rights (IACHR) observed that the Chávez regime frequently invoked a crime called "obstruction of work" against persons who engage in strike activity (IACHR 2011, 108). The regime adopted various penal statutes to impede the so-called "obstruction of work" and the right to strike. These include Article 192 of the Venezuelan Criminal Code, according to which, "anyone who, through violence or threats, in any way restricts or suppresses free commerce and industry shall face a penalty of imprisonment for one to ten months" (ibid.). Similarly, Articles 357 and 360 of the Penal Code limit peaceful demonstration and the right to strike in relation to labor demands (IACHR 2009, 281). Finally, Article 56 of the Organic Law on National Security establishes prison sentences of between five and ten years for those determined to have promoted conflict in the workplace of basic state industries. Based on information received by the IACHR, this article was invoked against labor activists seventy times in 2008 (ibid.). In 2011, 150 union members were subject to criminal prosecution for strike-related activities. Judges have exacerbated the deleterious impact of these criminal prosecutions against labor leaders by forbidding the accused from calling meetings or coming within a specified distance of companies where strike activity has been threatened or carried out (IACHR 2011, 32).

The case of Rúben González is perhaps the most illustrative example of the Chávez regime's employ of these penal statutes and punitive judicial practices to restrict strike and labor organization activity. González, secretary general of the Orinoco Iron Miners' Union (Sindicato de Trabajadores de Ferrominera Orinoco, SINTRAFERROMINERA), was arrested and taken into custody in September 2009 along with other union members after leading a work stoppage at the Orinoco Iron Mine Company to protest the company's failure to honor its collective bargaining commitments. The Attorney-General's Office charged González with committing crimes against public order, including incitement to break the law, unlawful association, restriction of the freedom of work, and non-compliance with special security zone regulations (ILO 2013, 310). The trial against González commenced on November 3, 2010; on February 28, 2011, the Sixth Tribunal of the State of Bolívar sentenced him to seven years in prison (311).

Subsequently, on March 3, 2011, the Criminal Chamber of the Supreme Tribunal of Justice overturned the original sentence, stating that it lacked sufficient grounds and declaring the original sentence null and void. The Supreme Tribunal transferred the case to another court in order to hold another trial. Although González was released from prison, the Supreme Tribunal required him to report to a judicial authority every two weeks and prohibited him from leaving the country (315). The ILO's Committee on Freedom of Association offered a stern rebuke to the Chávez regime's handling of the González case: "the charges against Rubén González do not justify the preventive detention and house arrest to which he was subjected . . . [the Committee] once again requests the Government that he be compensated for the damages suffered" (317).

While the Chávez regime's treatment of Rubén González is the most prominent case of its efforts to use judicial action to curtail union organizing and strike activity, it is by no means unique. According to the CTV, the government brought over 2,000 workers and labor leaders before the criminal courts under a "probationary system." Rather than being jailed, they were released but required to report regularly to judicial authorities and barred from engaging in any protest activities (ILO 2010b, 136). Through this type of action, the Chávez regime clearly intended to inhibit the willingness and ability of union leaders and rank-and-file members to challenge government labor policy.

The regime's failure to protect workers and union leaders from violence and assassination compounds the impact of this type of judicial action. The source of this violence originates from the nature of Venezuelan labor contracts. Labor contracts give unions the right to provide workers to enterprises. This contract stipulation gives corrupt union leaders incentives to sell jobs to workers for as much as $1000 per position. The lucrativeness of this practice has led to competition among unions for contracts, which in turn has led to the practice among union leaders of hiring body guards to protect them from threats from competing unions. Over time these body guards (or more precisely, hit men) began to eliminate union leaders in order to control for themselves the lucrative business of selling positions to workers.[10] Between 1997 and 2009, there were 240 union leaders and workers assassinated as a consequence of this competition for the sale of employment positions (IACHR 2009, 284). In 2012, there were 77 workers and labor leaders assassinated (PROVEA 2012, 143). The Chávez government prosecuted almost none of these crimes, leading to an environment of impunity for their perpetrators (IACHR 2009, 286; ILO 2010b, 136).

Conclusion

Despite its socialist rhetoric, the Chávez regime did little to strengthen the political and economic clout of Venezuelan workers or to establish a model of labor organization that transcends the problems of inequity and exploitation for which it has derided neoliberal labor regimes. Instead, it pursued policies that fragment and weaken organized labor, impede labor's autonomy, undermine collective bargaining, and exploit vulnerable workers in cooperatives through de facto flexibilization. Compounding the antilabor impact of its divisive institutional strategies, the Chávez regime utilized the penal code and judicial intervention and intimidation as means of thwarting collective action and bargaining on the part of union leaders and workers. Moreover, it failed to investigate and prosecute those responsible for violence against union leaders and workers, thereby allowing the perpetrators of these crimes to act with impunity. Finally, it utilized the politically targeted distribution of social welfare resources financed with oil rents to build support from the marginalized, unorganized masses and to thus compensate for its lack of support from organized labor.

When taken together, these various aspects of labor politics in contemporary Venezuela reveal the manner in which a charismatic leader like Chávez can utilize populist strategies to enhance his power while failing to promote avowed socialist goals of solidarity, equality, and autonomous popular participation, particularly for workers and the labor movement. Thus, the primary foible of the Chávez regime has not been its excessive or radical leftism as some of its most virulent critics claim; rather, its shortcoming has been its pursuit of populist control at the expense of an autonomous civil society and its self-proclaimed socialist ideals. Indeed, many leftist leaders in civil society believe the regime's socialist rhetoric belies its betrayal of socialism's core principles. These sentiments are expressed well by Orlando Chirino,[11] self-avowed Trotskyist, former Chavista and UNT member, and current leader of C-CURA:

> The goal of this government is to deepen state capitalism. It does not respect international labor conventions or union liberty—there is no union liberty in Venezuela! The businessmen aligned with the government, what I call "socialist entrepreneurs," take advantage of the credit and money the government offers to exploit workers, deny collective contracts; they take cover from their alliance with the government to deregulate labor relations. The intent of this flexibilization is to cheapen the cost of labor. What kind of socialism is this? It's neither socialism nor democracy!

Such criticisms have persisted since Hugo Chávez's death on March 13, 2013, under the government of his chosen successor, Nicolás Maduro. For example, a broad coalition of sixteen labor and human rights organizations, the Labor and Trade Union Action Unit (Unidad de Acción Sindical y Gremial, UASG),[12] issued a public proclamation on April 1, 2014, exactly one year after Maduro was elected president, strongly reinforcing the views expressed by Chirino:

> The only difference from previous governments is [this government's] deceptive and manipulative discourse. . . . The government discourages industrialization and agricultural production and in

> addition has created a crisis of low or paralyzed production in state enterprises, where the rights of workers are violated, collective contracts are not discussed and union autonomy is not respected. . . . Employment and the right to work depend increasingly on petroleum rents, which the government manipulates in an authoritarian and despotic manner. . . . Today more than ever, the state-as-employer promotes types of labor contracts at the margins of legality that put workers in situations of extreme vulnerability. . . . To this antidemocratic posture should be added the criminalization of labor and social protest. Through a shameful and biased use of the organs of justice many comrades and union leaders have been seized, indicted and prosecuted for nothing more than taking actions to defend their labor rights and demands.
>
> (My translation from original document in my possession)

These observations from a broad spectrum of labor organizations indicate the persistence of significant contradictions between regime rhetoric and policies. Such contradictions are likely to grow under President Maduro, given the steep decline in oil prices in recent months and thus the drastic decline in rents and social welfare resources his government can utilize to its political advantage. The opposition's substantial victory in the December 6, 2015, legislative elections appears to reflect these new circumstances.[13] If so, the regime's declining political fortunes suggest it is likely to resort to increasingly undemocratic means to maintain power, exacerbating further the already substantial contradictions between its socialist rhetoric and practice.[14]

Beyond examination of the Venezuelan case, such contradictions between left-wing rhetoric and practice raise a broader consideration regarding how one evaluates and conceptualizes so-called radical leftist regimes in Latin America. If one is to assess accurately the propensity and capacity of such regimes to promote desirable political and social welfare goals such as increased autonomy and reduced inequality for workers and marginalized groups more generally, one needs a more refined taxonomy than the present one. Mazzuca's conceptualization of rentier populism may be a useful starting point given its demonstration of common characteristics among the "radical" leftist regimes of Bolivia, Ecuador, and Venezuela: virtually unchecked presidential dominance of decision-making, gained through plebiscitarian support from the largely unorganized popular masses rather than the ranks of organized industrial workers, and cultivated through the distribution of social welfare benefits financed with rents generated from commodities exports.

Further research is needed to test the comparative utility of Mazzuca's concept in understanding Latin America's "radical" leftist regimes. In the meantime, analysis of contemporary labor politics in contemporary Venezuela indicates that the populist drive to concentrate political and economic power has subverted the leftist goals of eroding hierarchical forms of domination of marginalized popular sectors. Moreover, it is evident that despite its socialist rhetoric, the Chávez regime's political economy in general and its labor policies in particular have been highly antagonistic to workers' interests and mirror problems—flexibilized and precarious labor, vulnerability to global boom/bust cycles, the loss of a strong party advocate, and the internal fragmentation and lack of efficacy of organized labor—evident in other cases examined in this volume. As such, contrary to the proclamations of Chávez and now Maduro, the twenty-first-century "socialist" model of labor relations has failed to strengthen the political and economic clout of Venezuelan workers or to transcend the problems of inequity and exploitation for which it has denigrated neoliberal labor regimes.

An early version of this chapter appeared as "Laboring Under Chávez: Populism for the Twenty-first Century" by Paul W. Posner in *Latin American Politics and Society* 53, no. 3 (Fall 2016): 25–50.

8

Conclusion

The Historical Context of Contemporary Labor Politics in Latin America

As noted at the outset of this book, the structure and organization of labor have undergone profound changes across Latin America over the past four decades. Latin America's "golden era" of development, driven by state-led industrialization for nearly three decades after the end of the Second World War, witnessed the rise of labor movements and the expansion of labor rights across the region. However, this forward progress began to unravel with the decline of global economic conditions in the 1970s and the related deterioration of fragile domestic alliances among interventionist governments, producers, and organized labor.

Beginning with the ascendance of military regimes across much of the region in the 1960s and 1970s, followed by the painful neoliberal adjustment and the consolidation of structural reform through the 1980s and 1990s, workers in Latin America experienced substantial deterioration in both their labor rights and living standards. In some countries such as Chile, economic crisis, authoritarian repression, and flexibilizing labor legislation combined to precipitate a dramatic deterioration of labor rights and working conditions. In others, like Mexico, the preservation of protective labor regulations was no match for the destabilizing force of increasing global competition. In all countries across the region, IFIs such as the IMF and World Bank, promoted economic discourse and policies that legitimized the push to weaken unions and labor protections.

Through the market fundamentalism of the Washington Consensus, they asserted that such protections impeded economic growth and acted as barriers to the incorporation of greater numbers of workers into the formal economy.

However, over the course of the past several decades we have witnessed two important shifts in these trends. First, formerly authoritarian regimes have democratized. Subsequently, some of these democratic regimes moved, at least in rhetoric, to the left, adopting pro-poor, social justice agendas that directly challenge neoliberalism. Second, the failure of market orthodoxy to produce the increased formal sector employment and reduced inequality that its proponents promised has led IFIs and policymakers to reevaluate their adherence to the Washington Consensus. The combination of these shifts in political regime and economic discourse has opened the possibility for workers and worker organizations to reassert lost labor rights and to improve labor conditions, wages, and living standards. Yet, as our case studies demonstrate, while improvement for workers has not been entirely negligible, progress has been, at best, modest and uneven.

A Review of the Cases

On the whole, we see the pervasiveness of four negative, interrelated trends that cut across our case studies: (1) the adoption of labor flexibility practices, which increased the precariousness of labor; (2) the continued vulnerability of national economies to global competition and boom/bust cycles; (3) with the exception of Brazil, the significant weakening of party/union ties, leaving organized labor without strong, reliable political allies to help advance its interests; and (4) the internal fragmentation and attendant lack of efficacy of labor organizations in promoting positive reforms such as reducing flexibilization and increasing collective bargaining. Below we summarize how these trends manifest themselves in each of our five case studies.

Chile

Because Chile adopted flexibilizing labor reforms earlier and arguably more extensively than any other country in Latin America, it presents an ideal case by which to evaluate the pros and cons of flexibility. Following an acute and protracted economic crisis in the 1970s, the Augusto Pinochet regime under the guidance of the Chicago Boys, oversaw the institutionalization of a highly flexible labor market. In addition to restrictive labor policies, the regime controlled union activities through the threat and use of brutal repression. As such, labor organizations were unable to impede the adoption of the dictatorship's flexibilization reforms.

The nature of Chile's democratic transition facilitated the perpetuation of these reforms. In this transition, the military regime largely set the terms under which it would transfer power, the highly cohesive business community wielded substantial leverage with government, and the weak and fragmented labor movement was no longer able to depend on strong ties with its traditional party allies. Instead of reestablishing the close ties with labor that existed before the 1973 coup, the center-left parties that led the democratic opposition and that have made up the dominant political alliance since the transition, distanced themselves from the labor movement and failed to reverse the Pinochet regime's highly flexible labor reforms.

As detailed in chapter 3, these reforms have not produced the positive economic outcomes predicted by their proponents. Based on flexibility proponents' predictions, Chile should have experienced increased formal sector employment over time, particularly among the least skilled workers, as well as reduced wage inequality. Yet the rate of unemployment among Chile's least-skilled workers remains essentially unchanged since the democratic transition as does income inequality. These conditions persist despite a high degree of labor market flexibility. Thus, Chile's continued adherence to a flexibilized labor market should be understood not in terms of its capacity to reduce inequality or generate employment; rather, it should be understood as the product of several interrelated factors: (1) the business sector's ability to protect its interests; (2) the Concertación's limitation of threats to the business sector's interests; and (3) the weakness of organized labor, resulting from the perpetuation of the Pinochet-era labor regime and compounded by the decline in support from its traditional party allies.

The influence of global economic competition on Chile's political economy is a prominent variable in explaining these interrelationships. As other countries followed Chile's lead and lowered their trade barriers in the late 1980s and early 1990s, foreign firms at the upper end of the value chain were able to lower their prices by increasing their suppliers. This intensified global competition severely constrained the ability of Chilean export firms to raise prices and increase rents. Chilean firms selling to the domestic market faced a similar dynamic. With multinational firms aggressively pursuing expansion in the Chilean market, domestic producers were forced to keep prices low to maintain market share.

Thus, whether focused on export or domestic markets, Chilean firms confronted increased competitive pressures from free trade. They responded by reducing labor's share of rents, a goal accomplished in large measure by hiring subcontracted and temporary employees. As previously noted, temporary employees were prohibited from engaging in collective bargaining while subcontracted workers had limited collective bargaining rights, the exercise of which was ultimately dependent on the willingness of employers to negotiate. By imposing such constraints, the Pinochet-era labor code enabled Chilean employers to force the brunt of cost savings onto low-skilled workers. The flexibility provisions of the labor code have made such workers easily replaceable and have given them little leverage to increase job security or improve wages.

In a global economic environment of increasing competition, Chilean firms were determined to maintain this flexibility vis-à-vis workers. A well-organized and influential business sector, a weak and fragmented labor movement, and a center-left political alliance—at turns incapable or unwilling to fundamentally alter the balance of power between business and labor and the Pinochet-era labor code that sustains it—have ensured the perpetuation of the status quo. Thus, flexibility in Chile has been utilized by those in power to privilege the interests of business at the expense of workers. This finding challenges the understanding espoused by neoclassical economists that flexible labor reforms are merely tools by which to promote economic efficiency and growth. Yet it is a finding that applies to all the cases examined in this volume.

Mexico

For the most part, Mexico shied away from adopting in-depth formal labor code reforms but was still characterized by extensive de facto flexibilization during the time period under consideration. In Mexico, flexibilization resulted from the economic crisis of the 1980s and the subsequent implementation of wide-ranging neoliberal restructuring policies under PRI authoritarian rule. Successive Mexican governments since the late

1980s premised the resulting economic model in great part on keeping labor costs to a minimum in order for the country to gain a comparative advantage in terms of its labor force's competitiveness. Whereas labor rights were formally left untouched by this restructuring effort, an extensive de facto flexibilization process took place in parallel to the implementation of the main neoliberal reforms of the 1990s.

Indeed, the state refrained from implementing various provisions of the labor code during that period, effectively opening the door to the widespread adoption of flexibilizing practices by employers. Among other things, these measures resulted in increasing levels of informality and precariousness in the labor market, while the neoliberal economic model proved unable to guarantee stable and significant growth. The transition to democracy in 2000 changed these patterns very little, as the neoliberal model was continued and deepened under the two PAN governments. A limited reform of the labor code was adopted in 2012, which formalized some of the flexibilizing practices that had been allowed (and indeed encouraged) by the state in the past. Given this, the reform had only a limited impact on the labor market. As such, the degree of effective—that is, de facto and de jure—flexibility in Mexico is among the highest of our case studies, surpassed only by Chile.

Because of their direct institutional connection to the party in power, corporatist unions in Mexico were in an intrinsically disadvantageous position to resist flexibilization under the PRI's authoritarian regime. The economic restructuring of the 1990s as well as over two decades of de facto labor flexibilizing practices generated a considerable reduction of unionization rates and a congruent diminution of organized labor's mobilization and organization capabilities. This process affected ex-corporatist unions as well as independent unions. Indeed, the latter continued to be marginalized by the state even after the transition to democracy. This is particularly striking, as unionists, politicians, and observers generally considered that democratization of Mexico's regime would allow independent unions to assert themselves as the dominant segment of organized labor. This is due to the fact that independent unions represented the only subset of labor organizations offering a considerable degree of representativeness of their members' interests. It was believed that this would render independent unions more attractive to workers in a democratic context.

Yet, the PAN governments chose to continue marginalizing independent labor organizations, due to their resistance to the neoliberal model adopted by successive governments since 1988. In parallel to this, the corporatist unions either remained generally passive or supported flexibility in the post-transition period. They offered themselves as an appealing potential ally for the PAN governments in their efforts to deepen the neoliberal economic policies implemented by the PRI, given that ex-corporatist unions could still command the political support of a significant proportion of workers in the formal labor sector—or at least cause them to demobilize so that they did not represent an obstacle to the PAN's reformist agenda. This general context translated into labor quiescence and a significant flexibilization of the labor market, a tendency that was sustained and in fact deepened after the economic crisis of 2008–9. These dynamics continued after the return of the PRI to power at the end of 2012, with the main noticeable change being the realignment of the ex-corporatist unions with the PRI, after a 12-year informal alliance with the PAN while the latter was in government.

Argentina

Argentina and Brazil constitute middle-ground cases. Argentina underwent a period of significant labor code flexibilization under Carlos Menem's two administrations in the 1990s. These formal legal reforms followed the severe economic crisis of the 1980s—the Lost Decade—and were in keeping with neoliberal restructuring measures as well as existing employer practices that sought to circumvent labor code provisions deemed detrimental to their interests. Nonetheless, the pursuit of such reforms by the party that has historically represented workers in Argentina signified a momentous political transformation in the country.

The legal reforms under Menem were for the most part reversed toward the end of that decade, instituted again by the truncated Alliance administration and finally overturned during the more labor-friendly governments of Néstor and Cristina Kirchner, although some measures of flexibility still characterized Argentina in the 2000s. As in other cases, the trajectory of the country shows that notwithstanding the legal framework formally regulating labor markets, and given the weakness in enforcement the state still confronts, it is the pace of economic activity that becomes a key predictor of the effective power in the hands of workers to demand the exercise of their rights. But Argentina also shows that even high rates of economic growth can hardly generate the level of employment that will reinstate the structural power formal workers and their unions used to possess.

This is the conundrum for the corporatist CGT. During the Menem years its strategy revolved around defending its spheres of influence and the legislation that secured its organizational power: industry-wide collective agreements negotiated by the only union legally entitled to do so and control over the provision of health-care plans for its affiliates. While in many ways it was successful, the price paid was the gradual loss of cohesion, which eventually negatively impacted its political clout as well as its ability to negotiate with the state and private employers. Labor organizations outside the mainstream of the CGT, such as the breakaway CTA and the MTA, responded to the flexibilizing of the country's labor code through sustained and forceful collective actions, but to little avail.

Nonetheless, it was these organizations, along with organizations representing the unemployed, that took the lead in the social conflicts neoliberalism generated and that eventually resulted in its downfall. The CGT regained some of its mobilization capacity after the arrival to power of more labor friendly governing coalitions under Néstor Kirchner and Cristina Fernández, at a time when economic recovery favored the growth of formal employment. But these governments also courted other, less organized actors from marginalized sectors and newly created political organizations, and the Confederación was never able to regain its political prominence. Sectors of the CGT eventually grew to oppose Fernández's presidency, which contributed to its splintering into three organizations. This, along with the split of the CTA into two groups toward the end of Fernández's government, further divided the labor movement and reduced its ability to resist flexibilization policies and practices.

Like the other cases we have considered, labor markets in Argentina remained heavily marked by informality. The segmentation of labor markets, though, need not mean the segmentation of working-class strength or aspirations. The challenge lies in the foresight to organize around both development options that address the problem of employment generation and alternative forms of economic participation and forms of working-class organizations that are inclusive of the various forms work and production currently take. The CTA represented an attempt in this direction but, paradoxically, the advances achieved until 2002 were diluted in a political context that appeared considerably more receptive to the demands the organization had fought for during the challenging 1990s. The election of a government promoting very conservative corrective measures might bring unity to the organizations of the working class. However, this alone is not sufficient to address the several deficits labor confronts.

Brazil

As was the case for Argentina, flexibilization in Brazil was attained through a mix of formal/de jure as well as informal/de facto means. In both cases, the scope of labor flexibility was ultimately more limited than in the Chilean and Mexican cases. The Brazilian labor legislation was flexibilized mainly in the 1990s under the two Fernando Henrique Cardoso governments. This policy orientation was pursued in an attempt to deepen the restructuring of the country's economy, begun with the successful implementation of the Real Plan in response to the recession and hyperinflation that rocked Brazil in the 1980s and early 1990s. As in the Argentinean case, these legal transformations formalized some employer practices that had been common for years. The accession to power of Luiz Inácio Lula, an ex-labor leader from the militant "new unionism" movement, mitigated the implementation process of these measures, although it did not invalidate existing flexibilizing policies nor terminate flexibilizing employer practices.

Although Cardoso's administration was punctuated by economic difficulties, Lula's government coincided with an economic upturn in Brazil, caused among other things by a boom in commodity prices on the international market. This positive economic context allowed some leeway in developing more efficient and wider-focused social policies, both factors deemed central in the significant reduction of poverty and labor informality, as well as socioeconomic inequality that took place during 2003–10. Contrary to his predecessor, Lula's government favored the strengthening of collective workers' rights and created a context somewhat less conducive to labor market flexibilization. Yet, yearly growth rates were on average much higher than during the Cardoso years. Further substantiating what was indicated above in the case of Chile, this pattern tends to call into question the neoliberal dogma according to which economic growth and efficiency depend upon the implementation of in-depth labor market flexibilizing policies. Our analysis suggests instead that other factors may have a greater impact, such as transformations in the international economic context as well as variations in policy orientations between successive governing coalitions.

As concerns labor organizing in Brazil during the time period at hand, the Cardoso government aggressively confronted the more dynamic segments of organized labor (i.e., the new unionism movement led by the CUT), in order to impose his administration's flexibilizing priorities in the second half of the 1990s and early 2000s. Faced with an unyielding administration and with a delicate economic situation in which steady and significant growth remained elusive and job stability threatened, the CUT adopted a more defensive stance. It focused its actions on job preservation and tamed its efforts to derail the flexibilization of the country's labor legislation. For its part, Força Sindical, the CUT's main rival, whose creation had been fostered by the neoliberal government of Cardoso's predecessor, supported flexibilizing policies. This effectively divided the labor movement and weakened its cohesion and ability to resist the Cardoso administration's policy priorities.

The arrival of ex-CUT leader Lula to the head of Brazil's federal government changed the overall context in which the labor market and labor organizations operated and represented a source of hope for many unionists that the disequilibrium between workers and employers would be modified to favor the former. In fact, the Lula government was characterized by a fairly intimate relationship between the federal administration and the country's labor movement, in which the presidency assumed a clear leadership role and favored a top-down approach to settling labor-related issues. As such, the CUT—as well as the rest of the organized labor movement, for that matter—did not appear to recuperate its mobilization capacity during that time, and was unable to oppose some of Lula's most controversial reforms affecting unions (such as the pension reform of 2003). Furthermore, Lula's administration did not diverge from the fundamentals of the economic model implemented by Cardoso.

Nevertheless, the Lula government's overall policy orientation tended to create a labor market context more favorable to the interests of organized labor and furthered an enhancement of collective labor rights for both formal and informal sector workers. Indeed, the link between the PT government and major labor organizations—in particular, the CUT—remained strong during the Lula years, and continued—although in a weakened form—under Dilma Rousseff (2011–16). As such, the PT remained by and large a conduit for the demands of a significant segment of formal sector workers. Furthermore, the Constitutional reform of 2008 in fact strengthened ties between unions and parties—the latter at times sponsoring the creation of labor confederations such as in the case of the Communist Party of Brazil (Partido Comunista do Brasil, PCdoB) and the Brazilian Workers' Central (Central dos Trabalhadores e Trabalhadoras do Brasil, CTB). But it is worth noting that the Lula and Dilma administrations also made an effort to reach out to workers in the informal sector, supporting their organization and affording them improved legal protection, in order to ameliorate their interest representation and to bring them into the formal economy, among other things. This is fairly congruent with the PT's traditional ties with grassroots organizations, but it represents a significant—and positive—break with the manner in which the federal government had typically dealt with informal labor in Brazil.

Venezuela

In the Latin American context, and certainly among the cases examined here, Venezuela is considered as part of the radical or extreme left. However, as we have argued, the Venezuelan case is more accurately understood as predominately populist rather than leftist or socialist. Like other populist regimes, the Hugo Chávez regime has sought top-down control of civil society, though it diverged from classical populism by eschewing reliance on support from organized labor. Instead, consistent with the notion of rentier populism, it sought to build its political base among the unorganized masses. This project was facilitated by labor market changes—substantially increased informality and a related decline in unionization—precipitated by economic crisis and the adoption of neoliberal reforms under Punto Fijo.

By building its political base among the unorganized masses and eschewing reliance on support from organized labor, the Chávez regime was able to avoid constraints on its exercise of power. Thus, the structural adjustment policies carried out under Punto Fijo provided the foundation for Chávez's pursuit of rentier populism. To generate and maintain mass political support, the regime coupled Chávez's charismatic appeal with top-down control of popular organizations. This top-down control of popular organizations was, in turn, facilitated by the politically targeted distribution of material benefits to subaltern groups, financed with expanded state oil revenues. In other words, while the regime promoted a high level of mass mobilization, it did so in a manner that enhanced its control over the previously unorganized masses and facilitated favorable electoral outcomes.

While in rhetoric the regime vehemently rejected neoliberalism, in practice it promoted de facto flexibilized labor relations characteristic of neoliberalism through the creation of workers' cooperatives, which serve as sources of subcontracted labor, particularly for state-owned industries. In addition to exploiting vulnerable workers in cooperatives, it employed divisive institutional policies that fragment and weaken organized labor, impede its autonomy and undermine collective bargaining. Compounding the anti-labor impact of its divisive institutional strategies, the Chávez regime utilized the penal code and judicial intervention and intimidation as means of thwarting collective action and bargaining on the part of union leaders and workers. When considered in conjunction with the regime's co-optation of the unorganized masses through the politically targeted distribution of social welfare resources, these policies characterize a labor regime which is highly antagonistic to workers' interests and which mirrors problems—flexibilized and precarious labor, vulnerability to global boom/bust cycles, the loss of a strong party advocate, and the internal fragmentation and lack of efficacy of organized labor—evident in the other cases examined in this volume.

Comparative Analysis

As the preceding discussion suggests, there exist important similarities and differences among our cases. In this section, we attempt to make these similarities and differences more explicit and to bring into sharper focus general patterns that should serve as useful conceptual and theoretical guides when attempting to understand labor politics across the region. Among the most significant of our findings relates to the issue of flexibility. Analysis of our case studies provides scant support for claims regarding the purported benefits of flexibilization, particularly with respect to its promise of formal employment generation. Indeed, as chapter 3 illustrates, contrary to the predictions of labor flexibility's proponents (e.g., Cox Edwards 2007; Heckman and Pagés 2000, 2004; Sabatini and Farnsworth 2006), Chile's high degree of labor market flexibility—the highest among our five cases—has not led to increased levels of employment, particularly for Chile's poorest citizens. Moreover, despite high levels of labor market flexibility, empirical evidence indicates high and persistent income inequality in Chile, directly contradicting claims regarding flexibility's propensity to reduce inequality.

Mexico represents another case of high labor market flexibility, although flexibilization measures were implemented differently in Mexico than they were in Chile. Still, chapter 4 suggests that, as in Chile, labor flexibilization in Mexico failed to increase formal sector employment and revitalize economic growth. By comparison with Chile and Mexico, Brazil and Argentina achieved more moderate—although still considerable—levels of flexibilization. Similar to our findings in the Chilean case, chapter 6 shows that labor flexibilization measures implemented in Brazil during the Cardoso government did not yield the results expected by their proponents. In keeping with what was observed in Chile, levels of formal employment and economic growth showed little to no amelioration, and poverty as well as inequality rates remained the same, after the implementation of flexibilization in Brazil.

Far from enabling improvements in employment levels, the flexibilization of labor markets in Argentina, resulting from both legal reform and de facto market conditions, also produced a severe deterioration of working conditions including rising informality and precarity. The nature of the structural reforms Argentina followed during the 1990s restricted the options at the disposal of the government to respond to the challenging economic realities the country encountered as the decade progressed. Among these limited options, labor flexibilization acquired a growing importance even when, as chapter 5 shows, it was not always possible to achieve it through formal legal means. As in Mexico, de facto flexibilization was a key feature of labor markets during the decade, leading as it did in other countries of the region to unprecedented levels of informality, unemployment, poverty, and inequality.

In none of our case studies did the flexibilization of labor reduce levels of informality. At first glance, Brazil after Cardoso may seem to represent an exception to this pattern, since flexibilization measures adopted under Cardoso were for the most part continued under the PT governments, during which levels of informality diminished markedly. However, we have shown that the increase in formal sector employment experienced during the successive PT administrations is in fact not attributable to flexibilization measures. Rather, this change resulted from the implementation of a set of policies that aimed at strengthening the labor market, reducing unemployment and informality, and improving salaries as well as working conditions for workers. Thus, analysis of our case studies suggests that flexibilization is best understood, not as a means of reducing informality or inequality, but instead as a means of subverting the organizational strength of workers, thereby reducing both wage and nonwage costs for employers. In this sense, we argue that flexibility reforms shift the balance of power in favor of employers at the expense of workers.

Additionally, one of the central findings of our research is that there exist multiple ways in which labor flexibilization can be imposed. While some analysts focus on de jure protections of collective labor rights (Murillo and Schrank 2005) as evidence of improved organizational capacity for workers across Latin America, we observe that flexibilization—and thus the subversion of worker organizational capacity—has been achieved in ways other than legal reform of the labor code. As chapter 4's analysis of Mexico demonstrates most clearly, preserving labor legislation that ostensibly protects individual or collective labor rights does not necessarily prevent the flexibilization of labor relations. Firms imposed flexibilization at the plant level through negotiation of collective agreements, as occurred in Mexico and Argentina. Moreover, our case studies demonstrate that the economic consequences of structural adjustment—including poor rates of employment generation, rising unemployment, and, given the lack of a significant safety net, the parallel growth of the informal economy—were central to employers' capacity to impose extensive de facto flexibilization.

Our case studies also reveal that the imposition of flexibilization, whether de facto or de jure, has had a significant impact on labor organization and party-labor ties. In this regard, we observe a general pattern in which the more severe the structural adjustment and repression carried out pre-transition or pre-regime change:[1] (1) the weaker organized labor is post-transition or post-regime change; and (2) the weaker the linkage between organized labor and political parties, whether these be newly ascendant leftist parties such as the PSUV in Venezuela or historical allies of the labor movement such as the Socialist Party in Chile. As chapter 3 demonstrates, the severity of the Chilean military regime's structural adjustment policies and repression undermined the historical ties between organized labor and parties of the left and center. Since the return to democracy, these ties remain tenuous, reflecting a fundamental transformation of party-labor ties in Chile, which under the first four center-left governments left workers without sufficient political leverage to overturn the most egregious elements of the Pinochet regime's labor reforms.

As in Chile, structural reforms carried out under Mexican authoritarianism were perpetuated after the country's democratic transition. Indeed, the PAN maintained and deepened the neoliberal model post-transition and chose to continue the marginalization of independent labor organizations due to their resistance to this model. In this regard, Mexico experienced a transformation in party-labor ties as substantial as occurred in Chile. The main ex-corporatist unions effectively broke loyalty ties with the PRI, their historical ally, following the culmination of Mexico's democratic transition. These ex-corporatist unions then entered into a new clientelistic relationship, this time with the PAN in government.

Because these unions either supported or remained passive in the face of flexibility, they have been perceived by successive Mexican governments both before and after the country's transition to democracy as an effective tool of labor control. These unions therefore retained the bulk of their political importance after the transition, as they were actively courted by successive parties in power—whether the PAN (2000–2012) or the PRI (2012–18). As such, clientelistic state-labor relationships perpetuated and exacerbated flexibility in Mexico. Thus, despite differences between the Mexican and Chilean cases, chapter 4's analysis of Mexico indicates that, as was the case in Chile, the legacy of structural adjustment and authoritarianism persists post-transition and plays a significant part in compromising the position of labor vis-à-vis political parties under democracy.

In Argentina, the restoration of democracy gave organized labor a degree of leverage to shape the nature and extent of labor reform that the Chilean and Mexican labor movements did not share. Unlike its Chilean counterpart, the Argentine military's adoption of neoliberal reform was uneven at best, and its disgraced exit from power severely restricted its policy influence post-transition. As a result, organized labor in Argentina retained the capacity to protect rights that were at the core of its organizational power, even during the heyday of neoliberal reforms in the 1990s. Nonetheless, this partial victory was not sufficient to reduce the heavy organizational and political costs structural adjustment and labor flexibilization inflicted on unions and the CGT. The weakening of individual labor rights, along with growing unemployment and de facto flexibilization, reduced the structural power of unions while the search for political accommodation with the Menem administration undermined the CGT's legitimacy and produced deep divisions within the labor movement. The combined effects of these changes further weakened the position of the CGT within the Peronist Party.

As chapter 5 illustrates, the more labor-friendly Kirchner governments overturned the neoliberal labor reforms and fostered a process of economic growth that brought about substantial improvements in formal employment and, with it, new opportunities for union growth. Nonetheless, neoliberalism had produced a major restructuring of the economy, and, even with high rates of economic growth in the new century, informality and other forms of precarity remained very high. Therefore, while the CGT retained the bases of its considerable power, the existence of a large mass of unorganized workers continued to limit both the confederation's structural power and influence within the party. The weakening of the traditional ties between party and CGT was then the result of a complex set of circumstances, but labor's weak stance against the conditions that engendered informality and, in the face of it, its incapacity to devise organizational alternatives to encompass informal and precarious workers left these sectors of workers open to the political initiatives of other actors.

We observe similar dynamics at play in Venezuela. As chapter 7 demonstrates, economic crisis and the adoption of neoliberal reforms under the Punto Fijo regime during the 1980s and 1990s had the effect of undermining the regime's legitimacy, leading to its collapse and paving the way for Chávez's rise to power. By substantially increasing informality and producing a related decline in unionization, the economic crisis and subsequent adoption of neoliberal reforms under Punto Fijo precipitated a fundamental restructuring of party-labor ties in Venezuela. This restructuring deepened under the Chávez regime, as it pursued the unorganized masses that comprise the urban informal sector as its primary base of support. With a majority of workers in the informal sector, the Chávez regime realized that it could build a winning electoral block without relying on the organized labor movement, thereby freeing it from constraints the organized labor movement sought to impose on its power and policymaking.

Thus, as chapter 7 demonstrates, the Chávez (now Maduro) regime has neither re-created the corporatist labor relations that prevailed under Punto Fijo nor delivered on its promise to empower workers through some form of radical participatory democracy. Instead, it fragmented and weakened the labor movement and in the process fundamentally altered party-labor ties in Venezuela. These findings, along with the revelation of the Chávez regime's adoption of labor flexibility reforms through the use of contracted labor in workers cooperatives, contradict the regime's socialist rhetoric. As such, our analysis of the Chávez regime suggests the need to rethink the prevailing understanding of the relationship between populism and leftism. In this regard, our analysis challenges the prevailing debates in the literature, in which scholars either conflate populism and leftism (Castañeda 2006; Castañeda and Morales 2008; Weyland 2013; Weyland, Madrid, and Hunter 2010) or see them as distinct (Cameron and Hershberg 2010; French 2009; Levitsky and Roberts 2011). In contrast, we argue that, as the Venezuelan case demonstrates, populism and leftism are not only distinct but also in tension with one another. More precisely, we argue that analysis of labor politics in contemporary Venezuela indicates that the populist drive to concentrate political and economic power subverts the leftist goals of eroding hierarchical forms of domination of marginalized popular sectors. Accordingly, our analysis of labor politics in Venezuela offers insights that promise to deepen our understanding of other so-called radical leftist regimes in Bolivia and Ecuador.

Additionally, we observe in Venezuela a vicious cycle that is also evident in Chile and Argentina: the decline in the size and strength of organized labor—whether as a result of authoritarian repression, structural adjustment, or both—prompted parties historically aligned with labor to deemphasize this alliance and to shift their focus to unorganized workers in the informal sector. To the extent that this shift occurs, analysis of these case studies indicates that it is problematic for all workers since in none of these cases has the relative decline in influence of formal sector workers been accompanied by empowerment of the masses in the informal sector.

The analysis presented in chapter 6 indicates that Brazil is an exception to this pattern. In stark contrast to the Venezuelan case, our examination of the Brazilian case reveals the positive gains workers have experienced under a more moderate form of leftism. In this regard, Brazil is an outlier among our five case studies. For although organized labor saw some reduction of its mobilizing capacity since 1995, its membership remained essentially intact and it continued to be a central political actor with important ties to the PT and other political parties. Lula's top-down mode of resolving labor disputes and adherence to the economic model adopted by President Cardoso restricted organized labor's autonomy and ability to mobilize. This pattern of state-labor relations remained in place under the subsequent government led by Lula's protégé, Dilma. Nonetheless, relations between the federal government and major labor organizations such as the CUT remained by and large strong through the PT administrations, and the PT remained a key conduit for demands of significant segments of formal sector workers.

These positive party-labor relations were facilitated by institutional reforms adopted under the successive PT governments. For example, the 2008 Constitutional reform strengthened ties between unions and parties. In addition, Lula's administration modified the Brazilian labor code to advance workers' interest representation and implemented many policies demanded by labor organizations since the return to democracy—in particular, significant and steady increases in the real minimum salary. In contrast to the other cases examined in this volume, PT governments also supported the organizing and improved legal protections for informal sector workers. However, it is important to note that the political activation of segments of the informal sector did not change the fundamentals of the CUT-PT relationship.

Why has the labor movement experience been more positive in Brazil than in other cases examined in this volume? Our analysis of the Brazilian case reveals it to be the exception that affirms the general pattern noted above regarding the importance of the timing and nature of regime change and economic liberalization in determining the fate of labor reform and organization. In other words, if the Chilean and Mexican cases demonstrate the negative impact severe structural adjustment and repression under authoritarianism have on party-labor ties in the post-transition period, the Brazilian case demonstrates that adopting less extreme neoliberal reforms and adopting them in the post-transition period allows for the development of more positive party-labor ties. In this context, we see the interplay of a number of factors that serve to explain the uniqueness of the Brazilian experience. First, the perpetuation of ISI under the military regime maintained the economic importance and leverage of organized labor. Second, Brazil's more modest and relatively gradual adoption of neoliberal reforms after the democratic transition limited the negative repercussions of structural adjustment for the labor movement. Third, the democratic transition was spearheaded by new unionism—that is, the dynamic and significant noncorporatist segment of the Brazilian labor movement founded by Lula—among others. New unionism also played an essential role in the creation of both the CUT and the PT. As a result, it is not surprising that Lula and the PT continued to see labor as an important ally in the post-transition period. Hence, the Brazilian experience demonstrates the importance of the timing and nature of regime change and economic liberalization in determining the fate of labor reform and organization.

A key factor here appears to be the impact of structural reform on the size and related power and influence of the labor movement. As previously noted, in the Argentine, Chilean, and Venezuelan cases, where structural adjustment reduced substantially the size and strength of organized labor, labor's traditional party allies have reduced their focus on the organized labor movement and sought to cultivate support among unorganized workers in the informal sector. The result has been a significant reduction in the clout of organized labor without a commensurate increase in political or economic influence for workers in the informal sector.

The impact of flexibilization on informality and other characteristics of labor in contemporary Latin America reinforces the significance of this negative pattern. Specifically, our comparative analysis suggests that flexibilization does not reduce informality, improve employment, or reduce inequality. Rather, we conclude from our case study analyses that flexibility reforms shift the balance of power in favor of employers at the expense of workers. In this regard, we observe that implementation of flexibilization can be de facto or de jure. As such, labor laws that appear to protect the organizational rights and capacities may belie impediments to labor organization that exist in practice. Ultimately, whether de facto or de jure, our investigation indicates that flexibilization produces significant negative impacts on labor organization and party-labor ties.

Laboring in Latin America: A Pressing Agenda for Future Research

Our research has raised a number of issues that have not been the central focus of this study but which warrant investigation in the future. These include research to better understand intraregional migration, the relationship between economic growth and employment in Latin America, investigation into the conditions necessary to establish democratic unionism, and the role of politically targeted social welfare assistance in cultivating support among informal workers and thereby mitigating the need to build support from organized labor.

As noted in chapter 7, the Hugo Chávez regime utilized the politically targeted distribution of resources to cultivate support among the informal sector and other historically unorganized and disadvantaged segments of society. While in this volume we have not examined the use of this strategy outside of the Venezuelan case, exploring the extent to which this strategy has been utilized by other regimes across the region—particularly the other so-called radical leftist regimes in Bolivia and Ecuador—to cultivate support among the unorganized masses, promises to shed light on the challenges workers confront when the state has substantial rents at its disposal to distribute for political purposes. In this regard, we can reasonably hypothesize that: (1) the greater the level of informality and the weaker organized labor is post-transition or post-regime change; and (2) the weaker the linkage between organized labor and their historical party allies, then (3) the more political parties will rely on building a winning electoral strategy through cultivation of support via the informal sector; and (4) building this base of support within the unorganized masses will depend to a significant extent on the politically targeted distribution of social welfare resources.

Investigating these hypotheses promises to provide substantial insight into not only contemporary labor politics in Latin America but also the politics of social welfare distribution across the region. In particular, it promises to illuminate the interrelationship between labor and social welfare regimes. In the meantime, it seems evident that, in the context of liberalized economies and ever increasing global competition, reliance on labor flexibilization as a strategy for businesses to reduce costs and maintain profits and for some regimes to generate rents, is here to stay for the foreseeable future. Indeed, in the context of economic liberalization and global competition in export commodities, even avowed leftist parties appear reluctant to strengthen labor protections or weaken flexibility for fear of precipitating negative macroeconomic repercussions such as reduced foreign investment and growth as well as increased unemployment and inflation.

These macroeconomic concerns point to the need to better understand the relationship between economic growth and employment in Latin America. As our case studies show, even during a period of rapid economic growth in the new century, labor has remained structurally weak. Part of the problem lies in the high and enduring rates of informality in the region, a reflection of the inability of the region's economies to generate adequate employment in both quantitative and qualitative terms. This problem brings new urgency to the development of better theoretical and empirical tools through which to understand the relationship between economic growth and employment in a globalized Latin America. This is, in our view, a required step to better comprehend the challenges labor will face in the future to organize and to struggle for better working conditions. Pursuit of this research agenda is made all the more pressing by the steep downturn in primary export prices that Latin America has experienced in recent years.

In this challenging context, what economic strategies might generate the conditions in labor markets more favorable for labor organizing? Given the weakening bonds between labor and the parties that had previously given voice to its demands, what are the most effective ways in which labor can affect the course of development in the region? In particular, can labor become a more active ally in the struggles against the social and environmental costs of extractive industries?

Changing patterns in intraregional migration is another area that requires further exploration from the perspective of labor. The changes in labor markets our studies analyzed left many workers with few options other than finding a way out of the insecurity they face by migrating in search of better opportunities. While most of the migratory flow involves journeys toward the United States, Canada, and, increasingly over the last two decades, also Europe, a very sizeable portion of migrants remains within the region. Intraregional migratory flows in many cases feed the labor power required to sustain activities that are mostly labor intensive and require minimal skills. Regional migrants, often undocumented, are among the most vulnerable workers in the region, a vulnerability exacerbated by the lack of citizenship rights. Along with ways to better measure the presence of regional migrants, we also need a more thorough understanding of the way in which migrant workers impact the composition of specific sectors within the labor markets where they find their niche, particularly in terms of informalization and precarity.

Of course, as our analysis also suggests, labor's challenges are not exclusively external. Labor organizations confront fragmentation and internal weakness. Thus, we need a better understanding of the possibilities for the emergence of a more transparent, accountable, and democratic unionism. In this regard, it is imperative to further the analysis of legal reforms that might facilitate and strengthen this kind of unionism and the nature of the process through which agreement on reforms should be arrived at. A key question is whether more pluralistic processes for the selection of union authorities and recognition of unions can become a progressive tool to re-invigorate unionism or whether it will result in new divisions that can only benefit employers.

Our analysis suggests that highly centralized labor movements are not in themselves a guarantee of protection against reforms that harm workers. Furthermore, in many countries, this form of unionism has resulted in labor elites perpetuating their stay in power through undemocratic means, often at the cost of membership representativeness. However, some alternatives are equally dangerous for workers. In the name of greater union democracy, neoliberal labor code reforms have allegedly increased workers' freedoms by making it possible to choose their union or to refuse to belong to one. This effectively exacerbated competition between labor organizations vying to preserve and develop their membership. In turn, this has often led to the splintering of the labor movement and the reduction of its political influence.

What then is exactly the way forward? What should be the process to ensure the democratic renewal of labor unionism in Latin America? From where would the impetus for new and more inclusive forms of organizing come? Is the growing organization of the "social economy" the force that might inject new dynamism among the organizations of the working class broadly conceived?

Answers to these questions await future investigation. In the meantime, the findings of this research indicate that the challenges workers and labor organizations confront across Latin America as a result of the legacy of neoliberal reform—including flexibility, precarity, and acute vulnerability to the vagaries of the global market—are substantial and enduring. Indeed, even as regimes have remained democratic, and in some cases moved leftward, these challenges have persisted, and with the recent collapse of the commodities boom, intensified. As a result, the optimism that growing economies and the emergence of the pink tide across the region would empower workers and raise living standards has been shaken, if not shattered. Economic mismanagement and corruption have exacerbated the financial and fiscal crises precipitated by the commodities boom collapse.

Of course, such dire straits are not new to Latin America. Rather they are a recurring theme in the region's history. But this history also demonstrates that in periods of difficulty and crisis, leaders and citizens can be willing and capable of envisioning and adopting new solutions to perennial problems. The present moment offers such a historic opportunity. How will Latin America respond? Will leaders find new ways to pursue development that enhances the well-being of workers without sacrificing the region's cultural and natural resource endowments? We look forward to participating in the search for answers to these crucial questions.

Notes

Chapter 1. Introduction: Labor Politics in Latin America

1. The impact of globalization on labor rights and working-class power has given rise to a diverse body of literature providing critical insights into the very particular ways in which global forces have affected workers and their capacity to organize in various regions in the world (Anner 2008, 2011; Munck 2002; Ness 2015; Silver 2003; Stallings 2010; Wright 2000).

2. It is essential to note, as the authors do, that these "two designs are 'ideal types,' and the matching and contrasting of cases that they posit is never perfectly achieved in any real analysis" (Collier and Collier 1991, 15).

3. Among our five cases, Argentina, Brazil, Chile, and Mexico transitioned from authoritarianism to democracy while Venezuela underwent a change in regime from liberal democratic to left populist.

Chapter 2. Historical Overview

1. It was this heterogeneity, and the very high levels of inequality resulting from it, that according to Oxhorn (1998) explain the occurrence and recurrence of populism in the region.

2. Schmitter (1974, 99–103) suggested the need to differentiate between two variants of corporatism: societal and state corporatism. Scandinavian countries were a good example of corporatism in its first connotation, where societal corporatism or neocorporatism had facilitated processes of interest representation and policymaking that ensured a more autonomous involvement of labor. Under the state variant, on the contrary, corporatism can be conceptualized as a system of interest intermediation, where the state acquires the means to control and shape the demands emanating from the working class (Collier and Collier 1977). It is this particular understanding of corporatism that is utilized in this text. Some of the classical contributions on Latin American corporatism in the English literature are Chalmers (1991), Collier (1996), Collier and Collier (1977, 1991), and Malloy (1976).

3. The share of informal sector employment in total employment rose in the region from 42.8% in 1990 to 46.5% in 2002. Countries particularly affected by this trend during the 1990s were Brazil (where informal employment increased 5.4 percentage points), Colombia (9.9 percentage points), and Venezuela (13.8 percentage points) (ILO 2003, 33 and table 6-A, 101–4).

4. See, e.g., Lora and Pagés (1997) and Sabatini and Farnsworth (2006).

5. It has proven challenging to find a one- or two-word term to depict accurately the nature of the governments that have undertaken the process of change described in four of the book's case studies during the twenty-first century. Some governments had a more radical agenda of change, while others have worked through alliances incorporating forces not always connected to the left. Pink tide is in this sense a good shorthand to identify in general terms the emergence of governments that sought to respond to the challenges and failures neoliberalism had generated. In some cases, the terms "leftist," "progressive," and "radical" are used in this book, in full awareness that each one is inadequate in some way. However, the discussion in each chapter makes clear both the complex nature of political change in each case study and the difficulty in encapsulating these experiences in just one word.

6. This industry in China has been developed through investment from the same transnational corporations that previously produced soybean in Argentina (ADM, Bunge, and Cargill). These TNCs have now moved their investment to China, importing unprocessed seeds from Argentina. The centrality of TNCs in shifting patterns of investment and trade is also essential for understanding the growing importance of China as a U.S. trading partner (Jenkins 2010, 821 and 824).

7. Rising primary exports introduced new environmental challenges, both because of the expansion of the agricultural and mining frontiers and the methods employed. The growth of agricultural exports increased the value of productive land, leading to the displacement of both the traditional agricultural elite and large numbers of small producers. Similarly, the expansion of mining has taken place at the expense of local communities and at the risk of the environment, which has often brought these communities, in many cases indigenous communities as is the case in Ecuador, Bolivia, and Chile, into open opposition to both the transnational mining and petroleum industries and national states.

8. This is what critics referred to as "progressive neo-extractivism" (Gudynas 2012, 132).

Chapter 3. Labor Market Flexibility, Employment, and Inequality: Lessons from Chile

1. Economic efficiency is enhanced when the market price for labor is commensurate with demand, expressed in terms of the wages employers are willing to pay. Advocates of labor market flexibility argue that flexibility increases employment by lowering wages and labor costs, thereby making it more cost-effective for employers to hire more workers. Such hiring should, in turn, reduce informality, while the removal of job security protections should reduce wage disparities between those workers who enjoy such protections and those workers who do not.

2. Law 16,744, Article 15, obligated employers to pay social security taxes of 0.9% to 4.3% of workers' salaries to insure workers against injury. The higher rate is to cover workers in more dangerous occupations.

3. The Labor Bureau (Dirección del Trabajo) is the division within the Labor Ministry that monitors and oversees the enforcement of labor laws and works to resolve labor conflicts. See http://www.dt.gob.cl/1601/channel.html for further elaboration.

4. In 2011, the Chilean government changed the methodology utilized for the Encuesta CASEN, the National Socioeconomic Characterization Survey, from which data for this analysis are drawn. In the 2013 edition of the CASEN survey, the government provided income distribution calculations based on the traditional methodology as well as the new methodology. In the most recent CASEN survey, from 2015, however, only the new methodology is employed. As a result, income distribution data for this year are not comparable to earlier years and thus is not included in this analysis.

5. Fairfield and Jorratt arrive at slightly different figures, 15.1% for the unadjusted share of national income for Chile's top 1% and 21.7% to 23.0% for the adjusted rate (2014, 19).

6. The revised capital gains figures are based on estimates of retained profits, i.e., profits that the wealthiest Chileans don't declare in order to avoid paying capital gains taxes.

7. The Ministry of Social Development indicates on its website that survey data compiled after 2011 are based on a different methodology from data compiled for 1990 through 2011 (see http://observatorio.ministeriodesarrollosocial.gob.cl/casen/casen_convenios.php). Therefore, in order to ensure comparability, this analysis focuses only on those years for which comparable data are available. As noted in footnote 4, the data on income distribution are a partial exception to this rule as the 2013 CASEN Survey provides data on income distribution based on both the methodology utilized between 1990 and 2011 and the methodology employed in subsequent years.

8. The labor code adopted under the dictatorship and essentially maintained until the implementation of a new labor code in April 2017 stipulated that subcontracted workers could not unionize or engage in collective bargaining with employees of the primary enterprise. Exceptions were made for the formation of inter-enterprise unions in which the union of the employees of the principal enterprise and the union representing subcontracted employees join together. In instances where such inter-enterprise unions were formed, they were entitled to engage in collective bargaining with the principal enterprise. However, in all cases such negotiation remained completely voluntary on the part of employers. See Labor Bureau: http://www.dt.gob.cl/consultas/1613/w3-article-94227.html.

9. See Boeninger (1986) for one of the earliest expressions of this argument. Boeninger served as the coordinator of Political Relations and Government Programs for the pre-transition Concertación de Partidos por la Democracia (1988–89), minister secretary general of the presidency under President Aylwin (1990–94), and finally as a designated senator in the Chilean Congress.

10. The total value of the bond, or voucher, is equivalent to four *unidades de fomento* (UF) for each replacement worker hired. At the time of this writing, in August 2017, a UF was worth approximately 26,600 pesos; four times that amount at the current exchange rate would be approximately $163.00 (see http://valoruf.cl/ for the current UF value). The sum total of the bond is divided equally among all striking workers (see Article 381c, Labor Code, Tapia Guerrero and Domínguez Soto 2011, 170).

11. As Article 303 of the Labor Code states, "collective bargaining that affects more than one enterprise will always require prior agreement of the parties" (Tapia Guerrero and Domínguez Soto 2011, 139; my translation).

12. While the Bachelet government stated that it supports the expansion of collective bargaining rights, it made clear that it did not support inter-enterprise collective bargaining, or in other words, bargaining that extends beyond the plant level. In contrast, the CUT stated explicitly that it wants inter-enterprise collective bargaining rights.

13. Recent research suggests that the severe restrictions the current labor regime imposes on legal strike activity have led increasingly to illegal strike activity, particularly among public sector and subcontracted workers (both legally prohibited from striking) and increasingly outside the metropolitan region (Aguila and Armstrong 2011; Leiva 2013; Pérez, Medel, and Velásquez 2015). Further research is needed to determine if this increasing proclivity among some sectors of the labor force to engage in illegal strike activity represents a significant challenge to the established labor regime.

14. González Tapia, personal interview, June 28, 2011.

15. Destefani San Martín, personal interview, June 30, 2011.

16. At the time of this writing, in August 2017, the prospects for remedying the shortcomings in Bachelet's latest labor reforms appear remote, at least in the short term. The decision by the Christian Democratic Party to run its own candidate in the 2017 presidential election, thereby splitting the center-left vote, makes the right-wing candidate, former president Sebastián Piñera, the odds-on favorite to win reelection. If Piñera does, in fact, win reelection, his ties to the business community do not bode well for the prospects of amending the flaws in the newly implemented labor code in a manner favorable to Chilean workers.

Chapter 4. The Impact of Regime Change and Economic Restructuring on Mexico's Labor Relations, 1988–2012

1. Independent unions are generally considered to be more legitimate because more representative than their ex-corporatist counterparts (Middlebrook 1995). The main ex-corporatist labor confederation is the Labor Congress (Confederación del Trabajo, CT). The National Union of Workers (Unión Nacional de Trabajadores, UNT, Mexico) and, until the dissolution of the SME in 2009, the Mexican Union Front (Frente Sindical Mexicano, FSM) were the main confederations of independent unions (Mayer 2006, 10–11).

2. Strike petitions in Mexico do not necessarily result in strikes. They may be withdrawn, as is most often the case, and they may be rejected by the Labor Boards.

3. Protection contracts are collective agreements "that offer little or nothing to workers while protecting employers from real union representation." These contracts impose minimal obligations on employers and are often struck "without worker knowledge, reducing union representation to a legal fiction" (Tilly 2014, 176–77). Protection contracts also prevent other, arguably more representative, unions from attempting to replace the "white unions" (i.e., unions submissive to employers' priorities and demands) that generally agree to these contracts.

4. The CROM is the oldest workers' confederation in Mexico. It was instrumental in establishing the foundations of the PRI's governments but was later displaced by the CTM. The CROC was created in 1952 by the PRI in an attempt to divide—and thus facilitate control over—the "official" labor movement. Like the CTM, both confederations

have a reputation of corruption, cooptation, and lack of transparency in their functioning and leadership (Bensusán and Middlebrook 2012; Trejo Delabre 1976).

5. Soto Martínez, personal interview, August 15, 2012, my translation.

6. Rodríguez y Pacheco, personal interview, September 11, 2012, my translation.

7. Vega, personal interview, September 11, 2012, my translation.

8. Sánchez, personal interview, August 22, 2012, my translation.

9. Barrales, personal interview, August 23, 2012, my translation.

10. Rodríguez, personal interview, August 17, 2005, my translation.

11. Olivera, personal interview, August 16, 2012, my translation.

12. Martínez, personal interview, August 21, 2012, my translation.

13. Rodríguez y Pacheco, personal interview, September 11, 2012, my translation.

Chapter 5. Uncertain Transitions: Labor and the Politics of Reform in Argentina

1. The reader probably does not need reminding that, as in the case of Chile, the military dictatorship that ruled Argentina between 1976 and 1983 had already introduced some of the policies identified with neoliberalism.

2. As a high-ranking officer of the military regime publicly declared: "we seek to weaken the enormous power of the unions, which was one of the country's biggest problems" (cited by Andersen 1993, 178).

3. Two years after the military takeover, during the most violent phase of repression, left-leaning activists and shop-floor union leaders represented almost 40% of those who "disappeared" under the military's watch (Rock 1987, 368).

4. Carlos Alderete from the Light and Power (Luz y Fuerza) union was appointed the new minister of labor in 1987. He represented a union coalition known as the "Group of 15," an association closely connected to the orthodox wing of the Peronist party but at that time seeking accommodation with the Radical administration.

5. A good indication of this shift is the decline in wages and salaries as a proportion of the GDP from 34% in 1983 down to somewhere between 28 and 24% by 1989. Per capita GDP also shrank by almost 25% during the 1990s (Nun 1994, 108).

6. Cavallo had served since 1989 as the minister of foreign affairs. Previously, under the military dictatorship, he was the president of the Central Bank from 1982 to 1983. Later in 2001, during the last year of Fernando de la Rúa's presidency, as the country faced one of the deepest economic and political crises in its history, he would serve as economy minister once again.

7. The Convertibility Law was in effect until January 2002.

8. Greater flexibilization also implied a downgraded notion of formal employment, as more flexible working conditions were also more precarious in nature. Nonetheless, this was the alternative the government proposed as a way to control unregistered work.

9. The CTA's highly successful trajectory among the unemployed was in no small part the result of the charismatic presence of Luis D'Elía, one of the key figures in the movement during the 1990s.

10. The movement of the unemployed remained marginal to the organizational goals of the CGT during the period examined in this chapter. After 2010 there were some

initiatives on the part of the CGT to represent informal workers, for example, the National Federation of Unions with Workers in the Informal Economy (Federación Nacional de Sindicatos con Trabajadores en la Economía Informal, FENASTEI), but they have remained rather marginal to the main concerns of the confederation. It was only in 2016 that for the first time the CGT attempted to find ways of connecting with informal workers more forcefully, this time through some coordinated actions with the Confederation of Workers of the Popular Economy (Confederación de Trabajadores de la Economía Popular, CTEP).

11. Official data on changes in the consumer price index (CPI) from 2007 onward are notoriously unreliable, thus GDP growth may be overestimated.

12. Unfortunately, inflation became an ever-growing problem for the government, seriously undermining income gains and raising the stakes in the conflictive area of salary disputes.

13. Notwithstanding the significance of the legal reform, it is highly likely that, in stark contrast to the transformation in the 1990s, the consistent formalization of jobs might also be connected to an improving economy and not just changes to the law.

14. As mentioned in chapter 2, unregistered workers are those for whom the employer has not fulfilled the legal process of inscription in the pertinent register. As a consequence, these workers do not enjoy the protection extended to them by law and are denied access to social security coverage. Even after the critical period of very rapid growth, unregistered workers represented 35.8% of salaried workers in 2009, considerably higher than the 27.2% in 1990 (Neffa 2010, 68–70) and the 19% in 1980 (Chitarroni and Cimillo 2007, 6). Conditions for the self-employed were even worse: 58% were unregistered, a condition that considerably increased their vulnerability (Bertranou, Casanova, and Sarabia 2013, 5).

15. While a sector of the CTA found it less problematic to provide support to the FpV administrations, neither the organization as a whole nor its *oficialista* faction after 2010 were successful in gaining the legal recognition they had expected and that the ILO and the Argentinean Supreme Court had pressed the government to grant.

16. The national strike was eventually called off as the two CTAs decided to support instead the CGT's call to strike on April 6. Nonetheless, some of the unions within the CTA, in particular teachers, did maintain their strike for the day.

17. These included members of a significant group of cooperatives—worker-controlled companies, recycling cooperatives (known as *cartoneros* in Argentina) created under the auspices of social assistance programs, garment cooperatives—street vendors, and also small agricultural producers.

Chapter 6. The Limits of Labor Legislation Reforms: Rigidity, Growth, and Employment in Brazil, 1995–2010

1. Labor courts are populated by representatives of workers, employers, and the state—with the latter directing the courts' work. There are three levels of labor courts: local, regional/state, and national. Each has its own jurisdiction: local labor courts address grievances; regional/state labor courts settle contractual matters; and national

labor courts examine appeals from regional courts (Reis de Sousa and das Mercês Carneiro 2010, 20).

2. For more on this, see in particular, Boito (1994, 1998) and Riethof (2004).

3. Hyperinflation in Brazil originated from, among other things, the oil shocks-driven economic crisis of the 1970s and in deficit spending by successive Brazilian governments. The latter policy was implemented under the military regime (1964–85) but reached unparalleled levels after the country's transition to democracy. A series of four heterodox stabilization plans were adopted between 1986 and 1994, which failed to generate tangible results. Finally, the Real Plan was implemented in July 1994, which successfully tackled hyperinflation (Baer 2014, 80–95, 144–46).

4. The *Banco de Horas*, or Time Bank, is a management tool that may be utilized among other things to avoid granting financial compensation for overtime and facilitate utilization of the labor force. The *Banco de Horas* allows for the accumulation of hours worked in overtime by employees, so that this "banked time" can later be claimed as vacation time as opposed to being cashed out (CLT 2014, Art. 59, Para. 2).

5. Rodrigues de Azevedo, personal interview, April 12, 2010, Rio de Janeiro.

6. Berzoini, personal interview, May 5, 2010, Brasilia.

Chapter 7. Laboring under Chávez: Populism for the Twenty-First Century

1. Mazzuca (2013) includes Argentina among Latin America's rentier populist regimes. However, Argentina differs from Bolivia, Ecuador, and Venezuela in important ways. For example, Argentina's sources of commodity export rents such as soybeans are privately owned and profits do not go directly into state coffers as they do in the state-owned oil and gas industries in Bolivia, Ecuador, and Venezuela. Moreover, the Kirchners relied, in part, on organized labor for popular mobilization, a trait not found in the cases identified here as rentier populist. These distinct characteristics of Argentina under the Kirchners suggest that it does not fit neatly into the category of rentier populist regime, thus, it has not been categorized as such.

2. See Canache (2004) for survey data that substantiate the Chávez regime's reliance on the informal sector as a primary base of support.

3. Handlin notes, for example, that while the presence of a neighborhood Communal Council greatly increased the likelihood of a Chávez vote in the 2006 presidential election, the electoral impact depended heavily on material distribution. "Effects were extremely strong in communities receiving high levels of material spending under the program and nearly nonexistent in areas receiving little to no resources" (2016).

4. Note that the Venezuelan Communist Party (Partido Comunista Venezolano, PCV) was excluded from the Punto Fijo pact, which in all likelihood contributed to the emergence of a Communist insurgency in the 1960s.

5. The AD's decline is indicated by its limited influence in the National Assembly, where until the December 2015 election it held just 13 out of 162 seats. COPEI held an even more modest 6 seats. By contrast, the party most closely tied to the regime, the PSUV, held 95 seats. As a result of the 2015 elections, AD increased its representation to 25 seats while the COPEI won no seats. By comparison, in 1988, before the Punto Fijo

regime unraveled, AD controlled the presidency, AD and COPEI each held 24 seats in the 52-seat Senate, and AD held 97 seats in the 201-seat Chamber of Deputies, while COPEI held 67.

6. Ironically, Stalin Peréz Borges, one of the leaders of the *autonomista* faction of the UNT, is named after the Soviet leader, Joseph Stalin (Peréz Borges, personal interview, February 1, 2011).

7. During interviews in Caracas on February 1, 2011, Peréz Borges and Gómez of the UNT stated that they were in the process of "refounding and relaunching" the organization. At that time, the organization did not have its own offices.

8. Barrios, personal interview, February 23, 2011, Caracas.

9. Gómez, UNT National Coordinating Committee, personal interview, February 1, 2011, Caracas.

10. Aurelio Concheso, president FEDECAMARAS Labor Commission, personal interview, February 3, 2011, Caracas.

11. Chirino, leader C-CURA, personal interview, February 4, 2011, Caracas.

12. The sixteen organizations include: CTV, UNT, C-CURA, Confederation of Autonomous Trade Unions (Confederación de Sindicatos Autónomos, CODESA), CGT, Independent Trade Union Alliance (Alianza Sindical Independiente, ASI), Autonomous Employment Salary and Trade Union Defense Front (Frente Autónomo en Defensa del Empleo, el Salario y el Sindicato, FADESS), Trade Union Movement of the Base (Movimiento de Sindicatos de Base, MOBASE), Federation of University Professors of Venezuela (Federación de Asociaciones de Profesores Universitarios de Venezuela, FAPUV), National Federation of Retired Persons and Pensioners of Venezuela (Federación Nacional de Jubilados y Pensionados de Venezuela, FENAJUPV), Venezuelan Program of Education and Action in Human Rights (Programa Venezolano de Educación Acción en Derechos Humanos, PROVEA), National Union of Press Workers (Sindicato Nacional de Trabajadores de Prensa, SNTP), Public Services International (PSI), Interunion Transport Sector Command, Association of Professors of the Central University of Venezuela, and CNCA-ISP (*La Razón* 2014).

13. The opposition won 112 of 167 seats in the National Assembly, giving it precisely the number of seats necessary for a supermajority (Neuman and Torres 2015).

14. As evidence of this, the departing assembly appointed 13 new justices to the Supreme Court, which critics have attacked as an effort by the government to maintain its influence over the court. Subsequent to the election, the new court has allowed Socialist Party challenges to eight opposition-won seats, threatening the opposition's two-thirds majority (Neuman and Torres 2015). In addition, on February 11, 2016, the court approved the Maduro government's decree of economic emergency powers despite the opposition's rejection of the government's decree in January (Reuters 2016). Subsequently, the Maduro government usurped entirely the powers of the National Assembly through the creation of a Constituent Assembly, which it has tasked with rewriting the Constitution (Semple 2017b). In addition, it removed from office Attorney General Luisa Ortega, a prominent Maduro critic; she subsequently fled the country to Colombia and has promised to reveal widespread corruption within the government (Casey 2017). More

recently, the government held gubernatorial elections that the opposition criticized as severely flawed, if not fraudulent (Semple 2017a).

Chapter 8. Conclusion

1. As noted in chapter 1, among our five cases, Argentina, Brazil, Chile, and Mexico transitioned from authoritarianism to democracy while Venezuela underwent a change in regime from liberal democratic to left populist.

Bibliography

Abrahamer Rothstein, Frances. 2007. *Globalization in Rural Mexico: Three Decades of Change*. Austin: University of Texas Press.

Acosta, Alberto. 2013. "Extractivism and Neoextractivism: Two Sides of the Same Curse." In *Beyond Development: Alternative Visions from Latin America*, edited by Miriam Lang and Dunia Mokrani. Amsterdam: Rosa Luxemburg; Transnational Institute, 61–86.

Aguila, Rafael, and Alberto Armstrong. 2011. "Evolución de las huelgas laborales en Chile, 1979–2009." *Revista de Administración y Economía UC* 69: 13–17.

Aguilar García, Javier. 2010. "Tasa de sindicalización en México 2005–2008." *Análisis Político* (December): 5–17. http://library.fes.de/pdf-files/bueros/mexiko/08130.pdf.

———. 2012. *El sindicalismo mexicano en el siglo XXI*. Saarbrücken: Editorial Académica Española.

Albagli I., Elías, Pablo García S., and Jorge Restrepo L. 2004. "Evaluación del mercado laboral chileno desde una perspectiva internacional." *Revista Economía Chilena*, Banco Central 7, no. 2: 27–45.

Alcalde, Arturo. 2003. "Reforma laboral: Una iniciativa para favorecer al corporativismo." In *Reforma Laboral*, edited by Arturo Alcalde et al. Mexico City: Universidad Nacional Autónoma de México, 15–40.

———. 2012. "Reforma laboral: La agenda democrática." *La Jornada*, November 3. http://www.jornada.unam.mx/2012/11/03/opinion/013a2pol.

Alexander, Robert. 2003. *A History of Organized Labor in Brazil*. Westport: Praeger.

Álvarez, Sonia, ed. 2005. *Trabajo y producción de la pobreza en Latinoamérica y el Caribe: Estructuras, discursos y actores*. Buenos Aires: Consejo Latinoamericano de Ciencias Sociales (CLACSO).

Andersen, Martin Edwin. 1993. *Dossier Secreto: Argentina's Desaparecidos and the Myth of the "Dirty War."* Boulder: Westview Press.

Anner, Mark. 2008. "Meeting the Challenges of Industrial Restructuring: Labor Law Reform and Enforcement in Latin America." *Latin American Politics and Society* 50, no. 2: 33–65.

———. 2011. *Solidarity Transformed: Labor Responses to Globalization and Crisis in Latin America*. Ithaca, NY: Cornell University Press.

Ansell, Aaron. 2011. "Brazil's Social Safety Net under Lula." *NACLA* 44, no. 2: 23–26.

Arbache, Jorge Saba. 2001. *Unions and the Labor Market in Brazil*. Working Paper prepared for IPEA-World Bank Brazil Jobs Report 2002. http://papers.ssrn.com/sol3/papers.cfm?abstract_id=308564 (accessed December 12, 2015).

Arbache, Jorge Saba, and João Alberto de Negri. 2004. "Filiação industrial e diferencial de salários no Brasil." *Revista Brasileira de Economia* 58, no. 2: 159–84.

Arnold, Caroline E. 2010. "Where the Low Road and the High Road Meet: Flexible Employment in Global Value Chains." *Journal of Contemporary Asia* 40, no. 4: 612–37.

Aziz Nassif, Alberto. 1989. *El estado mexicano y la CTM*. Mexico City: Editorial La Casa Chata.

Baer, Werner. 2014. *The Brazilian Economy: Growth and Development*. 7th ed. Boulder: Lynne Rienner.

Banco Central do Brasil. 2015. *Series tamporais*. http://www.bcb.gov.br/?SERIETEMP (accessed June 12, 2015).

Banuri, Tariq, and Edward Amadeo. 1991. "Worlds within the Third World: Labour Market Institutions in Asia and Latin America." In *Economic Liberalization: No Panacea*, edited by Tariq Banuri. New York: Oxford University Press, 171–200.

Barrett, Patrick S. 2001. "Labour Policy, Labour-Business Relations and the Transition to Democracy in Chile." *Journal of Latin American Studies* 33: 561–97.

Barría Traverso, Diego, Eduardo Araya Moreno, and Oscar Drouillas. 2012. "Removed from the Bargaining Table: The CUT During the Bachelet Administration." *Latin American Perspectives* 39, no. 4: 85–101.

Basualdo, Victoria. 2010. "Los delegados y las comisiones internas en la historia argentina: 1943–2007." In *La industrial y el sindicalismo de base en la Argentina*, edited by Daniel Aspiazu, Martín Schorr, and Victoria Basualdo. Buenos Aires: Atuel, 81–157.

Behrman, Jere R., Nancy Birdsall, and Miguel Székely. 2007. "Economic Policy Changes and Wage Differentials in Latin America." *Economic Development and Cultural Change* 56, no. 1: 57–97.

Bensusán, Graciela. 1995. "Entre la tradición y el cambio: el corporativismo sindical en México." In *Sindicalismo latinoamericano: Entre la renovación y la resignación*, edited by Maria Silvia Portella de Castro and Achim Wachendorfer. Caracas: Editorial Nueva Sociedad, 67–81.

———. 2000. *El modelo mexicano de regulación laboral*. Mexico City: Plaza y Valdés.

———. 2006. "Las reformas laborales en América Latina." In *Teorias sociales y estudios del trabajo: Nuevos enfoques*, edited by Enrique de la Garza Toledo. Barcelona: Anthropos, 367–84.

———. 2007. "Los determinantes institucionales de los contratos de protección." In *Contratación colectiva de protección en México: Informe a la Organización Regional Interamericana de Trabajadores*, edited by Alfonzo Bouzas Ortiz and Luis Oliver Reyes Ramos. Mexico City: UNAM, 13–48.

Bensusán, Graciela, and Kevin Middlebrook. 2012. *Organized Labor and Politics in Mexico*. London: Institute for the Studies of the Americas.

Berg, Janine. 2004. *Miracle for Whom? Chilean Workers under Free Trade*. New York: Routledge.

Berg, Janine, and Dante Contreras. 2002. "Political-Economic Regime and the Wage

Curve: Evidence from Chile, 1957–1996." Schwartz Center for Economic Policy Analysis Working Paper Series 2002–10. New York: New School University.

Bertranou, Fabio, Luis Casanova, and Marianela Sarabia. 2013. "How, Why and in What Sectors Employment Informality Decreased in Argentina from 2003 to 2012." Paper presented at the Third Regulating for Decent Work Conference, "Regulating for Equitable and Job-Rich Growth." Geneva, July 3–5.

Biles, James. 2009. "Informal Work in Latin America: Competing Perspectives and Recent Debates." *Geography Compass* 3, no. 1: 214–36.

Bisio, Raúl H., Osvaldo R. Battistini, and Juan S. Montes Cató. 1999. "Transformaciones de la negociación colectiva durante la vigencia de gobiernos constitucionales a partir de 1973." In *Política y relaciones laborales en la transición democrática argentina*, edited by Arturo A. Fernández and Raúl Bisio. Buenos Aires: Editorial Lumen/Humanitas, 135–79.

Bizberg, Ilán. 1990. "La crisis del corporativismo mexicano." *Foro Internacional* 30, no. 4: 695–735.

Blanchflower, David G. 2006. *A Cross-Country Study of Union Membership*. IZA Discussion Paper Series, No. 2016. Bonn: Institute for the Study of Labor.

Blyde, Juan S., Christian Volpe Martincus, and Danielken Molina. 2014. *Fábricas sincronizadas: América Latina y el Caribe en la era de las Cadenas Globales de Valor.* Washington, DC: IDB Publications.

Boeninger, Edgardo. 1986. "The Chilean Road to Democracy." *Foreign Affairs* 64, no. 4: 812–32.

Boito, Armando Jr. 1991. *O sindicalismo de estado no Brasil—análise crítica da estrutura syndical.* São Paulo: UNICAMP Press.

———. 1994. "The State and Trade Unionism in Brazil." *Latin American Perspectives* 21, no. 1: 7–23.

———. 1998. "Neoliberal Hegemony and Unionism in Brazil." *Latin American Perspectives* 25, no. 1: 71–93.

Bonnet, Alberto. 2007. *La hegemonía menemista: El neoconservadurismo en Argentina, 1989–2001.* Buenos Aires: Prometeo Libros.

Bronstein, Arturo S. 1997. "Labour Law Reform in Latin America: Between State Protection and Flexibility." *International Labour Review* 136, no. 1 (Spring): 5–26.

Buchanan, Paul. 1995. *State, Labor, Capital: Democratizing Labor Relations in the Southern Cone.* Pittsburgh: University of Pittsburgh Press.

Burgess, Katrina. 2003. "Mexican Labor at a Crossroads." In *Mexico's Politics and Society in Transition*, edited by Joseph S. Tulchin and Andrew Selee. Boulder: Lynne Rienner, 73–108.

———. 2004. *Parties and Unions in the New Global Economy.* Pittsburgh: University of Pittsburgh Press.

Buxton, Julia. 2011. "Foreword: Venezuela's Bolivarian Democracy." In *Venezuela's Bolivarian Democracy: Participation, Politics, and Culture under Chávez*, edited by David Smilde and Daniel Hellinger. Durham, NC: Duke University Press, ix–xxii.

Cameron, Maxwell A., and Eric Hershberg, eds. 2010. *Latin America's Left Turns: Politics, Policies, and Trajectories of Change.* Boulder: Lynne Rienner.

Camp, Roderic. 2014. *Politics in Mexico.* 6th ed. New York: Oxford University Press.

Campero, Guillermo. 1991. "Entrepreneurs under the Military Regime." In *The Struggle for Democracy in Chile, 1982–1990*, edited by Paul W. Drake and Iván Jaksic. Lincoln: University of Nebraska Press, 128–58.

Canache, Damarys. 2004. "Urban Poor and Political Order." In *The Unraveling of Representative Democracy in Venezuela*, edited by Jennifer L. McCoy and David L. Myers. Baltimore, MD: Johns Hopkins University Press, 33–49.

Canuto, Otaviano, Matheus Cavallari, and José Guilherme Reis. 2013. "The Brazilian Competitiveness Cliff." *Economic Premise* 105. Washington, DC: World Bank.

Cárdenas, Ana. 2005. "El sujeto y el proceso de transformación en las condiciones de trabajo de Chile: Elementos teóricos y empíricos para la discusión." Santiago, Chile: Oficina Internacional del Trabajo, Oficina Subregional para el Cono Sur de América Latina.

Cardoso, Adalberto Moreira. 1999. *Sindicatos, trabalhadores e a coqueluche neoliberal: A era Vargas acabou?* Rio de Janeiro: Fundação Getulio Vargas.

———. 2004. *Industrial Relations, Social Dialogue and Employment in Argentina, Brazil and Mexico.* Employment Strategy Papers Series. Geneva: ILO.

Carmago, Ricardo. 2012. "Dealing with Income Inequality During the Bachelet Administration: A Critical Analysis of the Discourse of Chilean Political Elites." *Latin American Perspectives* 39, no. 4: 19–33.

Carneiro Araujo, Angela Maria, and Roberto Veras de Oliveira. 2011. "El sindicalismo brasileiro en la era de Lula." *Trabajo* 5, no. 8, 83–112.

Carrera, Nicolás Iñigo. 2013. "Democracia y movimiento sindical 1983–2013." *Voces en el Fénix* 4, no. 31 (December): 116–23.

Casey, Nicholas. 2017. "Venezuela's New, Powerful Assembly Takes Over Legislature's Duties." *New York Times*, online. August 18. https://www.nytimes.com/2017/08/18/world/americas/venezuela-constituent-assembly-maduro.htmlCastañeda, Jorge G. 2006. "Latin America's Left Turn." *Foreign Affairs* 85: 28.

Castañeda, Jorge G. 2006. "Latin America's Left Turn." *Foreign Affairs* 85, no. 3: 28–43.

Castañeda, Jorge G., and Marco A. Morales, eds. 2008. *Leftovers: Tales of the Latin American Left.* New York: Routledge.

Chalmers, Douglas A. 1991. "Corporatism and Comparative Politics." In *New Directions in Comparative Politics*, edited by Howard J. Wiarda. Boulder: Westview Press, 59–81.

Cheibub Figueiredo, Argelina. 2007. "Government Coalitions in Brazilian Democracy." *Brazilian Political Science Review* 1, no. 2: 182–216.

Chitarroni, Horacio, and Elsa Cimillo. 2007. "¿Resurge el sujeto histórico? Cambios en el colectivo del trabajo asalariado: 1974–2006." *Laboratorio. Estudios sobre Cambio Estructura y Desigualdad Social* 9, no. 21: 5–11.

CLT (Consolidação das Leis do Trabalho). 2014. http://www.planalto.gov.br/ccivil_03/decreto-lei/Del5452.htm (accessed March 8, 2015).

Collier, David. 1996. "Trajectory of a Concept: 'Corporatism' in the Study of Latin American Politics." In *Latin America in Comparative Perspective: New Approaches to Methods and Analysis*, edited by Peter Smith. Boulder: Westview Press, 135–62.

Collier, David, and Ruth Berins Collier. 1977. "Who Does What, to Whom, and How: Toward a Comparative Analysis of Latin America Corporatism." In *Authoritarianism and Corporatism in Latin America*, edited by James Malloy. Pittsburgh: University of Pittsburgh Press, 489–512.

Collier, Ruth Berins, and David Collier. 1991. *Shaping the Political Arena: Critical Junctures, the Labour Movement, and Regime Dynamics in Latin America*. Princeton: Princeton University Press.

Collier, Ruth Berins, and Samuel Handlin. 2009. *Reorganizing Popular Politics: Participation and the New Interest Regime in Latin America*. University Park: Penn State University Press.

Cook, Maria Lorena. 1995. "State-Labor Relations in Mexico: Old Tendencies and New Trends." In *Mexico Faces the 21st Century*, edited by Donald Schultz and Edward Williams. Westport: Praeger, 77–96.

———. 2007. *The Politics of Labor Reform in Latin America*. University Park: Penn State University Press.

Corradi, Juan Eugenio. 1978. "The Politics of Silence. Discourse, Text, and Social Conflict in South America." *Radical History Review* 18 (Fall): 38–57.

Corrales, Javier. 2010. "The Repeating Revolution: Chávez's New Politics and Old Economics." In *Leftist Governments in Latin America: Successes and Shortcomings*, edited by Kurt Weyland, Raúl L. Madrid, and Wendy Hunter. New York: Cambridge University Press, 28–56.

Corrales, Javier, and Michael Penfold-Becerra. 2007. "Crowding Out the Opposition." *Journal of Democracy* 18, no. 2: 99–113.

Cortázar, René. 1997. "Chile: The Evolution and Reform of the Labor Market." In *Labor Markets in Latin America: Combining Social Protection with Market Flexibility*, edited by Sebastian Edwards and Nora Claudia Lustig. Washington, D.C.: Brookings Institution Press, 235–60.

Cox Edwards, Alejandra. 1997. "Labor Market Regulation in Latin America: An Overview." In *Labor Markets in Latin America: Combining Social Protection with Market Flexibility*, edited by Sebastian Edwards and Nora Claudia Lustig. Washington, DC: Brookings Institution Press, 127–50.

———. 2007. *Labor Market Reforms in Latin America: Consequences and Costs*. Washington, DC: IADB.

Cypher, James M., and Raúl Delgado Wise. 2010. *Mexico's Economic Dilemma: The Developmental Failure of Neoliberalism*. Blue Ridge Summit, PA: Rowman and Littlefield.

Dabla-Norris, Era, Evridiki Tsounta, Kalpana Kochhar, Frantisek Ricka, and Nujin Suphaphiphat. 2015. *Causes and Consequences of Income Inequality: A Global Perspective*. Washington, DC: IMF.

Dal Morin, Naiara. 2011. "As reformas trabalhista e sindical no Brasil nos governos Cardoso e Lula: Conflitos e consensus." PhD diss., Programma de Pós-Graduação em Ciência Politica, Universidade Federal do Rio Grande do Sul.

Davis, Charles L., and Kenneth M. Coleman. 1989. "Political Control of Organized Labor in a Semi-Consociational Democracy: The Case of Venezuela." In *Labor Autonomy and the State in Latin America*, edited by Edward C. Epstein. Boston: Unwin Hyman, 247–73.

De Andrade Baltar, Paulo Eduardo, Anselmo Luís dos Santos, José Dari Krein, Eugenia Leone, Marcelo Weishaupt Proni, Amilton Moretto, Alexandre Gori Maia, and Carlos Salas. 2010. *Moving towards Decent Work. Labor in the Lula Government: Reflections on Recent Brazilian Experience*. Global Labour University Working Papers, no. 9 (May). http://www.global-labour-university.org/fileadmin/GLU_Working_Papers/GLU_WP_No.9.pdf (accessed October 5, 2014).

de la Garza Toledo, Enrique. 1998. "Sindicatos, Estado y economía en México." In *El sindicalismo ante los procesos de cambio económico y social en América Latina*, edited by Konrad Adenauer Stiftung. Buenos Aires: Grancharoff S.A., 183–237.

———, ed. 2003. *La situación del trabajo en México*. Mexico City: Plaza y Valdés.

de la O, Maria Eugenia, and Cirila Quintero, eds. 2001. *Globalización, trabajo y maquilas: Las nuevas y viejas fronteras en México*. Madrid: Plaza y Valdés.

de Oliveira, Francisco. 2006. "Lula in the Labyrinth." *New Left Review* 42: 5–22.

DIEESE (Departamento Intersindical de Estatísticas e Estudos Socioeconônicos). 2014. *Anuário do trabalho 2013*. https://www.dieese.org.br/anuario/2013/anuarioSebrae2013.html (accessed October 12, 2014).

Dirección del Trabajo. 2011. *ENCLA 2011: Informe de resultados. Séptima encuesta laboral*. Santiago: Departamento de Estudios, Dirección del Trabajo, Gobierno de Chile.

———. 2013. *Compendio de Series Estadísticas 1990–2012*. Santiago: Unidad de Análisis *Estadístico* del Departamento de Estudios, Dirección del Trabajo, Gobierno de Chile.

———. 2017. *Código del Trabajo*. Dirección del Trabajo, Gobierno de Chile.

Dömeland, Dörte, and Indermit S. Gill. 2002. "Labor Reform in Latin America during the 1990s." In *Crafting Labor Policy: Techniques and Lessons from Latin America*, edited by Indermit Gill, Claudio Montenegro, and Dörte Dömeland. New York: Oxford University Press, 1–32.

Drake, Paul W. 1996. *Labor Movements and Dictatorships: The Southern Cone in Comparative Perspective*. Baltimore: Johns Hopkins University Press.

Durán Sanhueza, Gonzalo. 2013. "Panorama sindical y de la negociación colectiva en el Chile de los US $22.655." *Revista de Derecho y Seguridad Social* 3: 85–96.

Echeverría, Magdalena, and Diego López. 2004. "Flexibilidad laboral en Chile: Las empresas y las personas." Santiago: Departamento de Estudios, Dirección del Trabajo, Gobierno de Chile.

ECLAC (Economic Commission for Latin America and the Caribbean). 2013. *Statistical Yearbook of Latin America and the Caribbean 2013*. http://www.cepal.org/en/publications/35864-anuario-estadistico-america-latina-caribe-2013-statistical-yearbook-latin-america (accessed May 15, 2015).

———. 2014a. "ECLAC Lowers Growth Forecast for the Region in 2014 to 2.2%." Press release, August 4.

———. 2014b. *Social Panorama of Latin America 2014*. http://www.cepal.org/en/publications/37626-social-panorama-latin-america-2014 (accessed May 15, 2015).

Edwards, Sebastian, and Nora Claudia Lustig. 1997. Introduction to *Labor Markets in Latin America: Combining Social Protection with Market Flexibility*, edited by Sebastian Edwards and Nora Claudia Lustig. Washington, DC: Brookings Institution Press, 1–26.

Ellner, Steve. 1993. *Organized Labor in Venezuela, 1958–1991: Behavior and Concerns in a Democratic Setting*. Wilmington, DE: Scholarly Resources.

———. 2005. "The Emergence of a New Trade Unionism in Venezuela with Vestiges of the Past." *Latin American Perspectives* 32, no. 2: 51–71.

———. 2008. *Rethinking Venezuelan Politics: Class, Conflict, and the Chávez Phenomenon*. Boulder: Lynne Rienner.

———. 2011. "Venezuela's Social-Based Democratic Model: Innovations and Limitations." *Journal of Latin American Studies* 43, no. 3: 421–49.

Ellner, Steve, and Miguel Tinker Salas, eds. 2007. *Venezuela: Hugo Chávez and the Decline of an Exceptional Democracy*. Lanham, MD: Rowman and Littlefield.

Epstein, Gerald A. 2005. "Introduction: Financialization and the World Economy." In *Financialization and the World Economy*, edited by Gerald A. Epstein. Northampton, MA: Edward Elgar, 3–16.

Erickson, Kenneth Paul. 1977. *The Brazilian Corporative State and Working-Class Politics*. Berkeley and Los Angeles: University of California Press.

Estevão, Marcello, and Irineu de Carvalho Filho. 2012. *Institutions, Informality, and Wage Flexibility: Evidence from Brazil*. IMF Working Paper Series. http://www.imf.org/external/pubs/ft/wp/2012/wp1284.pdf (accessed May 19, 2015).

Etchemendy, Sebastián. 2004. "Repression, Exclusion, and Inclusion: Government-Union Relations and Patterns of Labor Reform in Liberalizing Economies." *Comparative Politics* 36, no. 3: 273–90.

Etchemendy, Sebastián, and Ruth Berins Collier. 2007. "Down but Not Out: Union Resurgence and Segmented Neocorporatism in Argentina (2003–2007). *Politics and Society* 35, no. 3: 363–401.

Etchemendy, Sebastián, and Candelaria Garay. 2011. "Argentina: Left Populism in Comparative Perspective, 2003–2009." In *The Resurgence of the Latin American Left*, edited by Steven Levitsky and Kenneth M. Roberts. Baltimore, MD: Johns Hopkins University Press, 283–305.

Etchemendy, Sebastián, and Vicente Palermo. 1998. "Conflicto y concertación: Gobierno, congreso y organizaciones de interés en la reforma laboral del primer gobierno de Menem (1989–1995)." *Desarrollo Económico* 37, no. 148 (January–March): 559–90.

Fairfield, Tasha, and Michel Jorratt. 2014. "Top Income Shares, Business Profits and Effective Tax Rates in Contemporary Chile." International Center for Tax and Development, Working Paper 17: 1–48.

Fairris, David, and Edward Levine. 2004. "Declining Union Density in Mexico, 1984–2000." In *Monthly Labor Review* (September): 10–17.

Felder, Ruth, and Viviana Patroni. 2012. "Turbulent Times: Structural Reforms, Crisis, and Labour Policy in Argentina (1990s–2000s)." In *Comparative Public Policy in Latin America*, edited by Jordi Díez and Susan Franceschet. Toronto: University of Toronto Press, 78–101.

———. 2016. "Precarious Work in Recession and Growth: A New Structural Feature of Labor Markets in Argentina?" *Radical Review of Political Economics* July 7. http://

journals.sagepub.com/doi/abs/10.1177/0486613416635053. Print: vol. 50, no. 1 (2018): 44–65.

———. 2017. "Organizing the "Unorganizable": The Case of Popular Economy Workers in Argentina." Paper presented at the XXXV International Congress of the Latin American Studies Association, Lima, Peru, April 29–May 1.

Fernandes, Sujatha. 2011. "Radio Bemba in an Age of Electronic Media: The Dynamics of Popular Communication in Chávez's Venezuela." In *Venezuela's Bolivarian Democracy: Participation, Politics, and Culture under Chávez*, edited by David Smilde and Daniel Hellinger. Durham, NC: Duke University Press, 131–56.

Fernández S., María Eugenia. 2008. "La protección social de los trabajadores asociados en cooperativas en Venezuela." *Revista Gaceta Laboral* 14, no. 2: 171–92.

Frank, Volker. 2002. "The Elusive Goal in Democratic Chile: Reforming the Pinochet Labor Legislation." *Latin American Politics and Society* 44, no. 1: 35–68.

French, John D. 1992. *The Brazilian Workers' ABC: Class Conflict and Alliances in Modern São Paulo*. Chapel Hill: University of North Carolina Press.

———. 2004. *Drowning in Laws: Labor Law and Brazilian Political Culture*. Chapel Hill: University of North Carolina Press.

———. 2009. "Understanding the Politics of Latin America's Plural Lefts (Chavez/Lula): Social Democracy, Populism and Convergence on the Path to a Post-Neoliberal World." *Third World Quarterly* 30, no. 2: 349–70.

Galvão, Andréia. 2003. "Neoliberalismo e reforma trabalhista no Brasil." PhD diss. Campinas: UNICAMP.

———. 2008. "A reconfiguração do movimento sindical no governo Lula." *Revista Outubro* 19: 175–97.

Gammage, Sarah, Thomás Alburquerque, and Gonzálo Durán. 2014. "Poverty, Inequality and Employment in Chile." Conditions of Work and Employment Series No. 46. Geneva: ILO.

Garcia, Cyro. 2008. "Partido dos Trabalhadores: Da ruptura com a lógica da diferença á sustentação da ordem." PhD diss., Programa de Pos-Graduação em Historia, Universidade Federal Fluminense.

García Villanueva, Carlos, and Alfred Stoll. 1995. "Las relaciones laborales en México y su contexto económico y social." In *Ruptura en las relaciones laborales*, edited by Manfred Wanaffel. Caracas: Nueva Sociedad, 213–47.

García-Guadilla, María Pilar. 2011. "Urban Land Committees: Co-optation, Autonomy, and Protagonism." In *Venezuela's Bolivarian Democracy: Participation, Politics, and Culture under Chávez*, edited by David Smilde and Daniel Hellinger. Durham, NC: Duke University Press, 80–103.

Garretón, Manuel Antonio M. 1989. "Popular Mobilization and the Military Regime in Chile: The Complexities of the Invisible Transition." In *Power and Popular Protest: Latin American Social Movements*, edited by Susan Eckstein. Berkeley and Los Angeles: University of California Press, 259–77.

Gereffi, Gary. 2014. "Global Value Chains in a Post-Washington Consensus World." *Review of International Political Economy* 1, no. 21: 9–37.

Gerring, John. 2007. *Case Study Research: Principles and Practices*. New York: Cambridge University Press.

Gill, Indermit, and Claudio Montenegro. 2002. "Some Guidelines for the New Decades: Summary and Conclusions." In *Crafting Labor Policy: Techniques and Lessons from Latin America*, edited by Indermit Gill, Claudio Montenegro, and Dörte Dömeland, 215–36. New York: Oxford University Press.

Goldfrank, Benjamin. 2011. "The Left and Participatory Democracy: Brazil, Uruguay, and Venezuela." In *The Resurgence of the Latin American Left*, edited by Steven Levitsky and Kenneth M. Roberts, 162–83. Baltimore, MD: Johns Hopkins University Press.

González Moya, Carlos A., ed. 1991. *Nuevo código del trabajo*. Santiago, Chile: Editora Jurídica Manuel Montt S.A.

Gootenberg, Paul. 2010. "Latin American Inequalities: New Perspectives from History, Politics, and Culture." In *Indelible Inequalities in Latin America: Insights from History, Politics, and Culture*, edited by Paul Gootenberg and Luis Reygadas, 3–22. Durham, NC: Duke University Press.

Grayson, George. 1989. *The Mexican Labor Machine: Power, Politics, and Patronage*. Washington, DC: CSIS.

Gudynas, Eduardo. 2010. "The New Extractivism of the 21st Century: Ten Urgent Theses about Extractivism in Relation to Current South American Progressivism." *Americas Program Report*. Washington, DC: Center for International Policy, January 21.

———. 2012. "Estado compensador y nuevos extractivismos: Las ambivalencias del progresismo sudamericano." *Nueva Sociedad* 237: 128–46.

Haagh, Louise. 2002a. *Citizenship, Labour Markets and Democratization: Chile and the Modern Sequence*. New York: Palgrave.

———. 2002b. "The Emperor's New Clothes: Labor Reform and Social Democratization in Chile." *Studies in Comparative International Development* 37, no. 1: 86–115.

Haber, Stephen, Herbert Klein, Noel Maurer, and Kevin Middlebrook. 2008. *Mexico Since 1980*. New York: Cambridge University Press.

Haggard, Stephan, and Robert Kaufman. 1995. *The Political Economy of Democratic Transitions*. Princeton: Princeton University Press.

Hamilton, Nora, and Sunhyuk Kim. 2004. "Democratization, Economic Liberalization, and Labor Politics: Mexico and Korea." *Comparative Sociology* 3, no. 1: 67–92.

Handlin, Samuel. 2016. "Mass Organization and the Durability of Competitive Authoritarian Regimes: Evidence from Venezuela." *Comparative Political Studies* 49, no. 9: 1238–69.

Harrison, Bennett. 1997. *Lean and Mean: Why Large Corporations Will Continue to Dominate the Global Economy*. New York: Guildford Press.

Harrison, Graham. 2005. "Economic Faith, Social Project and a Misreading of African Society: The Travails of Neoliberalism in Africa." *Third World Quarterly* 26, no. 8: 1303–20.

Hawkins, Kirk A. 2010a. *Venezuela's Chavismo and Populism in Comparative Perspective*. New York: Cambridge University Press.

———. 2010b. "Who Mobilizes? Participatory Democracy in Chávez's Bolivarian Revolution." *Latin American Politics and Society* 52, no. 3: 31–66.

Hawkins, Kirk A., and David R. Hansen. 2006. "Dependent Civil Society: The Círculos Bolivarianos in Venezuela." *Latin American Research Review* 41, no. 1: 102–32.

Hawkins, Kurt, Guillermo Rosas, and Michael E. Johnson. 2011. "The Misiones of the Chávez Government." In *Venezuela's Bolivarian Democracy: Participation, Politics, and Culture under Chávez*, edited by David Smilde and Daniel Hellinger, 186–218. Durham, NC: Duke University Press.

Heckman, James, and Carmen Pagés. 2000. *The Cost of Job Security Regulation: Evidence from Latin American Labor Markets*. Inter-American Development Bank Working Paper No. 430. Washington, DC: IADB.

———. 2004. *Law and Employment: Lessons from Latin America and the Caribbean*. Chicago: University of Chicago Press.

Hellinger, Daniel. 2009. "Venezuela." In *Politics of Latin America: The Power Game*, edited by Harry E. Vanden and Gary Prevost, 462–93. 3rd ed. New York: Oxford University Press.

Hernández Alvarez, Oscar, and Antonio Romero Milano. 2008. "Temas relevantes de las relaciones laborales contemporáneas en Venezuela." *Revista Gaceta Laboral* 14, no. 3: 392–426.

Hoffman, Kelly, and Miguel Angel Centeno. 2003. "The Lopsided Continent: Inequality in Latin America." *Annual Review of Sociology* 29: 363–90.

Huber, Evelyn, and John D. Stephens. 2012. *Democracy and the Left: Social Policy and Inequality in Latin America*. Chicago: University of Chicago Press.

Human Rights Watch. 2008. *A Decade Under Chávez: Political Intolerance and Lost Opportunities for Advancing Human Rights in Venezuela*. New York: Human Rights Watch.

Hunter, Wendy. 2014. "Making Citizens: Brazilian Social Policy from Getúlio to Lula." *Journal of Politics in Latin America* 6, no. 3: 15–37. http://journals.sub.uni-hamburg.de/giga/jpla/article/view/792/793 (accessed March 4, 2016).

IACHR (Inter-American Commission on Human Rights). 2009. *Democracy and Human Rights in Venezuela*. http://www.cidh.org/countryrep/Venezuela2009eng/VE09.TOC.eng.htm.

———. 2011. *Annual Report of the Inter-American Commission on Human Rights 2011*. Chapter IV, Venezuela. http://www.oas.org/en/iachr/docs/annual/2011/TOC.asp.

IADB (Inter-American Development Bank). 1997. *Latin America after a Decade of Reforms: Economic and Social Progress*. Washington, DC: IADB.

———. 1998. *Facing Up to Inequality in Latin America*. Washington, DC: IADB.

IBGE (Instituto Brasileiro de Geografía e Estatísticas). 2012. *Anuário estatestico do Brasil* 72. http://biblioteca.ibge.gov.br/visualizacao/periodicos/20/aeb_2012.pdf (accessed April 7, 2015).

ILO (International Labor Organization). ILO Convention 87. http://blue.lim.ilo.org/cariblex/pdfs/ILO_Convention_87.pdf.

———. Venezuela. http://www.ilo.org/wcmsp5/groups/public/---ed_dialogue/---actrav/documents/publication/wcms_111426.pdf.

———. 2003. *Labour Overview: Latin America and the Caribbean*. Ithaca, NY: Regional Office for Latin America and the Caribbean, ILO.

———. 2004. *Report of the Committee of Experts on the Application of Conventions and Recommendations*. International Labor Conference, 92nd session. Geneva, Switzerland: ILO.

———. 2005. *Labour Overview: Latin America and the Caribbean* (First Semester Advanced Report). http://www.ilo.org/wcmsp5/groups/public/---dgreports/---dcomm/---publ/documents/publication/wcms_publ_9221175693_en.pdf.

———. 2010a. *Global Job Pact: Promoting Jobs, Protecting People*. Geneva: ILO.

———. 2010b. *Conference Committee on the Application of Standards*. International Labor Conference, 99th session. Geneva, Switzerland: ILO.

———. 2011. *Brazil: An Innovative Income-Led Strategy*. http://www.ilo.org/wcmsp5/groups/public/---dgreports/---dcomm/---publ/documents/publication/wcms_153768.pdf (accessed August 8, 2014).

———. 2012. *World of Work Report 2012: Better Jobs for a Better Economy*. Geneva: International Institute for Labour Studies.

———. 2013. Governing Body, 317th Session, Reports of the Committee on Freedom of Association, 367th Report of the Committee on Freedom of Association. Geneva, Switzerland: ILO.

———. 2014. *LABORSTA Database on Labor Statistics* (now ILOSTAT). http://www.ilo.org/ilostat/faces/wcnav_defaultSelection;ILOSTATCOOKIE=Zoj-bnbcNdv4t4RIZGeY_j6pSN01elvVU30i0sibM4Gc59F-9SXxL!613767086?_afrLoop=269005642893663&_afrWindowMode=0&_afrWindowId=null#!%40%40%3F_afrWindowId%3Dnull%26_afrLoop%3D269005642893663%26_afrWindowMode%3D0%26_adf.ctrl-state%3Dapa7avv7c_4 (accessed May 23, 2015).

IMF (International Monetary Fund). 2009. "Spotlight: Latin America's Debt." *Finance and Development* 46, no. 1 (March): 56.

———. 2015. *World Economic Outlook: Uneven Growth—Short- and Long-Term Factors* (April). Washington: IMF.

Instituto Nacional de Estadísticas y Geografía (INEGI). 2018. *Encuesta Nacional de Ocupación y Empleo*. http://www.beta.inegi.org.mx/proyectos/enchogares/regulares/enoe/.

IPEA (Instituto de Pesquisa Econômica Aplicada). 2014. *Boletim de mercado de trabalho*. http://www.ipea.gov.br/portal/index.php?option=com_content&view=article&id=21560&Itemid=9 (accessed April 7, 2015).

Jaime, Edna. 2004. "Fox's Economic Agenda: An Incomplete Transition." In *Mexico Under Fox*, edited by Luis Rubio and Susan Kaufman Purcell, 35–64. Boulder: Lynne Rienner.

Jaumotte, Florence, and Carolina Osorio Buitron. 2015. "Power from the People." *Finance and Development* 52, no. 1 (March): 29–31.

Jenkins, Rhys. 2010. "China's Global Expansion and Latin America." *Journal of Latin American Studies* 42: 809–37.

Katz, Harry C., and Owen Darbishire. 2000. *Converging Divergences: Worldwide Changes in Employment Systems*. Ithaca, NY: ILR Press/Cornell University Press.

Kay, Cristóbal, and Robert N. Gwynne. 2000. "Relevance of Structuralist and Dependency Theories in the Neoliberal Period: A Latin American Perspective." *Journal of Developing Societies* 16, no. 1: 49–69.

Klasen, Stephan, and Felicitas Nowak-Lehmann. 2008. *Poverty, Inequality, and Policy in Latin America*. Cambridge, MA: MIT Press.

Kliass, Paulo. 2011. "Lula's Political Economy: Crisis and Continuity." *NACLA* 44, no. 2: 19–22.

Kopinak, K., ed. 2004. *The Social Costs of Industrial Growth in Northern Mexico*. San Diego: Center for US-Mexican Studies, UCSD.

Kornblith, Miriam. 2013. "Chavismo after Chávez?" *Journal of Democracy* 24, no. 3: 47–61.

Kugler, Adriana, and Maurice Kugler. 2009. "Labor Market Effects of Payroll Taxes in Developing Countries." *Economic Development and Cultural Change* 57, no. 2: 335–58.

La Razón. 2014. "16 sindicatos piden cambios en lo económico." https://www.larazon.net/2014/04/16-sindicatos-piden-cambios-en-lo-economico/.

La Tercera (Santiago) online. 2003. "Presidente de la CUT: Estoy defraudado." May 21.

LaBotz, Dan. 1992. *Mask of Democracy: Labor Suppression in Mexico Today*. Boston: South End Press.

Leiva, Fernando Ignacio. 2006. "Neoliberal and Neostructuralist Perspectives on Labour Flexibility, Poverty and Inequality: A Critical Appraisal." *New Political Economy* 11, no. 3: 337–59.

———. 2008. *Latin American Neostructuralism: The Contradictions of Post-Neoliberal Development*. Minneapolis: University of Minnesota Press.

———. 2012. "Flexible Workers, Gender, and Contending Strategies for Confronting the Crisis of Labor in Chile." *Latin American Perspectives* 39, no. 4: 102–28.

———. 2013. "Chile's Labor Movement 1990–2012: Ensnared in the Past and Absent from the Struggles to Democratize Society?" Paper presented at the 2013 Congress of the Latin American Studies Association, Washington, DC, May 29–June 1.

Levine, Robert. 1999. *The History of Brazil*. New York: Palgrave McMillan.

Levinsohn, James. 1999. "Employment Responses to International Liberalization in Chile." *Journal of International Economics* 47: 321–44.

Levitsky, Steven, and Kenneth M. Roberts, eds. 2011. *The Resurgence of the Latin American Left*. Baltimore, MD: Johns Hopkins University Press.

Lindenboim, Javier, Damián Kennedy, and Juan M. Graña. 2010. "El debate sobre la distribución funcional del ingreso." *Desarrollo Económico* 49, no. 196 (January–March): 541–71.

Lisbôa Romão, Frederico. 2006. "A greve do fim do mundo: Petroleiros 1995, a expressão fenomênica da crise fordista no Brasil." PhD diss. Instituto de Filosofia e Ciências Humanas: Universidade Estadual de Campinas.

López, Ramón, Eugenio Figueroa B., and Pablo Gutiérrez C. 2013. "La 'parte del león': Nuevas estimaciones de la participación de los súper ricos en el ingreso de Chile."

Serie de Documentos de Trabajo 379, March. Santiago: Departamento de Economía, Universidad de Chile.

López Maya, Margarita. 2011. "Hugo Chávez and the Populist Left." In *The Resurgence of the Latin American Left*, edited by Steven Levitsky and Kenneth M. Roberts. Baltimore, MD: Johns Hopkins University Press, 213–37.

López Maya, Margarita, and Luis E. Lander. 2011. "Participatory Democracy in Venezuela: Origin, Ideas, and Implementation." In *Venezuela's Bolivarian Democracy: Participation, Politics, and Culture under Chávez*, edited by David Smilde and Daniel Hellinger, 58–79. Durham, NC: Duke University Press.

López Sánchez, Roberto. 2012. "El movimiento de trabajadores en la Venezuela bolivariana: Configuración de tendencias: autonomistas contra leninistas." *Espacio Abierto* 21, no. 1: 145–81.

Lora, Eduardo, and Carmen Pagés. 1997. "La legislación laboral en el proceso de reformas estructurales de América Latina y el Caribe." Working Paper No. 343. IADB, Office of the Chief Economist.

Malloy, James, ed. 1977. *Authoritarianism and Corporatism in Latin America*. Pittsburgh: University of Pittsburgh Press.

Maloney, William, and Jairo Nuñez. 2004. "Measuring the Impact of Minimum Wages: Evidence from Latin America." In *Law and Employment: Lessons from Latin America and the Caribbean*, edited by James Heckman and Carmen Pagés. Chicago: University of Chicago Press.

Mancebo, Marta. 1998. "El nuevo bloque de poder y el nuevo modelo de dominación (1976–1996)." In *La economía argentina a fin de siglo: Fragmentación presente y desarrollo ausente*, edited by Hugo Notcheff, 169–202. Buenos Aires: Eudeba.

March, Luke. 2007. "From Vanguard of the Proletariat to Vox Populi: Left-populism as a 'Shadow' of Contemporary Socialism." *SAIS Review* 27, no. 1: 63–77.

Marques, Rosa Maria, and Áquilas Mendes. 2004. "O governo Lula e a contra-reforma previdenciária." *São Paulo Perspectiva* 18, no. 3: 3–15.

Márquez, Gustavo, and Carmen Pagés. 1998. *Ties that Bind: Employment Protection and Labor Markets Outcome in Latin America.* Washington, DC: IADB.

Marshall, Adriana. 2004. "Labour Market Policies and Regulations in Argentina, Brazil and Mexico: Programmes and Impacts." International Labor Organization Employment Strategy Paper 13. Geneva: ILO. http://www.ilo.org/wcmsp5/groups/public/---ed_emp/---emp_elm/documents/publication/wcms_114302.pdf.

Marticorena, Clara. 2015. "Avances en el estudio de la relación entre sindicalismo y kirchnerismo." *Sociohistorica* 36. http://www.sociohistorica.fahce.unlp.edu.ar/article/view/SH2015n36a04.

Martínez, Javier, and Alvaro Díaz. 1996. *Chile: The Great Transformation*. Washington, DC: Brookings Institution.

Mayer, Jean François. 2006. "Changes in Relations between the State and Independent Unions? Mexico Under the Fox Presidency." *Canadian Journal of Latin American and Caribbean Studies* 31, no. 61: 9–35.

Mayer, Jean François, and Patrik Marier. 2006. "Unions and Pension Reforms in Mexico:

The Impact of Democratic Governance." *Journal of Iberian and Latin American Studies* 11, no. 2: 29–52.

Mazali, Antonio Alberto, and José Angelo Divino. 2010. "Real Wage Rigidity and the New Phillips Curve: The Brazilian Case." *Revista Brasileira de Economia* 64, no. 3: 291–306.

Mazzuca, Sebastián L. 2013. "The Rise of Rentier Populism." *Journal of Democracy* 24, no. 2: 108–22.

McCoy, Jennifer L. 2004. "From Representative to Participatory Democracy? Regime Transformation in Venezuela." In *The Unraveling of Representative Democracy in Venezuela*, edited by Jennifer L. McCoy and David L. Myers, 263–95. Baltimore: Johns Hopkins University Press.

———. 2010. "Venezuela under Chávez: Beyond Liberalism." In *Latin America's Left Turns: Politics, Policies, and Trajectories of Change*, edited by Maxwell A. Cameron and Eric Hershberg, 81–100. Boulder: Lynne Rienner.

Meeks, John. 1999. "Wages, Employment and Workers' Rights in Latin America, 1970–98." *International Labour Review* 138, no. 2: 151–69.

Mericle, Kenneth. 1977. "Corporatist Control of the Working Class: Authoritarian Brazil since 1964." In *Authoritarianism and Corporatism in Latin America*, edited by James Malloy, 303–39. Pittsburgh: University of Pittsburgh Press.

Middlebrook, Kevin J. 1995. *The Paradox of Revolution: Labor, the State, and Authoritarianism in Mexico*. Baltimore: Johns Hopkins University Press.

Middlebrook, Kevin, and Eduardo Zepeda. 2003. On the Political Economy of Mexican Development Policy. In *Confronting Development*, edited by Kevin J. Middlebrook and Eduardo Zepeda, 3–54. Stanford: Stanford University Press.

Ministerio de Desarrollo Social. 2011. *CASEN 2011: Encuesta de caracterización socioeconómica nacional*. Santiago: Gobierno de Chile.

———. 2013. *CASEN 2013: Evolución y distribución del ingreso de los hogares (2006–2013)*. Santiago: Gobierno de Chile.

Ministerio de Planificación. 2006. *CASEN 2006: Encuesta de caracterización socioeconómica nacional*. Santiago: Gobierno de Chile.

Ministerio del Trabajo y Previsión Social. 2006. "Ley No. 20.123." *Agenda Laboral* 28: 1–8. Santiago: Gobierno de Chile.

MLNA (*Mexican Labor News and Analysis*). Various issues and years. http://www.ueinternational.org/MLNA/.

Morais, Lecio, and Alfredo Saad-Filho. 2011. "Da economia política à política econômica: O novo-desenvolvimentismo e o governo Lula." *Revista de Economia Política* 31, no. 4, 507–27.

Munck, Ronaldo. 2002. *Globalization and Labour: The New Great Transformation*. London: Zed Books.

———. 2004. Introduction to *Latin American Perspectives* 31, no. 4: 3–31.

Muñoz Ríos, Patricia, 2007. "Desbandada masiva de afiliados have languidecer a las centrales sindicales." *La Jornada*, June 4. http://www.jornada.unam.mx/2007/06/04/index.php?section=sociedad&article=043n1soc.

Murillo, María Victoria. 2000. "From Populism to Neoliberalism: Labor Unions and Market Reforms in Latin America." *World Politics* 52, no. 2: 135–74.

———. 2001. *Labor Unions, Partisan Coalitions, and Market Reforms in Latin America.* New York: Cambridge University Press.

———. 2005. "Partisanship Amidst Convergence: The Politics of Labor Reform in Latin America." *Comparative Politics* 37, no. 4: 441–58.

———. 2013. "Cambio y continuidad del sindicalismo en democracia." *Revista SAAP* 7, no. 2 (November): 339–48.

Murillo, Maria Victoria, and Andrew Schrank. 2005. "With a Little Help from My Friends: Partisan Politics, Transnational Alliances, and Labor Rights in Latin America." *Comparative Political Studies* 38, no. 8: 971–99.

Murmis, Miguel, and Juan Carlos Portantiero. 1971. *Estudios sobre los orígenes del Peronismo.* Buenos Aires: Siglo Veintiuno.

Nakoa Nakahodo, Sidney, and José Roberto Savoia. 2008. "A reforma da previdência no Brasil: Estudo comparative dos governos Fernando Henrique Cardoso e Lula." *Revista Brasileira de Ciências Sociais* 23, no. 66: 45–58.

Neffa, Julio César. 2010. "El trabajo no registrado como modalidad límite de precariedad." In *La corrosión del trabajo: Estudios sobre informalidad y precariedad laboral,* edited by Mariana Busso and Pablo Pérez, 51–77. Buenos Aires: Miño y Dávila.

Neffa, Julio César, and Demián T. Panigo. 2010. "Modelos productivos y sus impactos sobre la relación salarial: Reflexiones a partir del caso argentino: Primera parte." In *Trabajo y modelos productivos en América Latina: Argentina, Brasil, Colombia, México, y Venezuela luego de las crisis del modo de desarrollo neoliberal,* edited by Enrique de la Garza Toledo y Julio César Neffa. Buenos Aires: Consejo Latinoamericano de Ciencias Sociales (CLACSO), 261–87.

Ness, Immanuel. 2015. *Southern Insurgency: The Coming of the Global Working Class.* London: Pluto Press.

Neuman, William, and Patricia Torres. 2015. "Venezuelan Courts Block 4 Lawmakers." *New York Times* online. December 31. http://www.nytimes.com/2015/12/31/world/americas/venezuelan-court-blocks-4-lawmakers.html?emc=etal&_r=0.

Notimex. 2010. "Perderá UNT un tercio de su membresía sin el sindicato del IMSS." *NTR Zacatecas,* April 17. http://ntrzacatecas.com/2010/04/17/perdera-unt-un-tercio-de-su-membresia-sin-el-sindicato-del-imss/.

Novick, Marta, Miguel Lengyel, and Marianela Sarabia. 2009. "From Social Protection to Vulnerability: Argentina's Neo-Liberal Reforms of the 1990s." *International Labour Review* 148, no. 3: 235–52.

Nun, José. 1994. "Populismo, representación y menemismo." *Sociedad* 5 (October): 93–121.

Olivera, Diego. 2008. "Nace la central socialista de trabajadores." *Agencia Latinoamericana de Información.* http://alainet.org/active/25606&lang=es.

Orlando, Maria Beatriz. 2001. "The Informal Sector in Venezuela: Catalyst or Hindrance to Poverty Reduction?" Instituto de Investigaciones Económicas y Sociales, Universidad Católica Andrés Bello, Caracas, Venezuela.

Orovitz Sanmartino, Jorge. 2010. "Crisis, acumulación y forma de estado en la Argentina post-neoliberal." *Cuestiones de Sociología*, 5–6.

Ortega, Manuel, and Ana Alicia Solís de Alba. 1999. *Estado, crisis y reorganización sindical*. Mexico City: Itaca.

Ostry, Jonathan D., Andrew Berg, and Charalambos G. Tsangarides. 2014. *Redistribution, Inequality, and Growth*. IMF Staff Discussion Note 14/02. Washington: IMF Research Department.

Otis, John, 2012. "How Mexico's Pro-Industry Unions Undermine Workers' Rights." *Global Post*, March 21. http://www.globalpost.com/dispatch/news/regions/americas/mexico/120320/no-protection-how-mexicos-pro-industry-unions-undermine.

Oxhorn, Philip. 1998. "The Social Foundations of Latin America's Recurrent Populism: Problems of Popular Sector Class Formation and Collective Action." *Journal of Historical Sociology* 11, no. 2 (June): 212–46.

Paczyńska, Agnieszka. 2009. *State, Labor, and the Transition to a Market Economy: Egypt, Poland, Mexico, and the Czech Republic*. University Park: Penn State University Press.

Palacios-Valladares, Indira. 2010. "From Militancy to Clientelism: Labor Union Strategies and Membership Trajectories in Contemporary Chile." *Latin America Politics and Society* 52, no. 2: 73–98.

Palomino, Héctor. 2011. "La renovada presencia de los sindicatos en la Argentina contemporánea." *Voces en el Fénix* 2, no. 6: 24–31.

Panigo, Demian, and Julio César Neffa. 2009. *El mercado de trabajo argentino en el nuevo modelo de desarrollo*. Dirección Nacional de Programación Macroeconómica Dirección de Modelos y Proyecciones, Ministerio de Economía, República Argentina.

Patroni, Viviana. 2001. "The Decline and Fall of Corporatism? Labor Legislation Reform in Mexico and Argentina during the 1990s." *Canadian Journal of Political Science* 34, no. 2: 249–74.

Penfold-Becerra, Michael. 2007. "Clientelism and Social Funds: Evidence from Chávez's Misiones." *Latin American Politics and Society* 49, no. 4: 63–84.

Pereira da Silva, Arthur Simão, and Sandro Eduardo Monsueto. 2012. *Flexibilidade do Mercado de Trabalho: Uma Análise Comparativa Entre Segmentos Socioeconómicos no Brasil (2002–2009)*. Working Paper, Associação Nacional dos Centros de Pós-Graduação em Economia (ANPEC). www.anpec.org.br/encontro/2012/inscricao/files_I/i12-351de703e4da2073e562bebdf5fd0981.pdf (accessed May 19, 2015).

Pérez, Domingo, Rodrigo Medel, and Diego Velásquez. 2015. "El desarrollo de la huelga ilegal en el Chile contemporáneo (1990–2009)." Paper presented at 2015 Congress of the Latin American Studies Association, San Juan, PR, May 27–30.

Pichler, Walter Arno. 2011. "Tendências da sindicalização no Brasil: 1992–2009." *Indicadores Econômicos FEE* 38, no. 3: 37–46.

Piñeiro, Camila. 2009. "Workplace Democracy and Social Consciousness: A Study of Venezuelan Cooperatives." *Science and Society* 73, no. 3: 309–39.

Portes, Alejandro, and Kelly Hoffman. 2003. "Latin American Class Structures: Their Composition and Change during the Neoliberal Era." *Latin American Research Review* 38, no. 1: 41–82.

Posner, Paul W. 2008. *State, Market, and Democracy in Chile: The Constraint of Popular Participation*. Basingstoke, UK: Palgrave Macmillan.

Power, Timothy J., and Mahrukh Doctor. 2004. "Beyond the Century of Corporatism? Continuity and Change in Brazil." In *Authoritarianism and Corporatism in Latin America Revisited*, edited by Howard J. Wiarda, 218–41. Gainesville: University Press of Florida.

PROVEA. 2012. Situación de los derechos humanos en Venezuela. Informe annual enero/diciembre 2012, derechos laborales. https://www.derechos.org.ve/web/wp-content/uploads/07Laborales-1.pdf.

Radio Cooperativa (Santiago) online. 2007a. "Presidenta Bachelet creará Consejo Asesor sobre equidad social." August 20.

———. 2007b. "CUT: Más que decepción, hay indignación con la Presidenta Bachelet." August 24.

———. 2008a. "Finalizó la heulga de los subcontratados de Codelco." May 5.

———. 2008b. "Corte Suprema: Codelco no está obligada a incorporar a subcontratados." May 12.

———. 2008c. "Subcontratados: Fallo de la Suprema deja sin facultades a Dirección del Trabajo." May 13.

Ramirez, Miguel D. 1993. "Stabilization and Adjustment in Latin America: A Neostructuralist Perspective." *Journal of Economic Issues* 27, no. 4: 1015–40.

Reis de Sousa, Otávio Augusto, and Ricardo José das Mercês Carneiro. 2010. "Estrutura e organização da Justica do Trabalho." *Revista do TST* 67, no. 4: 15–27.

Reuters. 2016. "Venezuelan Top Court Grants Maduro Emergency Powers, Opposition Cries Foul. http://www.reuters.com/article/us-venezuela-politics-idUSKCN0VL0AE.

Reygadas, Luis. 2010. "The Construction of Latin American Inequalities." In *Indelible Inequalities in Latin America: Insights from History, Politics, and Culture*, edited by Paul Gootenberg and Luis Reygadas, 23–49. Durham, NC: Duke University Press.

Riethof, Marieke. 2004. "Changing Strategies of the Brazilian Labor Movement." *Latin American Perspectives* 31, no. 6: 31–47.

Roberts, Kenneth M. 1996. "Neoliberalism and the Transformation of Populism in Latin America: The Peruvian Case." *World Politics* 48, no. 1: 82–116.

———. 1998. *Deepening Democracy: The Modern Left and Social Movements in Chile and Peru*. Stanford: Stanford University Press.

———. 2002. "Social Inequalities without Class Cleavages in Latin America's Neoliberal Era." *Studies in Comparative International Development* 36, no. 4: 3–33.

———. 2007a. "The Crisis of Labor Politics in Latin America: Parties and Labor Movements during the Transition to Neoliberalism." *International Labor and Working-Class History* 72 (Fall): 116–33.

———. 2007b. "Latin America's Populist Revival." *SAIS Review* 27, no. 1: 3–15.

Robinson, William I. 2003. *Transnational Conflicts: Central America, Social Change, and Globalization*. New York: Verso.

———. 2012. "Latin America in the New Global Capitalism." *NACLA Report on the Americas* 45, no. 2: 13–18.

Robles, Jorge. 2011. "Breve historia (no oficial) de la UNT." *Rojo y Negro* (blog), February 25. http://rojoynego.blogspot.ca/2011/02/breve-historia-no-oficial-de-la-unt.html.

Rock, David. 1987. *Argentina, 1516–1987: From Spanish Colonization to Alfonsín*. Berkeley and Los Angeles: University of California Press.

Rodríguez, Francisco. 2008. "Venezuela's Revolution in Decline: Beware the Wounded Tiger." *World Policy Journal* 25, no. 1: 45–58.

Roman, Richard, and Edur Velasco Arregui. 2006. "The State, the Bourgeoisie, and the Unions." *Latin American Perspectives* 33, no. 2: 95–103.

Roxborough, Ian. 1998. "Urban Labour Movements in Latin America since 1930s." In *Latin America: Politics and Society since 1930*, edited by Leslie Bethell. New York: Cambridge University Press, 219–90.

Rubio, Luis. 2004. "Democratic Politics in Mexico: New Complexities." In *Mexico Under Fox*, edited by Luis Rubio and Susan Kaufman Purcell. Boulder: Lynne Rienner, 5–36.

Ruiz-Tagle, Jaime. 1989. "Trade Unionism and the State under the Chilean Military Regime." In *Labor Autonomy and the State in Latin America*, edited by Edward C. Epstein. Boston: Unwin Hyman, 73–100.

Saad-Filho, Alfredo, and Maria de Lourdes R. Mollo. 2002. "Inflation and Stabilization in Brazil: A Political Economy Analysis." *Review of Radical Political Economics* 34: 109–35.

Sabatini, Christopher, and Eric Farnsworth. 2006. "A 'Left Turn' in Latin America? The Urgent Need for Labor Law Reform." *Journal of Democracy* 17, no. 4: 50–64.

Salas, Carlos, and Eduardo Zepeda. 2003. "Employment and Wages: Enduring the Costs of Liberalization and Economic Reforms." In *Confronting Development*, edited by Kevin J. Middlebrook and Eduardo Zepeda. Stanford: Stanford University Press, 522–58.

Samstad, James G. 2002. "Corporation and Democratic Transition." *Latin American Politics and Society* 44, no. 4: 1–28.

Santiso, Javier, and Jeff Dayton-Johnson. 2012. *The Oxford Handbook of Latin American Political Economy.* New York: Oxford University Press.

Santos Azuela, Hector. 1989. "La libertad sindical en México." In *Modernidad y legislación laboral*, edited by Graciela Bensusán and Carlos García. Mexico: FES Editors, 30–52.

Schamis, Hector E. 2002. *Re-Forming the State: The Politics of Privatization in Latin America and Europe*. Ann Arbor: University of Michigan Press.

Schiller, Naomi. 2011. "Catia Sees You: Community Television, Clientelism, and the State in the Chávez Era." In *Venezuela's Bolivarian Democracy: Participation, Politics, and Culture under Chávez*, edited by David Smilde and Daniel Hellinger. Durham, NC: Duke University Press, 104–30.

Schipani, Andrés. 2012. "Los motivos de la fractura." *Le Monde Diplomatique* 157 (July).

Schmitter, Philippe C. 1974. "Still the Century of Corporatism?" *Review of Politics* 36, no. 1: 85–131.

———. 1982. "Reflections on Where the Theory of Neo-Corporatism Has Gone and Where the Praxis of Neo-Corporatism May Be Going." In *Patterns of Corporatist Policy-Making*, edited by Gerhard Lehmbruch and Philippe C. Schmitter. Beverly Hills: Sage, 259–79.

Schneider, Ben R. 2013. *Hierarchical Capitalism in Latin America: Business, Labor, and the Challenges of Equitable Development*. New York: Cambridge University Press.

Scolnik, Fernando. 2014. "El movimiento obrero argentino entre dos crisis: Las organizaciones de base antiburocráticas en el área metropolitana de Buenos Aires durante el período 2003–2007." *Conflicto Social* 2, no. 2: 224–55.

Secretaría del Trabajo y Previsión Social. 2015. *Estadísticas del sector*. http://www.stps.gob.mx/bp/secciones/conoce/areas_atencion/areas_atencion/web/menu_infsector.html.

Selee, Andrew, and Jacqueline Peschard. 2010. "Mexico's Democratic Challenges." In *Mexico's Democratic Challenges: Politics, Government, and Society*, edited by Andrew Selee and Jacqueline Peschard. Washington, DC: Woodrow Wilson Center Press, 1–28.

Semple, Kirk. 2017a. "Venezuelan Opposition Denounces Latest Vote as Ruling Party Makes Gains." *New York Times*, online. October 16. https://www.nytimes.com/2017/10/16/world/americas/venezuela-opposition-maduro-elections.html.

———. 2017b. "Venezuelan's Two Legislatures Duel, but Only One Has Ammunition." *New York Times*, online. November 3. https://www.nytimes.com/2017/11/03/world/americas/venezuela-national-assembly-maduro.html

Siavelis, Peter. 2016. "Bachelet's Labor Policy Leaves No One Happy in Chile." *World Politics Review* (November 29). http://www.worldpoliticsreview.com/trend-lines/20564/bachelet-s-labor-policy-leaves-no-one-happy-in-chile (accessed August 9, 2017).

Sidicaro, Ricardo. 2002. *Los tres peronismos: Estado y poder económico 1946–55/1973–76/1989–99*. Buenos Aires: Siglo veintiuno.

Silva, Eduardo. 1996. "From Dictatorship to Democracy: The Business-State Nexus in Chile's Economic Transformation, 1975–1994." *Comparative Politics* 28, no. 3: 299–320.

Silver, Beverly. 2003. *Forces of Labour: Workers' Movements and Globalization since 1870*. Cambridge, New York: Cambridge University Press.

Skidmore, Thomas. 2010. *Brazil: Five Centuries of Change*. 2nd ed. New York: Oxford University Press.

Smilde, David. 2011. "Introduction: Participation, Politics, and Culture—Emerging Fragments of Venezuela's Bolivarian Democracy." In *Venezuela's Bolivarian Democracy: Participation, Politics, and Culture under Chávez*, edited by David Smilde and Daniel Hellinger. Durham, NC: Duke University Press, 1–27.

Smith, William C. 1991. *Authoritarianism and the Crisis of the Argentine Political Economy*. Stanford: Stanford University Press.

Solimano, Andrés. 2007. "Employment Creation, Real Wages and Job Quality: How Much Aggregate Economic Growth Delivers? The Case of Chile." Working Paper 79, Policy Integration Department. Geneva: ILO.

Stallings, Barbara. 1978. *Class Conflict and Economic Development in Chile, 1958–1973*. Stanford: Stanford University Press.

———. 1992. "International Influence and Economic Policy: Debt, Stabilization, and Policy Reform." In *The Politics of Economic Adjustment*, edited by Stephan Haggard and Robert Kaufman. Princeton: Princeton University Press, 41–88.

——. 2010. "Globalization and Labor in Four Developing Regions: An Institutional Approach." *Studies in Comparative International Development* 45: 127–50

Standing, Guy. 1999. *Global Labor Flexibility: Seeking Distributive Justice*. Houndmills, Basingstoke, UK: Palgrave Macmillan.

Stokes, Susan C., Thad Dunning, Marcelo Nazareno, and Valeria Brusco. 2013. *Brokers, Voters, and Clientelism: The Puzzle of Distributive Politics*. New York: Cambridge University Press.

Svampa, Maristella, and Mirta A. Antonelli, eds. 2009. *Minería transnacional, narrativas del desarrollo y resistencias sociales*. Buenos Aires: Editorial Biblos.

Svampa, Maristella, and Sebastián Pereyra. 2003. *Entre la ruta y el barrio: La experiencia de las organizaciones piqueteras*. Buenos Aires: Biblos.

Tapia Guerrero, Francisco, and Carmen Elena Domínguez Soto, eds. 2011. *Código del Trabajo, undécima edición*. Santiago, Chile: Legal Publishing Chile.

Thelen, Kathleen, and James Mahoney. 2015. "Comparative-Historical Analysis in Contemporary Political Science." In *Advances in Comparative-Historical Analysis*, edited by James Mahoney and Kathleen Thelen. New York: Cambridge University Press, 3–36.

Thomas, Jim. 1996. "The New Economic Model and Labour Markets in Latin America." In *The New Economic Model in Latin America and Its Impact on Income Distribution and Poverty*, edited by V. Bulmer-Thomas. London: Macmillan, 79–102.

Thompson, Andrés. 1993. "De la primavera populista al invierno conservador: El sindicalismo peronista entre 1973 y 1989." In *Desafíos para el sindicalismo en la Argentina*, edited by Omar Moreno. Buenos Aires: Legasa, 81–92.

Tilly, Chris. 2014. "Beyond *Contratos de Protección*: Strong and Weak Unionism in Mexican Retail Enterprises." *Latin American Research Review* 49, no. 3: 176–98.

Tissera, Silvana, Juan Martín Bustos, Fernando Sciarrotta, Juliana Persia, Gonzalo Herrera Gallo, Natalia Cillis, Verónica Garcia Allegrone, and Agustín Salvia. 2000. "Reformas laborales y precarización del trabajo asalariado (Argentina 1990–2000)." Lindemboin, *Cuadernos del CEPED* 4. Buenos Aires: CEPED. https://www.aacademica.org/agustin.salvia/218.

Trabajo y Equidad. 2008. "Hacia un Chile más justo: trabajo, salario, competitividad y equidad social." http://www.cnid.cl/wp-content/uploads/2008/10/Hacia-un-Chile-m%C3%A1s-justo_2008.pdf.

Trejo Delabre, Raúl. 1976. "The Mexican Labor Movement: 1917–1975." *Latin American Perspectives* 3, no. 1: 133–53.

——. 1990. *Crónica del sindicalismo en México (1976–1988)*. Mexico City: Siglo 21.

United Nations. 2015. *Transforming Our World: The 2030 Agenda for Sustainable Development*. General Assembly's Seventieth Session, Resolution adopted by the General Assembly on September 25, 2015. http://www.un.org/ga/search/view_doc.asp?symbol=A/RES/70/1&Lang=E.

Valenzuela, Arturo. 1978. *The Breakdown of Democratic Regimes: Chile*. Baltimore: Johns Hopkins University Press.

——. 1995. "Chile: Origins and Consolidation of a Latin American Democracy." In *Politics in Developing Countries: Comparing Experiences with Democracy*, edited by

Larry Diamond, Juan J. Linz, and Seymour Martin Lipset. 2nd ed. Boulder: Lynne Rienner, 67–118.

Vega Ruíz, María Luz. 2005. *La reforma laboral en América Latina: 15 años después*. Lima: Oficina Internacional del Trabajo, Oficina Regional para América Latina y el Caribe.

Veras Soares, Fábio, Rafael Perez Ribas, and Rafael Guerreiro Osório. 2010. "Evaluating the Impact of Brazil's Bolsa Família." *Latin American Research Review* 45, no. 2: 173–90.

Walker, Ignacio. 1990. *Socialismo y democracía: Chile y Europa en perspectiva comparada*. Santiago de Chile: Cieplan-Hachette.

Weaver, Frederick Stirton. 2000. *Latin America in the World Economy: Mercantile Colonialism to Global Capitalism*. Boulder: Westview Press.

Weffort, Francisco. 1989. "Why Democracy." In *Democratizing Brazil*, edited by Alfred Stepan. Oxford: Oxford University Press, 327–50.

Weyland, Kurt. 2001. "Clarifying a Contested Concept: Populism in the Study of Latin American Politics." *Comparative Politics* 34, no. 1: 1–22.

———. 2003. "Neopopulism and Neoliberalism in Latin America: How Much Affinity?" *Third World Quarterly* 24, no. 6: 1095–1115.

———. 2013. "The Threat from the Populist Left." *Journal of Democracy* 24, no. 3: 18–32.

Weyland, Kurt, Raúl L. Madrid, and Wendy Hunter, eds. 2010. *Leftist Governments in Latin America: Successes and Shortcomings*. New York: Cambridge University Press.

Winn, Peter. 2004. *Victims of the Chilean Miracle: Workers and Neoliberalism in the Pinochet Era, 1973–2002*. Durham, NC: Duke University Press.

World Bank. 2012. *The World Development Report 2013: Jobs*. Washington: World Bank.

———. 2014. GDP Per Capita. Available from http://data.worldbank.org/indicator/NY.GDP.PCAP.PP.CD?page=4.

World Bank Databank. 2013. *World Bank Databank*. http://databank.worldbank.org/ddp/editReport?REQUEST_SOURCE=search&CNO=2&country=BRA&series=&period (accessed July 19, 2014).

———. 2015. *World Bank Databank*. http://databank.worldbank.org/data/home.aspx.

Wright, Erik O. 2000. "Working-Class Power, Capitalist-Class Interests, and Class Compromise." *American Journal of Sociology* 105, no. 4 (January): 957–1002.

Zapata, Francisco. 1995. *El sindicalismo mexicano frente a la reestructuración*. Mexico City: El Colegio de México

———. 1998. "Trade Unions and the Corporatist System in Mexico." In *What Kind of Democracy? What Kind of Market?* edited by Philip Oxhorn and Graciela Ducatenzeiler. University Park: Penn State University Press, 151–68.

———. 2006. "La negociación de las reformas a la Ley Federal del Trabajo (1989–2005)." *Foro Internacional* 46, no. 1: 81–102.

Index

Page numbers followed by *f* indicate an illustration; page numbers followed by *t* indicate a table.

Paul W. Posner is associate professor in the Department of Political Science at Clark University in Worcester, Massachusetts. His current research focuses on democratization and political participation in Latin America. In particular, he is interested in the impact of economic globalization and related state reforms on social organization and collective action in the region. Current projects examine labor politics, the politics of social welfare resource distribution, the New Left and populism in Latin America, with specific focus on Chile, Ecuador, and Venezuela. His work has been published in the *Journal of Interamerican Studies and World Affairs*; *Democratization*; *Latin American Politics and Society*; *Political Power and Social Theory*; *International Journal of Urban and Regional Research*; and *New Political Economy*. His book, *State, Market, and Democracy in Chile: The Constraint of Popular Participation*, assesses the impact neoliberal reform has had on the ability of Chile's urban poor to organize and represent their interests in the political arena.

Viviana Patroni is associate professor in the Department of Social Science at York University, where she teaches in the International Development Studies program. Her research focuses on the political economy of Latin America, the transformation of the world of work in this region since the 1980s, the centrality of labor struggles in shaping patterns of development, and the transformation of labor markets in Argentina since the 1990s. She has also contributed to the study of the impact of Canadian investment in the Latin American mining sector and, as a codirector of a Canadian-funded initiative, to a program of activities aimed at supporting the development of a Latin American network for human rights education and research. Her work has been published in the *Canadian Journal of Political Science*; *Canadian Journal of Latin American and Caribbean Studies*; *Radical Review of Political Economics*; and the *Journal of Socialist Studies*. Her most recent work includes an interest in the rise of organizations of informal workers and their challenge to prevalent views within labor movements about their understanding of work and working class. Between 2000 and 2007 she was the director of the Centre for Research on Latin America and the Caribbean, also at York University.

Jean François Mayer specializes in comparative politics and political ethnography. His research expertise is on social movements, labor markets, and organization, as well as state-society relations in Latin America, with a particular emphasis on Brazil and Mexico. His current work focuses on the formal and informal strategies of resistance used by people working in precarious and informal environments; the sociopolitical impacts of precarious and informal labor contexts (namely insecurity, marginalization, poverty, and violence); and, more broadly, the manner in which poor people organize to defend and advance their labor and social rights. Mayer has published in a wide variety of academic journals, including the *Journal of Politics in Latin America*; *Journal of Social Policy*; *Bulletin of Latin American Research*; *Latin Americanist*; and the *Journal of Iberian and Latin American Research*. Mayer has held numerous research grants, among which an Insight Development Grant and a Standard Research Grant from the Social Sciences and Humanities Research Council of Canada (SSHRC), as well as a research grant from the International Development Research Center of Canada (IDRC).

www.ingramcontent.com/pod-product-compliance
Lightning Source LLC
Chambersburg PA
CBHW031817080825
30823CB00002B/78

9781683400455